SKILLS & STRATEGIES FOR
WINNING
RACQUETBALL

SKILLS & STRATEGIES FOR
WINNING
RACQUETBALL

Ed Turner, PhD
Appalachian State University

Marty Hogan
Professional Racquetball Player

Leisure Press
Champaign, Illinois

Developmental Editor: Steve Houseworth
Copy Editor: Patrick O'Hayer
Assistant Editor: JoAnne Cline
Production Director: Ernie Noa
Projects Manager: Lezli Harris
Typesetter: Sonnie Bowman
Text Design: Keith Blomberg
Text Layout: Terry Kohler
Cover Design: Conundrum Designs
Cover Photo: Marty Hogan, Courtesy of Leader Sport Products,
 Manufacturers
Illustrations By: Terry Kohler
Printed By: Versa Press

ISBN: 0-88011-289-1

Copyright © 1988 by Edward T. Turner

Library of Congress Cataloging-in-Publication Data

Turner, Edward T.
 Skills and strategies for winning racquetball.

 Includes index.
 1. Racquetball. I. Hogan, Marty. II. Title.
GV1003.34.T87   1988   796.34'3   87-2736
ISBN 0-88011-289-1

Printed in the United States of America

10 9 8 7 6 5 4 3 2

Leisure Press
A division of Human Kinetics Publishers, Inc.
Box 5076, Champaign, IL 61820
1-800-DIAL-HKP
1-800-334-3665 (in Illinois)

Dedication

This text is dedicated to George Kramer for his provoking thoughts and friendship and to Luke and Matt for being themselves. Thanks.

Acknowledgments

The authors are indebted and wish to express sincere gratitude to Mick Kreszock and Mike Hypes for the photos in this book. We would also like to thank *Racquetball Illustrated* magazine for sharing photos and articles. A special thanks is given to Ms. Emily Risewick for the preliminary typing of the manuscript. We would also like to recognize Murray Broome for sharing his ideas in chapter 15. The authors would also like to thank Boone Sports for providing equipment used in the text. For their photogenic characteristics the authors thank Lowell Furman, Beth Guice, Mel Gruensfelder, Eric Gentry, and Jin Yang.

Contents

Preface

After a decade and a half of rapid growth the sport of racquetball is here to stay. Many books have been written about racquetball, yet no comprehensive book on the sport has been produced. This book, then, is an attempt to give the player—whether beginning, intermediate, or advanced—a complete guide to racquetball. *This book is designed for the player.*

This text is divided into three basic sections: "Getting Ready," "Skills and Strategies," and "Advancing Your Skills." In the "Getting Ready" section attention is given to history, equipment, places to play, safety and conditioning, and the players. The "Skills and Strategy" section of the text includes information on grips, power supplies, hitting position, types of shots, volleys, serves, and the return of serves. The final section of the book looks at more complicated shots, diving, movement patterns, footwork, anticipation, half-volleys, angles, spin, basic errors and corrections, strategies, doubles, courts and court games, terminology, rules and resources.

Although this book is broad in scope, each chapter gives specific highlights in lists of key ideas, and all skills chapters have separate sections on key information, common problems, and drills. We hope that this text will be enjoyable and worthwhile to all players and advocates of the sport of racquetball. Good reading and good knowledge can make a better player. Good luck!

Ed Turner
Marty Hogan

Figure Key

H = Hitter

O = Opponent

L = Left

R = Right or Receiver

S = Server

B = Bounce

X = Player

• = Ball

------- = Path of ball

❙❙ = Foot placement

Part I

Getting Ready to
Play Racquetball

CHAPTER 1
History and Growth
of Racquetball

The roots of racquetball are varied. Modern racquetball grew out of a number of contemporary sports, including handball, paddleball, squash, and tennis. The beginning complexities of early ball-hitting games, however, date back to jai alai in Spain during the seventh century, in which a ball was hurled with a type of racquet. In the thirteenth century, a game was played in both European courtyards and monasteries that was a form of handball in which the ball was both tossed and hit with the hand. By the fifteenth and sixteenth centuries, very primitive forms of racquets were used to hit balls in Europe, and this seems to be the start of the racquet sport era. By the eighteenth century, the English were playing a game called "racquets," the forerunner of tennis. The Irish game of handball, which developed from courtyard handball, also had some bearing on the development of racquetball as it is played today. The roots of racquetball are intertwined with the long historical development of tennis, squash racquets, Irish handball, and other early ball-hitting games.

More recently, the game of paddleball was developed in the late 1920s at the University of Michigan by Earl Riskey. For years, Riskey had watched tennis players practicing tennis in handball courts during the inclement weather months. From this, Riskey's ideas for the game of paddleball evolved. Paddleball was played with a wooden paddle similar to a table tennis paddle, but about twice its size, with a number of holes drilled through the hitting surface. Paddleball slowly grew in popularity through the 1930s in both YMCAs and universities, and during the early 1940s it was used as conditioning training for our armed forces. For one reason or another, however, paddleball was slow to gain widespread popularity. It wasn't until 1961 that the first national paddleball tournament was held, in Madison, Wisconsin.

In 1950 Joe Sobek, a tennis and squash player in Greenwich, Connecticut, developed a new sport called "paddle rackets" that was the actual beginning of racquetball. Sobek developed paddle rackets as a result of his disgust that he had no one to play squash with, that it was winter and too cold to play tennis, and that paddleball was such a dull game. He began to formulate a new gaming concept by developing a paddle racket with a string face rather than a wooden one. At the same time he looked for a faster ball than the sponge ball used in paddleball. He found some Spalding red and blue play balls in a local store and used those. Sobek's rules for paddle rackets were drawn from squash, handball, and paddleball rules. Thus "paddle rackets" was invented. Like Riskey's paddleball, the growth of paddle rackets was slow during the 1950s and 1960s.

The upswing in the popularity of paddle rackets began in 1968 with the first national paddle rackets championships held in St. Louis, Missouri, and in 1969 when the first international paddle rackets championships were held in that same city. At this time the name of the game was changed to racquetball and the International Racquetball Association (IRA) was founded. In 1973 the National Racquetball Club (NRC), a new professional racquetball association, was founded. When the NRC became the organization for professional players, the United States Racquetball Association (USRA) was formed as an amateur, player organization.

During this time Dr. Bud Muehleisen, one of the founding fathers of racquetball, began promoting the game by holding clinics across the country. This clinical exposure plus racquetball's first professional tournament, held at the Houston, Texas, YMCA on September 27–30, 1973, gave needed impetus to the development of the game.

During the mid-1970s the American Amateur Racquetball Association (AARA) came into existence out of the roots of the defunct IRA to compete with both the professional NRC and the amateur USRA. For a few

Figure 1-1. Brumfield in action against Hogan (Courtesy Racquetball Illustrated)

years there was chaos in the racquetball world because of disagreement over which organization was really the national governing body. In 1981 the USRA and the NRC ceased to exist, and the AARA became the official governing body for amateur racquetball.

From its small beginnings in Joe Sobek's Greenwich, Connecticut YMCA, where no thought was even given to national recognition, the sport of racquetball now has over 11 million competing players. The largest growth period in the development of racquetball was from 1976–1979, when participation in the sport increased 283 percent. Racquetball seems to have plateaued in the early 1980s, with about a 5–6 percent increase in players per year. During this time the market has been flooded with new, more sophisticated equipment, better courts, more advanced players, and many new publications. Racquetball has settled in as one of America's favorite leisuretime activities. The development of sophisticated racquetball clubs has helped spawn more enthusiasm and interest in racquetball participation. (The one area in which racquetball has not developed is in the mass media market, especially television.) Clearly, racquetball is here to stay, and it is great to be a part of it both as a player and a contributor to its players.

CHAPTER 2
Selecting Equipment

Even though much specific information is included in this chapter on equipment, four general rules dictate equipment selection. First, equipment selection should be based on each individual's own preferences. Second, it should be based on the type of play—the power or touch with which you play. Your equipment purchase should also be based on your racquetball skill level and on the style of your play, including movement patterns, shot selection, and other variables.

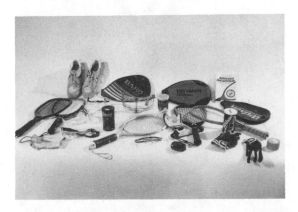

Figure 2-1. The racquetball market is flooded with a variety of equipment

Equipment is constantly being changed and improved. Many new items of equipment will be on the market before this book appears in print. If you use the information provided in this chapter and purchase with sound reasoning, you will obtain usable, quality equipment that fits your needs.

Racquets and Grips

With the growth of any sport come major changes in equipment employed in that sport. Initially the racquetball racquet was made of wood and was not aerodynamically designed. The first racquets were heavy, bulky, non-flexible and club-like compared to the sophisticated racquets used today. In selecting a racquet, you must consider size, grip, shape, price, manufacturer, weight, material, prototypes, and string qualities. Each of these considerations is very important in selecting the racquet best suited for your type, style, and level of play. The selection of the racquet must also be considered as a financial investment. So, consider each of these factors as you decide on the racquet that is right for you.

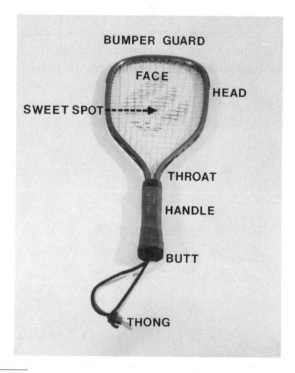

Figure 2-2. Racquet terminology

Size

The rules of racquetball stipulate that the total length and width of the racquet may not exceed 21 inches. Today's racquets normally vary in length from 17-3/4 inches to 21 inches. Everything else being equal, the longer the racquet the more power and reach you have, but you lose some amount of control with a longer racquet. The variance of one and one-quarter inches does not make an appreciable playing difference for most beginning- or intermediate-level racquetball players, but it does significantly affect play at the advanced level. Today's oversized and midsized racquets are still in the neophyte stages of development. Playing with a larger racquet has many advantages, as seen in tennis, but it is still too early to comment on the future of oversized racquets. The most important aspect of racquet size is the size of the grip (the circumference of the grip measured in inches and fractions of inches). Newcomers to racquetball have a tendency to select a racquet with too large a grip. In tennis, large-circumference grips are employed for helping maintain wrist stability. However, in racquetball, which employs major wrist action, a smaller grip size should be used. Racquetball grip sizes range in inches from three and eleven-sixteenths (super small), three and fifteen-sixteenths (extra-small), four and one-eighth (small), and four and five-sixteenths (medium) to four and one-half (large).

The surest technique to determine your grip size is to use different racquets of varying grip sizes until you can select the size that feels best to you. A rule of thumb is that a smaller grip is best for individuals who need extra power and who have a small- to average-size hand. Generally, the smaller your racquet grip, the more flexion-rotation, or wrist-snap, you can obtain, thus increasing your power. The proper grip size is important

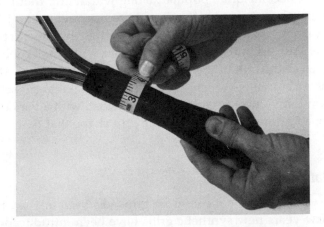

Figure 2-3. Measuring the grip size

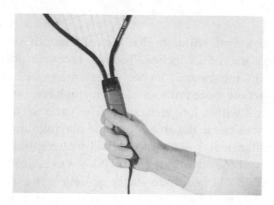

Figure 2-4. The correct grip size as indicated by the position of the middle finger and the base of the thumb

in controlling your racquet. An improper grip size can cause the racquet handle to turn in your hand, bringing about a loss of control.

Grip Shapes

The basic shape of the racquetball racquet grip, as in most racquet sports, is equal in circumference from the top of the grip area to the butt end of the grip, where a raised end section affords a resting stop for the side of the hand. The purpose of the raised or knurled butt-end is to enable the hitter to keep better control of the racquet by stopping the racquet from sliding out of the hand.

With the increase in innovative ideas in the fast-growing racquetball industry, the grip has been subject to change, and now there are a variety of new grips. A flared grip that is narrower at the top and wider at the base has become quite popular, along with a grip that is bent at an angle so that the racquet head is in a more natural position. If they are not yet available, soon there will be grips with finger indentations, grips with larger knurled butts, and probably grips with small rubber stabilizers attached to the butt of the handle to help absorb shock. All these innovations are currently available in other racquet sports to meet the needs of different individuals. Again, hit a racquetball with a variety of differently shaped grips in order to find the grip shape that best suits you as a player.

Grip Materials

Over the years the basic material for grips has been leather, but within the last few years new synthetic grips have been introduced. The new synthetics have all the qualities of leather and are marketed as being less affected by perspiration than leather so they can be gripped more tightly and provide more control without slippage. In both quality leather and quality synthetic grips, a tacky or sticky feeling is quite important in racquet control because it affords a firmer grip with the fingers and hands. Usually, the less expensive the grip, the less tacky the grip feels. The rubber grips on the market do not compare favorably with leather and synthetic grips. Leather grips should be made of top-quality leather and should be perforated with small holes to increase absorption of perspiration.

Grips may either be flat or have raised ridges spiraling around the handle. The raised spiral gives the hitter a rougher surface to grip, which allows for a firmer grasp on the racquet. One problem with the raised spiral is that it can be worn down by players who are consistent with their grips. Thus a worn pattern develops on the spiral and, if the player does not get his or her fingers into the worn grooves when changing grips, the grip may be uncomfortable and difficult to control. Some players, however, prefer the raised spiral grip, and many are beginning to use a self-made gauze

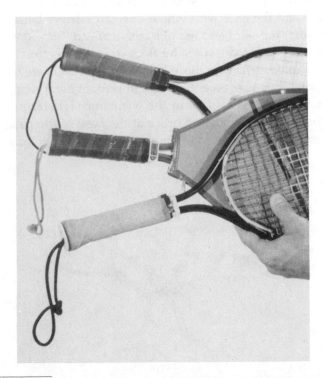

Figure 2-5. Three types of grips. Top to bottom: smooth, spiral, and gauze.

or tacky wrap on their handles that provides a super-tacky grip. The gauze or tacky wrap can be purchased in tennis and racquetball shops. One problem with the tacky wrap is that it increases the circumference of the grip, which may be a negative factor for some individuals. If you buy your grip smaller than usual, then you can build it up with the gauze or tacky wrap.

Shape

When racquetball first began all racquets were oval- or round-headed. Today, many differently shaped racquets are available, but most racquet heads fall between teardrop and rectangular shapes. The head shape determines to some degree the location of the center of percussion, or sweet spot, size and shape of the sweet spot, flexibility of the racquet, torque of the racquet, and the ease with which you can retrieve balls along the walls.

Different head shapes (Figure 2-6), along with the other factors listed in this chapter, dictate the actual state of the majority of these factors. Head shape alone provides ease of retrieving balls along the wall (wallpaper shots) and the ease with which one can retrieve balls low to the floor. The flatter the sides and top of a racquet head, the more string surface the player can get closer to the floor or wall; therefore, the player gets more racquet surface on more balls when the balls are hugging the walls or floors. The most recent change in racquet head shape concerns string patterning and is evident in the wishbone-style racquet head. In the wishbone design there is no brace at the base of the head, and the strings extend almost down to the handle of the racquet. This design of

Figure 2-6. The transition of racquets

elongated strings and more string surface changes control, flex, sweet spots, and racquet torque.

Price and Manufacturer

As racquetball has become more sophisticated so has the equipment. Today the manufacturing of racquetball racquets has become a science. The Ektelon manufacturing company has done more for the scientific refinement of the racquetball racquet than any other. Ektelon was the first company to manufacture only racquetball equipment, and they helped develop the production of sophisticated racquets greatly. There are a large number of brand-name companies, including Ektelon, D.P., AMF-Head, AMF-Voit, Marty Hogan Racquetball, Omega, Richcraft, and Wilson that offer a wide selection of quality racquets. Other companies in the racquetball racquet industry produce only a few select racquets, such as Geostar, Olympian, and EST. All of these companies manufacture quality products.

There are also many companies that manufacture racquets with little emphasis on quality control and therefore sell their products much more cheaply than name-brand racquets. We suggest that you buy a brand name product to ensure that you have a quality racquet. However, we are constantly amazed to find top-flight open players using inferior quality racquets with great success. Prices vary greatly in a range from $20.00 to $200.00 for quality racquets. You can purchase other racquets from $5.00 on up.

Materials and Weight

The original racquetball racquet was wooden. Today, racquets are made of metals, such as steel or aluminum, or graphite-fiberglass-ceramic composites. Obviously, if you buy a racquet made of cheap material, the chances of its lasting for a reasonable length of time are slight. The life of the racquet also depends on how hard you hit the ball, how often you play, and how often you hit the walls and floor with the racquet. The harder and more often these practices occur, the shorter the racquet's life expectancy. To withstand the constant impact of the ball hitting the racquet and the racquet hitting the walls and floor, quality aluminum racquets should be in the 5,000-, 6,000-, or 7,000-series grade.

The extruded form or special shape into which the aluminum is molded gives strength to the aluminum and thus to the racquet. There are I beam, H beam, A beam, channel, flat channel, and flat I beam extrusions on the market. If you were to cut through the aluminum in a racquet head, the cross-section would be in the design shape of the extrusion process, such as H-shaped or I-shaped. Titanium is a lightweight, strong metal similar to aluminum that is used successfully in a few racquets.

The graphite-fiberglass racquets have cornered a large portion of the racquetball market. These racquets are actually composite racquets, meaning that they are made from two or more products rather than from just one product. Graphite has become very popular because it is exceedingly strong and lightweight and can be stiff or flexible depending on the materials with which it is combined. Graphite racquets are quite expensive. Some of the materials that are mixed with graphite are fiberglass, boron, Zytel, Kelvar, nylon, ceramic, and carbon. Your individual preference will determine whether to buy a metal or a composite racquet. Most of the qualities of each material can be manufactured into other materials, thus metal or composite racquets can be made to be durable, flexible, or stiff, and light or heavy.

Racquet weights have changed drastically since the beginning of racquetball. The racquetball racquet has become progressively lighter, and today racquets weigh from 230 to 285 grams. A range of 230 to 245 grams is considered a light racquet, 245 to 260 grams is a medium-weight racquet, and above 260 grams is a heavy racquet. In general, the lighter the racquet, the more control a player has, but with decreased weight some power is lost.

The balance of the racquet is also an important consideration when purchasing a product. Most racquets are balanced evenly from the head to the handle, but some are heavier in the head. A head-heavy racquet gives the hitter more power, but it also takes more strength to control the racquet. As long as the material is of high quality your choice should be based upon personal preference.

Figure 2-7. Metal and composite racquets

Prototypes

As racquetball has become more popular, racquet designs have been developed. The shape of the racquet head is constantly changing, string designs with the wishbone frame have changed the hitting surface and new string density and design patterns have been developed. Racquet handles have been changed too; new grips such as the hourglass-shaped grip and angled handles have been introduced. The grip itself has undergone many changes. New synthetics available that absorb perspiration are sold in a variety of colors and textures. The throat area of the racquet, designed either with no brace, with a floating brace, or with some differently shaped brace, has been given much attention in the racquet industry. The first oversized racquets have been introduced. These are some two inches longer and three inches wider than standard-sized racquets, providing over 30 square inches more hitting area with little added weight. Also available are ceramic composite racquets with strong, lightweight ceramic strings that absorb shock exceedingly well.

As racquetball continues to grow, new prototype racquets will constantly be on the market. Most of these new racquets are untested over long periods of time. Many prototype racquets have come and gone during the past decade. The player must understand that each manufacturer is attempting to gain a portion of the equipment market by introducing a new racquet, so don't assume a prototype racquet must be an improvement. Find out how other players who have used the new racquet feel about it, and try to play with the prototype racquet to see how it feels before you purchase it. The player can also ask racquetball pros their opinions about a new racquet.

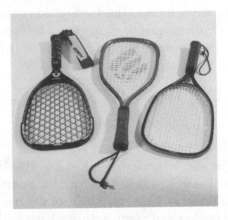

Figure 2-8. Different string patterns. From left to right: Geodesic, Wishbone (Sunburst), and Normal.

String Characteristics

Strings, like other parts of the racquet, have undergone much change. Strings are made from either nylon or gut. Strings with special textures, thicknesses, and resiliency are designed specifically for racquetball. Gauge indicates the thickness of the string; the higher the gauge, the thinner the string. Most racquets are strung with 16-gauge strings, the best hitting resiliency for most racquets. Nylon strings take many forms, from standard monofilament to graphite-impregnated to square strings. Gut strings, which are made from the intestines of cattle, pigs, and sheep, have changed little over the years. Gut strings give a different rebound action on the ball than do nylon strings, and gut strings are much more expensive. The string material that is best suited to your game should be determined by your personal preference.

Stringing patterns have changed from the standard, evenly spaced vertical and horizontal string pattern to an infinite number of new patterns, including geodesic string patterns, wishbone patterns, sunburst patterns, and denser stringing patterns on part or all of the string surface. Once again you must play with racquets designed with these new stringing techniques before you decide which type and design of string pattern to buy.

String tension is also an important factor for the player. Racquetball racquets are generally strung at a much lower poundage than tennis racquets. The lower range of string tension is 18 to 22 pounds, and the higher range of string tension is 23 to 34 pounds. Normally, all other factors being equal, the looser the strings the more power and the less control the player has in hitting. Because of different head shapes, racquet designs, racquet materials, string designs, and string materials, the optimal string tension will vary from racquet to racquet and from player to player. For example, certain racquet designs call for lower string tension than others solely because of the design.

Balls

Racquetball design has also gone through changes during the last ten years but has now been standardized. Pressurized, nonpressurized, vividly colored, and multicolored balls, and balls of different textures have all appeared on the market, but manufacturers have settled on a blue, nonpressurized ball. A nonpressurized ball obtains its bounce from the rubber from which it is made, rather than from air pressure within its hollow core.

Racquetballs must meet official standards of size, bounce, and weight, and these standards should be indicated on the package. Although many lesser-known racquetball brands still circulate on the market, Penn, Ektelon, AMF-Voit, Ram, and Wilson are the leading manufacturers of racquetballs. Penn racquetballs are the standard of the industry and are used most in tournaments. All of these leading manufacturers produce quality products. Balls usually sell for $3.00 to $5.00 for a can of two.

Gloves

The racquetball glove has gained a large section of the market as an integral piece of sports equipment. When shopping for a racquetball glove, you should look for two major qualities: finger style and the material from which the glove is constructed.

You have a choice between partial-finger or full-finger racquetball gloves. Some players prefer partial-finger gloves because they can grip better and can get a better feel on their grip when the fingers come in contact directly with the grip of the racquet. Others prefer full-finger gloves because the purpose of the glove is to keep the hand dry and to prevent blisters, and they feel partial-finger gloves do not afford the dryness or protection of a full glove. If you are going to play serious racquetball you need a glove; which type to select is up to your individual taste.

The second major consideration in glove selection is the material from which the glove is made. Originally gloves were made only from cowhide,

Figure 2-9. A variety of gloves

but it was found that cowhide gloves got stiff very quickly from the salts in sweat and they could not be washed effectively to rid them of these salts. Next the deerskin glove, which stayed supple longer and could be washed, was marketed. Deerskin racquetball gloves are still a leader in sales. A few companies are making gloves with other leathers such as goat skin and pig skin, but the only real challenge to deerskin seems to be coming from the synthetic materials currently being used in manufacturing racquetball gloves. A synthetic suede leather that is soft, does not stiffen as readily from salts, and can be washed is now on the market.

When washing a glove use a mild soap and lukewarm water and wash the glove by hand. Rinse your glove thoroughly a number of times and then allow it to dry flat on a towel or similar absorbing surface. Sometimes it is helpful to slip the glove onto your hand to form it to your hand before it totally dries. Remember that after you wash your glove it will never feel the same or be as soft as when it was new, but it will usually be better than it was before washing.

When you buy a racquetball glove, choose one that forms to your hand and fingers. It should be neither too tight nor too loose. The glove should have tucked-in seams for comfort, and all seams should be reinforced in the stress areas at the finger base and the back of the hand closure. Almost all gloves have large velcro closures, and these are excellent. Another important feature you need to look for in a glove is the amount of ventilation it affords to the hand. Look at the back and the fingers of the glove to determine if holes and/or mesh are provided for air to get to your skin.

You have a choice of various glove colors and various glove manufacturers from which to pick. A few of the better-known racquetball glove companies are Champion, Trophy, SAI, Saranac, and Ektelon. The price range of a glove varies from around $8.00 to about $16.00. A glove is essential for the serious player, so take some time in the selection process. If you can borrow and try different types of gloves from friends, do so. Hitting with a glove to see how it feels and grips is the best method of determining which is the best glove for you.

Shoes

Over the last few years the racquetball shoe industry has peaked, and there are fewer shoes on the market today than before. The racquetball shoe is designed especially for quick starts and rapid changes of motion. In order to serve this purpose, the shoe must have gum rubber soles and reinforced uppers to withstand great forces. Shoes should also be light-weight and have well-built insoles and midsoles. The uppers may be made of nylon, nylon mesh, or leather. The leading manufacturers of racquet-ball shoes are Adidas, Bata, Brooks, Converse, Envoy, USA, Foot-Joy, Pony, and Tred-2. The price range of racquetball shoes is usually between $27.00 and $40.00.

Shoe fit is very important. Of course, as a potential shoe buyer you cannot test the shoe by playing racquetball in it; however, you can wear the socks to the shoestore that you would wear when playing, which will give you a truer sense of fit. You can also run, stop, push off, and change directions rapidly to assess the shoe in the store. Most racquetball shoes maintain their size and will not stretch after you play in them, so "if the shoe fits, wear it" is a good policy to follow. All racquetball shoes are durable if worn inside on court-type floors. If the racquetball shoe is worn on a rough surface, such as macadem, the sole will wear out quickly.

It is a good idea to walk (inside) in your new shoes for a few days be-fore playing in them. When you do go to the court, it would be helpful to take your old shoes and some adhesive bandages with you in case you get hot spots and blisters. Even with quality new shoes the stress from racquetball's sudden and quick movements can cause foot problems. It might be a good policy to play in new shoes for one game and then switch to your old shoes as a preventive measure.

To enhance your best playing and to keep injuries to a minimum, do not wear other sport-specific shoes when playing racquetball. A running shoe, tennis shoe, or other sport specific shoe is designed for its own sport, not for racquetball.

Figure 2-10. Shoes, shoes, and more shoes

Eyeguards

Eyeguards should be worn by all racquetball players. Most clubs provide eyeguards on request, and many clubs require eyeguards to be worn by all players. There are many types of eyeguards on the market today, and they can be divided into three basic groups: open plastic guards, closed plastic guards, and full-faced guards for those players who wear glasses. According to many articles and research investigations, the safest guards are the closed-lens plastic ones. The investigations state that with direct frontal impacts from balls traveling at speeds of as low as 40 miles per hour, open guards allow the ball to penetrate into the eye socket. These reported findings have stopped some players from wearing open plastic guards. However, because open plastic guards are the most readily available and also the least expensive, many players wear no eyeguards in lieu of the expense and unavailability of the other types of eyeguards.

The problem with the research findings is that all are based on direct frontal impacts, which very seldom happen in racquetball. The majority of impacts to the eye area are glancing blows, and the open eyeguard affords good protection from glancing blows. Open eyeguards are not foolproof, but they are certainly better than no eyeguards at all. The closed plastic and the full-faced guards also afford excellent protection for the eyes. The problem with closed guards is that the lenses get dirty and scratched, and perspiration forms more readily around the eyes, creating some visual acuity problems. Most open eyeguards range from $6.00 to $10.00, and most closed and full-faced guards range from $10.00 to $30.00. However, cost should be of little concern for preservation of eyesight. An eye injury can be devastating, and, in the case of high-speed racquetball, prevention is worth everything.

Miscellaneous Racquetball Accessories and Equipment

Although you might be interested in purchasing one or more of the racquetball accessories listed in this section, it is important to note that none of these items is necessary for playing successful racquetball. They are just what the title suggests—accessories.

An item that some players like is the wrist tether, which serves two basic purposes. It is a sweatband and a means of comfortably attaching the thong of the racquet to the wrist. The concept is sound, and some players prefer the wrist tether to the racquet thong alone attached to their wrists.

If you are interested in a racquetball mechanical throwing machine there are a few on the market. If you are taking lessons you might consider the availability of a throwing machine to speed up your skill acquisition. The machines are very accurate, and the trajectory and force with which they propel the ball can be adjusted. Two machines currently available are the Racqueteer and the Lob Ster. These machines are similar to the tennis ball throwers that have been on the market for a number of years, and they give constant, accurate throws. These machines are expensive, however, so check if they are available for members' use at your racquetball club.

If you are working on hitting skills you might consider a racquetball hopper that will carry your racquetballs and be helpful in retrieving the balls. These are especially useful if you are going to hit a large number of balls before retrieving them. The hopper allows you to pick up loose balls efficiently.

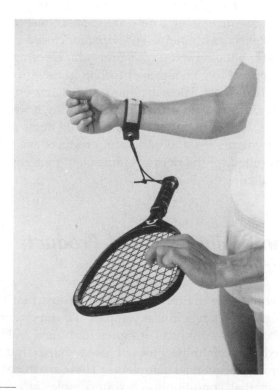

Figure 2-11. The wrist tether

Another racquetball item that is used by many players is a carrying bag for clothes, racquets, and other playing gear. Some carrying bags are designed solely for racquetball, but you may choose to purchase a general sports bag. A few major characteristics to look for in a carrying bag are size, shape, number of compartments, and construction techniques. Obtain a bag large enough for all the items you are likely to carry; think in terms of seasonal changes and warm-ups. Carrying bags come in a number of shapes, but the tube shape is probably the most common today. The compartments within a bag are important for organizing your gear as well as for keeping wet items away from other items (in a separate waterproof area) and for housing your racquet. All carrying bags should have reinforced construction around the seams and the handle area stress points. Other points to consider when you select a carrying bag are color, ventilation, type of handle or straps for carrying, and closures. Do you need a shoulder strap, handles, or both? Do you want a zippered or velcro closure?

There are some other unique racquetball accessories on the market that we will mention just to give you an idea of how many new products continually appear on the market. There are special small towels for use in the courts, a wrist score keeper, a lens wiper for closed eyeguards, a key ring with clips for hanging wet gloves from your carrying bag, grip grabbers that are applied to give a tackier feeling to the grip, and matching headband-wristband sets. There are many other items on the market that are specifically designed for racquetball, including a whole line of racquetball clothes, but these previously mentioned items should give you a sense of the uniqueness and variety of products available. Clothing, as long as it is suited for the rigorous movement patterns of racquetball, is an individual choice.

Fitness and Injury-Related Products and Equipment

With the great increase in fitness concern and now that many racquetball courts are part of a larger fitness complex, it is important to have some knowledge about those products designed for fitness and injury that relate to racquetball. Weight machines of many shapes and sizes are now available in many racquetball complexes. These machines are excellent to use for racquetball conditioning. If your complex offers both machine weights and free weights, try them both. Machines are safer, but they afford less balance work than do free weights. Machines also enable the participant to obtain a quick workout in a short time period, whereas free weights are more versatile but usually require longer workouts.

The marketplace is also flooded with new nutritional items. Vitamins, natural foods, special drinks, proteins, and diet supplements are available at most racquetball complexes. These nutritional items can be beneficial as long as you take them as directed. The typical club player probably obtains all of the needed nutrients in his or her everyday diet, so these supplements are not actually necessary.

With the general increase in sports participation, and the specific increase in racquetball participation, comes the increased awareness of injury in the sport. Various supportive devices such as elbow and wrist bands, ice bands, ankle and knee braces, and many more items are available to the injured player. As far as most of the supportive apparatuses are concerned, it would probably be best to buy these only if your physician or orthopedic surgeon recommends them to you. Most supportive items are very expensive and many offer nothing but a psychological value.

This is just a small sampling of accessories and products that are available to the racquetball player. Many of the products mentioned have merit and are very practical, but you must also remember that all these products are on the market to make money. With this in mind the racquetball consumer should carefully investigate any claims made by any product manufacturer before buying the product. The product-accessory market will continue to expand and grow as long as racquetball continues to be an important fitness-related sport in this country.

Figure 2-12. Big money even in the racquetball injury business

Keys for Selecting Racquetball Equipment

- A smaller grip size, rather than a larger grip size, affords better control and power for the player.
- Hitting with a variety of racquets and grip sizes is the best method of determining the correct racquet and grip size for each individual player.
- A racquet with flat sides and top makes it easier to play balls hugging the wall and floor because you can get more of the racquet surface closer to the ball.
- Buy brand name racquetball products because these items are of quality construction and thus are a better investment.
- Lightweight racquets are more advantageous for the control player and heavyweight racquets are more advantageous for the power player. The light racquet can be maneuvered more easily but the heavier racquet imparts more force on the ball.
- Be aware and use caution when purchasing any ''new'' product on the racquetball market. Remember new products are introduced to make money, not because they have proven qualities.
- Use lower string tension for more power and tighter strings for more control.
- Eye injuries are a risk in racquetball. Wear eyeguards!
- Wear a racquetball glove to prevent blisters and to keep perspiration off your racquet hand. Purchase gloves without full fingers if you want to have more feel on your grip.
- Wear sport-specific racquetball shoes that enhance your movement skills and prevent injuries. Do not wear other sport-specific shoes when playing racquetball (e.g., running shoes).

CHAPTER 3
Selecting a Racquetball Facility

You may very possibly have only one racquetball facility in your area. Thus your decision on where to play may be based solely on the availability of courts. However, you might have some choice between commercial clubs, either private or public, YWCAs and YMCAs, local college courts, or a private noncommercial court.

If possible, choose a racquetball facility by visiting facilities and asking questions about the club. Talk to employees and club members to find out what they have to say about the facility. If you know someone who is a member, talk with him or her before you visit the club. From this point on your selection will probably be based on your individual needs and wants. There are many factors to consider in selecting a place to play, and this chapter will discuss the ones to think about before making a club membership decision.

Your first major decision is whether or not to join a club solely for racquetball or to look for a club that provides other ingredients and offerings along with racquetball. Some facilities cater to nothing but racquetball players, and others cater to persons seeking a wide range of fitness and socially oriented activities, including racquetball.

Selecting a Facility Strictly for Racquetball

Some of the major considerations for selecting a facility solely for racquetball include cost, courts, waiting time, tournaments, and instructor-pro availability. Cost concerns include the size of the initial membership fee—a one-time payment when first joining—and that of the yearly, semiyearly, or monthly membership fee as well as court-time fees. The type of court and court accessories should be a major consideration in your selection process. Type of construction, such as panel walls, block walls, wood walls, cement walls, and glass walls, makes a difference in ball rebounding and general play. The amount of time one needs to call in advance or to wait for court availability is also a factor in considering facility selection.

Cost

The cost for each facility may vary from club to club. Initiation fees can run from $100 to $1000 and up, and yearly fees might be in the $200 to $500 range. Court-time fees might range from $2.00 an hour per person to $10.00 an hour per person. Court fees also vary with time of day and day of week, so you need to have an idea of when you will be playing most of your matches. Evening and weekend court fees are usually higher than morning-afternoon and weekday fees. You should also consider other cost items such as instructor-pro fees; guest fees; service fees for towels, hair dryers, and locker rental; tournament entry fees; parking fees; and discount-cost factors for family and/or group memberships. If your club is professionally managed, the more you pay, the more benefits you receive. Various clubs are managed differently, however, and it is in your best interest to check cost factors closely before selecting a club.

Type of Courts

Panel walls give the most consistent rebounding patterns if they are installed properly. You can check the seams between panels and the screw hole plugs on each panel for flushness by running your hand over the faces of the panels. If the faces of the panels and the seams of the panels are smooth you will get consistent rebounding action on the racquetball. Block walls and cement walls deteriorate more rapidly than other wall construction. Look for small holes and cracks that will give inconsistent rebounding to the racquetball. Wood walls are uncommon, but if you encounter wood courts, check for flushness of the individual pieces of wood. The more flush, the more consistent is the rebounding action of the ball. Glass walls are very nice and very expensive to install. It is also very difficult to visually follow the rebounding action of the racquetball in a glass-walled court.

The floor surface is also important, and usually you will have to choose between a wood or synthetic floor. Wood floors seem to be much more amenable to racquetball movement patterns than synthetic floors. You can slide much more easily on wood floors than on synthetic floors and because sliding is important in racquetball playing, wood floors are preferable.

Several aspects of court lighting should be considered, including total illumination of the court, spot brightness problems, glare problems, and light color. Checking total illumination involves being sure that there is ample lighting in the court as well as equal lighting in both the front and the back sections of the court. If the court is not well lighted or is not consistently lighted throughout, you will have trouble visually following the racquetball as it moves through the court. Spot brightness and glare go hand-in-hand because each deals with lighting in a specific spot or spots within a court. Spot brightness involves one area being excessively bright. For instance, if you look into the lights on the ceiling and they are so bright that you lose sight of the ball, this makes for poor playing conditions. Glare, or excessive brightness, on the floor or walls can also interfere with your watching and following the racquetball in a game situation. Light colors vary with the type of lighting system employed in the court. Fluorescent lights give a white light, incandescent lights give an off-white light, metal halide lights give a bluish to pinkish light, and sodium lights give a yellowish light. Lighting color is a matter of individual preference. However, if your court has a distinct hue to it, you may have difficulty adjusting to other courts with other lighting systems when you play in tournament competition.

Court ventilation is very important to control moisture and odor. If ventilation and construction are not adequate, moisture forms on the walls and the courts become unplayable. When the racquetball hits the moisture spots, it becomes too fast and too erratic to play, thus making returning the ball during the rally impossible. Proper ventilation also keeps the court cooler so that perspiration is minimized and wet spots on the floor caused by drips of sweat are prevented that might otherwise create both ball bounce inconsistencies and slippery spots for the players' feet. A well-ventilated court also keeps playing conditions comfortable by preventing the air in the court from getting too hot and stale. One other moisture-related condition to check for is leakage problems in the courts. Water leakage in the courts causes the same problems as moisture from improper court ventilation. You don't want to have to cancel indoor racquetball playing time because of rain.

A few other items to look for in courts are the use of glass on the walls for viewing and instruction purposes and the flushness of all edges such as door jambs, light fixtures, and air vents. Unflush surfaces make for erratic play. The location of vents and doors is also important; vents should not be in the ceiling close to the front wall where they would impede accurate ceiling shots, and doors should not be on the sides of back walls near the corners because corners are where most balls should be ultimately hit in rallies. A last item to consider is the availability of equipment storage either inside or outside of the court for your warm-up clothing, extra racquets, and/or valuables. With the cost of equipment and clothing today you cannot afford to lose too many racquets, warm-ups, *or* wallets because of insufficient and unsafe court storage areas.

Playing on Glass-Walled Courts

At one time or another most players will play on a glass-walled court. The most common glass wall design is the back wall followed by the side wall. Either the total wall or just a portion of it may be glass. There are also two- and three-walled glass courts and some courts with front glass walls. Almost all of these glass walls are tempered glass ranging from one half to five eighths of an inch thick. Some clear polycarbonate plastic-walled courts also exist.

The first major difference in playing on a glass-walled court is that you need to concentrate on the ball even more than when playing in courts with other types of walls. Playing on a glass court is much more difficult because it is easier to be distracted by people, your own reflection, ball reflection, and losing the ball in the darker glass wall. Further, the ball has a tendency to grab and slip on glass. Most racquetball players anticipate where a ball will end, but on glass walls you cannot anticipate—you must be patient and wait until the ball leaves the glass and then react to it. So two major adjustments are required when you play off glass: Your concentration needs upgrading, and you must wait for rather than anticipate the angle of the ball's bounce. Depth perception can also be somewhat altered when looking into the glass. Beginners have more problems with glass wall surfaces than do advanced players.

Different strategies should be used for playing in courts with different glass walls depending upon the location of the glass wall. In a court with a back glass wall, force your opponent to look into the glass. Hit drives, ceilings, lobs, Z serves, and around-the-wall shots. On front wall glass, use drives, cross-court shots, and down-the-line passing shots. Don't play the ball high or low on the front glass wall because you lose the effect of the differentiated background. On one glass side wall play serves and shots to that glass wall. Hitting pinch shots and splat shots into the glass has a tendency to momentarily freeze your opponent, so take advantage of that freezing action. If you play on two- or three-glass-sided courts, go for the corners with pinches along with down-the-line passes. Some players like to use cross-court shots to make their opponents follow the ball off and on to two-glass walls.

If you are going to play on glass take some time to practice on glass in order to learn to concentrate, be patient, and become familiar with how the ball plays off glass. Your aim should be to take advantage of the glass play and the busy backgrounds behind the glass to make the glass a disadvantage to your opponent. When you walk into a glass-walled court your strategy should be to make use of the glass to your advantage and not to allow the glass to be a hindrance to you.

Time

With today's fast pace and limited amount of time for lunch and exercise breaks, quick court occupancy is paramount. Can you call the morning of the day that you wish to play or do you have to call a week in advance? How long you are allowed to play at a given time should also be taken into consideration. For example, if you have 1 hour in which to play racquetball at lunch time, can you be assured of obtaining a court at your allocated time in order to ensure a full hour's play or must you wait 10 or 15 minutes before you can play? Also, will you have to quit playing in the middle of a tight game to allow the next waiting players to move onto the court? All of these questions concerning time should be answered to your satisfaction before you select a racquetball club.

Tournaments

The tournament offerings a facility affords are certainly a consideration in the selection process. Does the club afford regular tournaments in-house, and do they sponsor state, regional, and national tournaments? Does the club provide tournaments for all players—for novice or C-level to open divisions? Are there tournaments for women, seniors, masters, and children? Are there doubles and mixed doubles tournaments, and does the facility provide a challenge court(s) for club members? If so, when is it available?

The cost effectiveness of the answers to the tournament questions might be an important consideration in your club choice. For the tournament-oriented player the membership cost may be offset by being able to play in large numbers of tournaments. For the beginning player the cost of membership and court fees may be prohibitive since the beginner will play in only a few or no tournaments.

Professional Instruction

The last major area of concern in the court selection process would be to determine the availability of instruction from the club pro. Is there a pro, is the instruction good, is the pro's background strong in racquetball? Are modern teaching aids such as ball machines, videotape units, and computer analysis available? Is there an extra cost for lessons, and, if so, what are the prices?

All of these questions deal directly with selection of a facility in which to play racquetball only. Since many racquetball players are looking for other aspects in a club we will now discuss some other items to consider in club selection. Some of the following items might seem unimportant to some racquetball players, but it must be remembered that with such a great number of players of all levels a wide variety of diversified non-playing interests become evident.

Selecting a Club for Purposes Other Than Racquetball

Other important fitness attributes of the club complex concern the availability of specialized areas, such as free weights, machine weights, swimming pools, and jogging tracks. Instruction in these areas as well as sessions in aerobic dancing, jazzercize, yoga, and self-defense are integral aspects of the development of an individual fitness program. You may wish to check whether the instructors and fitness director are trained specialists with backgrounds in physical education or exercise physiology. Does the club offer complete physiological fitness testing for its members, and, if so, is there an additional cost for this service?

Relaxation is another prime reason why individuals select a club. Is there a whirlpool, sauna, Jacuzzi, steam room, suntan booth, background music, and a large screen TV? What type of food services are provided (such as snack bar, full-fledged restaurant, juice bar, regular bar, or health food area)? Eating or dining at a club is a great way for many people to relax.

One might also look closely at the pro shop, the selection of equipment it has to offer, when it is open, and the availability of the club pro for consultation in purchasing equipment. You should also ask about the other programs the club offers for family activities, singles activities, child care, celebrity appearances, clinics, equipment rentals, and parking. Two final items contributing to your club choice are the policies of the club and its cleanliness and upkeep. What are the policies concerning signing in, guests, membership cards, locker-room services, and general management attitude toward members? Cleanliness and upkeep speak for themselves, and these are areas in which clubs differ greatly. To some racquetball players general club cleanliness is important, although to other players this is not of paramount concern.

The selection of a club should be made carefully, over a period of time, so that when you do join the club it will provide the majority of items that are important to you as an individual, as a player, and as a club member.

Keys for Club Selection Checklist

Check those items that are important to you as a prospective club member and then see how many and to what degree your needs can be met at a club. First decide if you are looking at clubs specifically for racquetball or also for other club activities and offerings.

_____ Courts (including number in the area, condition, type, lighting, and ventilation)

_____ Cost (including fees for courts, instruction, membership, and guests)

_____ Availability of instructor-pro

_____ Competent instructor-pro

_____ Swimming pool (including depth, diving area, lap swimming, and temperature)

_____ Aerobics and aerobic dance instruction and programs

_____ Instruction and participation available in:

_____ handball _____ squash _____ wallyball _____ yoga _____ weight lifting _____ self-defense _____ jazzercize _____ heavy hands _____ other areas

_____ Availability of fitness equipment including:

_____ track _____ free weights _____ machine weights _____ stationary bicycles _____ treadmill _____ hydrostatic weighing tank _____ others

_____ Locker-room services and conditions (including locker types, size and location, towel and laundry policies, and the availability of soap, hair dryers, shampoo, and other cosmetic paraphernalia)

_____ Relaxing atmosphere including:

_____ whirlpool   _____ steam room   _____ sauna   _____ music _____ large screen TV   _____ suntan booth   _____ others

_____ Tournaments held at club

_____ Social activities including:

_____ wet bar   _____ restaurant   _____ snack bar   _____ juice bar _____ family activities   _____ singles activities   _____ others

_____ Health food availabilities

_____ Pro shop (including hours, equipment, rentals, and instructional tips)

_____ Clinics offered in a variety of activities

_____ General cleanliness and club upkeep

_____ Availability of child care

_____ Parking conditions (including amount, extra cost, and proximity to club)

_____ General club policies

_____ Attitude of management to club members

_____ Other specific individual needs (you list)

_____   _____   _____

CHAPTER 4
Safety, Warm-Ups, Injuries, and Conditioning

Racquetball players should concentrate on preventing injuries, rather than treating them. Preventing injury requires attention, good judgment, and thorough preparation. Using protective equipment, wisely selecting a racquet, and applying common sense and courtesy on the racquetball court are all simple means of preventing injuries. This chapter will focus on a variety of measures you can take to avoid common racquetball injuries.

Safety

Common injuries in racquetball are eye injuries from being hit by a ball, body injuries from being hit by a ball or a racquet, ankle and foot injuries such as sprains and blisters from stopping and starting, elbow injuries from racquet vibration, and lower back pain from bending repeatedly.

Eye Safety

Eye injuries are often caused by getting hit by the ball or by the opponent's racquet. The key to reducing the number of eye injuries is to wear some form of eyeguard. Eyeguards offer some needed protection against both ball blows and racquet blows.

If you have read any recent commentaries on eyeguard studies, you might think that *not* wearing eyeguards is as good as wearing some of the eyeguards on the market. For example, a student recently went to a local sporting goods store to purchase a pair of open-type eyeguards. The salesman said that, although he had the open-type eyeguard, he would not sell one to the student because he had just read an article stating that open eyeguards do not stop a ball from doing eye damage. Was the salesman right or wrong? Let's discuss the various types of eyeguards and their safety properties.

A number of laboratory experiments have been used to test the safety of various types of eyeguards. A mannequin wearing the eyeguard being studied would face a ball machine throwing racquetballs at it from a given direction and with a given velocity. Almost all of these studies concluded that open eyeguards cannot prevent eye damage from a direct frontal hit by a ball with a speed of 40 miles per hour or more. Because almost anyone can hit a ball at that rate, should open eyeguards be removed from the market? No, they shouldn't. Unfortunately, all of the studies examined the results of direct frontal impacts. How often in racquetball would you get a direct frontal hit from a ball? The answer is very few times because most ball blows are glancing. Either the head is moving slightly or turning as the ball hits or else the ball is coming from an angle as it strikes. As a result, even open eyeguards afford a great deal of protection. They

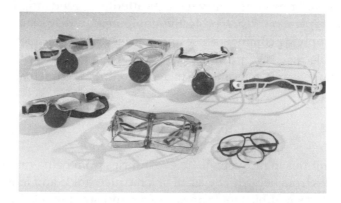

Figure 4-1. Eyeguards—your decision!

are not foolproof but they will protect against most glancing ball blows—and, to repeat, most ball blows in racquetball are glancing blows.

Hinged eyeguards were also tested. The studies reported that hinged eyeguards have a tendency to break under impact with resulting eye injury caused by plastic or metal pieces of the guard imbedding in the eye. Most of the studies recommend that racquetball players wear one-piece, closed-lens eyeguards. These are fine but they are more expensive than open eyeguards, and perspiration tends to get on the lenses.

We recommend wearing one of the various types of eyeguards without hinges. If you wear glasses you can obtain cage eyeguards to wear over them. A warning: Don't wear your glasses in place of eyeguards. Eyeglasses are hinged and are probably not made of polycarbonate, the strong plastic from which most eyeguards are constructed.

You may know some top players who do not wear eyeguards and wonder, "Why should I?" Failure to use eyeguards is *their* problem. If your eyes are important to you, wear some type of eyeguard whenever you step into the court. You should also remember that beginners are more likely to be hit by balls than either intermediate or advanced players because beginners have little control over their shots, and the nonhitter is often out of position. These two factors make it even more important for the beginning racquetball player to wear eyeguards.

As you advance in skill you will be turning your head more often to watch your opponent get set for his or her shot so that you can get a jump on the return. Here are a few safety hints on turning to watch your opponent. First, turn only your head, not your whole body, and turn it only far enough to see your opponent. If you were to get hit, this strategy ensures that you would receive mostly glancing blows. Second, you can help shield your eyes with the forearm on the side toward which you turn. As your head turns, you should raise your arm and keep your forearm parallel to the ground. Your forearm becomes an extra eye shield as you watch your opponent play. Take care of your eyes; they cannot be replaced at any cost.

Body Safety

Another very common injury in racquetball is the laceration or bruise caused by being hit with your opponent's racquet. This should never happen if both players are thinking about safety and courtesy on the court. Scoring points in a game is not worth being hit or hitting someone with a racquet. When you know your opponent is nearby, either let up on your swing, which might include the follow-through as well as the backswing,

A

B

Figure 4-2. Two methods of securing the thong: (A) Twist method, (B) Slip knot method

or stop your swing altogether, call a hinder, and replay the point. Don't swing recklessly when you know your opponent is nearby.

You must also remember always to attach the racquet thong to your wrist so that the racquet will not fly out of your hand and hit your opponent. Wearing a racquetball glove also helps to keep a good grip on the racquet. But if your glove gets wet, you should replace it with a dry glove immediately.

Another important safety item is to switch to a slower swing when attempting to play a ball that is close to the wall or in a corner. Think of a sweeping or scraping action rather than a hitting action. This will pre-

Figure 4-3. Oops—Get out of my way! Brumfield and Peck (Courtesy Racquet ball Illustrated)

vent injuries caused by your racquet rebounding off the wall and hitting you and will also eliminate stress on your arm from a hard, direct racquet-wall impact.

Try to stay out of your opponent's way not only with your racquet but also with your body. Once again, prevent collisions before they occur. Don't crowd or bump your opponent. If you plan ahead and anticipate a possible injury situation, you can select the proper movements to avoid injury.

Ankle and Foot Safety

Another major type of injury in racquetball is the ankle injury. One important precaution is to keep the court floor dry. If undue amounts of perspiration accumulate on the floor, take some time to wipe it up or change courts. If one of the players dives or falls on the court, wipe the floor with a towel and get all of the moisture up. Wet spots are one of the most common causes of ankle injuries on the court. Improper shoes also increase the risk of ankle injury. Don't wear running shoes or other sport shoes for racquetball; use a shoe designed specifically for racquetball. Refer to the equipment section in chapter 2 for more information about racquetball shoes.

If you know you have ankle problems, you might want to wear high-top shoes to give your ankles a little more support. Also, if you are just recovering from an injury or know you have a slight injury to your ankle, have your ankle taped with athletic tape by a knowledgeable taper. Don't use an Ace bandage ankle wrap instead of taping. An ankle wrap affords little protection to a weak or injured ankle. An ankle wrap, however, can be used like a high-top shoe to help prevent certain ankle injuries. If you should sprain an ankle, keep your shoe on until you can get ice on the injury and can elevate the injured ankle. Apply the ice and elevate the injured ankle immediately, keep your weight off the injured ankle, and have it X-rayed and attended to by a physician as soon as possible.

A less serious but rather incapacitating injury is the blister. Beginners who are not used to the continuous stopping, starting, and sliding movements of racquetball are prime candidates for blisters on the feet. Wearing proper shoes with two pairs of socks and keeping your shoes and socks dry will help prevent blisters on the feet. Foot powder can be helpful on the feet, between pairs of socks as well as in your shoes. Make sure your socks fit with no folds or creases, and don't wear tube socks. The lack of a heel makes the tube sock ride up and down. Your shoes need to fit properly—not too big or too small. Blisters are caused by the friction of the quick and powerful stopping and starting patterns of racquetball play. If you know you have a painful spot, pad it carefully with a Band-Aid, athletic tape, or "donut" pad or use petroleum jelly to help cut down friction on that spot. Eventually, callouses will form on your feet and you will not get blisters.

Blisters can develop on the racquet hand from the twisting and rotating of the racquet handle. Using a glove, Band-Aids, athletic tape, or donut pad can help to prevent blisters on the racquet hand. Check your racquet handle and grip to ensure that nothing out of the ordinary is causing the blister. Again, with more playing over a period of time your hand will become calloused.

Elbow Safety

Damage to elbows is another common racquetball injury. Common elbow injuries include inflamed or torn tendons and ligaments within the elbow joint. Hitting with a faulty technique, using an improper racquet, and hitting too hard for long periods of time can cause elbow injuries. The hitting technique problem can be corrected by bending your arm slightly on ball-racquet contact rather than having the arm fully extended or rigid upon contact. Remember, racquets vary in their flex, weight, and vibration. If you are having an elbow problem, try a racquet that is more (or less) flexible or lighter or that vibrates less than your current racquet. Finally, remember that you don't need to overhit on every ball.

This in itself will help save your elbow. Strong forearms will also help to alleviate many racquetball elbow problems.

If your elbow is injured, allow it to rest; if it is still painful when you resume play, rest it more. If it continues to be a problem, see an orthopedic surgeon for treatment.

Back Safety

Lower back problems are more prevalent among beginners and intermediate players than advanced players who are used to bending and staying low. When you are not accustomed to bending as you must do in racquetball in order to keep the ball low, you can put undue strain on your lower back and thus get lower back pain. There is not much you can do to prevent lower back pain other than bending and staying low as much as possible when playing racquetball.

Safety Playing Tips

Here are some other preventive measures you can take to help reduce racquetball injuries. Wear proper clothing in order to bend and move easily. Replace wet clothing and broken equipment, keep your shoes tied, and dry a wet ball. Always try to watch the ball. Control your emotions— don't throw your racquet or bang it into the wall; it may rebound and hit you or your opponent. As a receiver, don't hit fault serves and don't hit the ball out of frustration after the rally is finished; use good court etiquette. When you are close to the front wall, don't hit the ball as hard as you can; you may not have time to move out of the way of the rebounding ball. Be careful about hitting yourself with your racquet—think about what you are doing. Not only can it hurt and cause serious injury, but hitting yourself with the racquet is also downright embarrassing. Finally, two important safety measures in racquetball are to warm up sufficiently and to condition yourself properly.

Warm-ups

Warming up is an interesting phenomenon that is really specific to the individual player. Warm-ups can be considered as aiding performance or as preventing injury or both. The research on the benefits of warming up to improve performance is a little nebulous. Although some investigations have shown that warming up enhances performance, other studies have shown no difference in performance with or without warm-ups. Research has demonstrated that warming up stretches and actually warms the muscles because of an increase in blood flow to the muscles. Therefore, it makes sense to warm up to increase the elasticity of muscles and to provide increased circulation of blood to the muscles. This "warming" of the muscles can help to prevent muscle strain and certain injuries.

Because warming up is very specific to each individual player and specific sport, the types of warm-up may vary. Some players, for example, hit a variety of shots easily and then hit them progressively harder. Other players stretch, do calisthenics, run in place, or run around the court. Still other players do many different types of warm-ups.

Warm-ups may have psychological as well as physiological benefits. If the player *thinks* the warm-up is helping to improve skill performance, then it may actually improve performance. In any case, warm-up at your own pace. Do what feels good for you. Think about the forearms, shoulders, lower back, and legs as the prime movers in the skills of racquetball and incorporate these areas into your warm-up routines. Whether warm-ups are helpful physiologically, psychologically or both, they can benefit you and may help prevent injury.

Conditioning

Conditioning for racquetball, like any other sport, serves two basic functions. First, conditioning is a great way to prevent injuries, and, second, conditioning properly done can improve your skill level. Conditioning for racquetball should be specific to the skills and demands of the game. In considering conditioning for racquetball, analyze the basic movement and skill patterns of the game and condition accordingly.

Racquetball takes a great deal of energy and some degree of cardio-respiratory endurance. The skills that are used are varied yet repetitive; therefore, specific muscular endurance is needed. The major body parts involved in racquetball are the legs for bending, stretching, stopping, and starting; the arm, especially the forearm, for wrist action; and the shoulder for arm action in the backswing, swing, and follow-through. Those are the basic, specific body parts to think about in conditioning for racquetball. However, it is important to remember that many other areas of the body come into play in racquetball as in any other sport skill. Cardio-respiratory conditioning, flexibility, muscular endurance, skills training, and a strength and power program are all necessary.

Cardiorespiratory Conditioning

The cardiorespiratory phase of the program would consist of running, swimming, or bicycling, as well as playing racquetball, for long periods of time. In running, swimming, or bicycling, one may strive for distance alone or combine sprinting with distance work.

Flexibility

Flexibility can be attained and/or maintained by static stretching, that is, by stretching and holding the stretch position. Do not bounce when you stretch. Leg stretching, lower back stretching, torso stretching, and arm-shoulder stretching should be combined in your program.

Muscular Endurance

Muscular endurance specifically for racquetball can be attained in two ways. First, muscular endurance can be achieved by practicing the skills of racquetball. You can hit 100 ceiling shots, 100 kills, 50 Z serves, and so forth. Use both forehands and backhands because slightly different muscle groups are used for each technique. Hit the skills in succession. A second way to attain muscular endurance is through weight training. In lifting weights for endurance you should do 3 to 5 sets of 12 to 15 repetitions each. Later in this chapter we will give you some specific weight training exercises to be used for racquetball.

Skills Training

Racquetball skills can be enhanced by practicing each skill either in strict practice sessions or in game situations. You should make sure to include both in your conditioning program. It becomes very easy only to play practice games and never, or rarely, to practice just the skills. You need to do both. Both are specific, and you cannot attain total skill conditioning with one without the other.

Strength and Power

The last aspect of specific conditioning for racquetball is strength and power, two of the major concerns of all racquetball players. The best way to increase strength and power is to offer resistance to your muscles over a distance or through a range of motion. This is the basic "overload" principle, and weight training can best complete this portion of your conditioning program.

Let's look first at the legs. Squats are excellent for the legs. Do them at an even pace and do not bounce when you are fully squatted. Leg extensions and leg flexions on a leg machine work very well on both upper and lower legs. The leg press on a weight machine is similar to the squat exercise and gives a good workout to the upper front of the leg. Toe raises also help to build the calf area of the lower leg.

Next, let's look at some shoulder weight-training activities. Any type of press, including the military and bench press, is excellent for shoulder development. Pull-ups and dips, on a pull-up bar or parallel bars, are also very good exercises for the shoulder. Bicep curls put significant stress on the shoulders, so they should be included in the racquetball conditioning program.

An important part of the weight-training conditioning program for racquetball is the development of the forearms. The forearms control the wrist and finger actions. Strong wrists and fingers are a necessity for playing racquetball well. The hitting wrist action involves all three major muscle groups in the forearm: the flexor muscles on the inside of your forearm, the extensor muscles on the back of your forearm, and the rotator muscles on both sides of your forearm. A weight conditioning program for the forearms must develop each of these three muscle groups. Dumbbells or barbells can be employed in prone and supine wrist curls. The supine wrist curl (flexors—flexing the wrist) and the prone wrist curl (extensors—laying the wrist back) adequately develop these two sets of muscles. Wrist rotation muscles can be strengthened by using dumbbells in the supine position and rotating the dumbbell inward and back to the starting position. Bicep curls significantly stress the forearm, so they serve a dual purpose for both shoulder and forearm conditioning.

We mentioned lower back and ankle problems in the safety portion of this chapter. Here are some conditioning tips that can help prevent these problems. For the lower back, lie flat on your back with arms on the floor, palms down, and feet flat on the floor with the knees bent. Reach and grasp one knee at a time and pull the knee toward the chest. The knee always stays bent. After doing the same with the other knee, you can pull both knees simultaneously to the chest. Remember, knees stay bent throughout this exercise. The ankles can be strengthened by doing toe and heel raises with the body weight or with weights. Stand erect, roll up to your toes, hold, and then do the same onto your heels. You can also rotate your feet in, out, up, and down and hold. You can do this exercise sitting or standing; however, the standing position puts more stress on your ankles. These exercises can be done with foot weights when sitting.

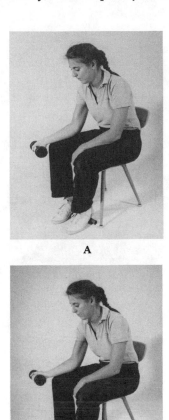

A

B

C

Figure 4-4. Supine dumbbell curls for wrist flexor development

A

B

Figure 4-5. Supine barbell curls for wrist flexor development

A

B

Figure 4-6. Prone dumbbell curls for wrist extensor development

A

B

Figure 4-7. Prone barbell curls for wrist extensor development

A

B

Figure 4-8.   Wrist rotation dumbbell curls for forearm rotator development

Figure 4-9. Rolling a rope for forearm development

Weight training for strength should consist of three sets of five repetitions each. These routines are done with the maximum weight in order to barely complete the three sets of five. Finishing with any activities for the forearms and fingers such as rolling a rope, fingertip push-ups, finger wrist curls, and squeezing exercises can round out your program.

A new weight-training concept called "periodization" has recently proven to be an effective strength-gaining regimen. It is basically set up with three weeks of doing three sets of five repetitions each, three weeks of doing five sets of ten repetitions each, and one week of three sets of two repetitions each. In each period maximum weight is employed in order to just barely complete the routine. With periodization, after the seven weeks of training, you take a week off and then you begin all over again. One desirable aspect of periodization technique is that it can build you to a peak. For example, if you begin training seven weeks prior to a tournament, you peak for the tournament. The program encompasses both strength and endurance.

Diet and psychological conditioning are also important dimensions of a racquetball conditioning program. Your diet should be well rounded with the proper intake of vitamins, minerals, carbohydrates, fats, and proteins. With a well-balanced diet, no supplements need to be taken.

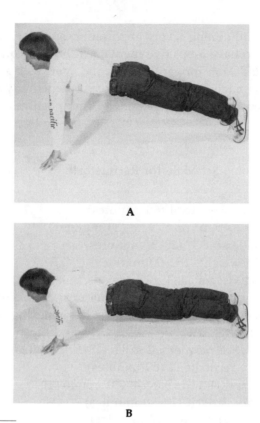

A

B

Figure 4-10. Fingertip push-ups for finger and forearm development

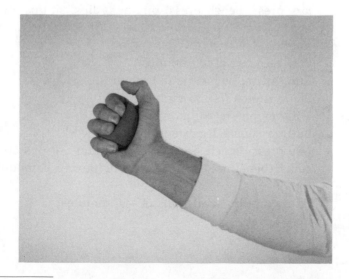

Figure 4-11. Squeezing a racquetball for finger and forearm development

Psychological conditioning is very important to successfully play racquetball. You need to have a positive mental set. First, racquetball is something you should look forward to. Second, you will play better with positive mental imagery and enjoy your sport whether you win or lose, whether you are practicing or playing. Think positive.

Sample Conditioning Schedule for Racquetball

Monday	Play racquetball (60 minutes)
	Run, swim, or bicycle (30 minutes)
	Static stretch (20–30 minutes)
Tuesday	Lift weights (60–90 minutes)
	Include: squats, leg extensions, ankle work, bicep curls, military press, bench press, pull-ups, dips, sit-ups on incline bench (bent knee), and wrist work (flexing, extending, and rotating)
	Practice racquetball skills (45–60 minutes)
Wednesday	Play racquetball (60 minutes)
	Run, swim, or bicycle (30 minutes)
	Static stretch (20–30 minutes)
Thursday	Lift weights (60–90 minutes)
	Include: squats, leg extensions, ankle work, bicep curls, military press, bench press, pull-ups, dips, sit-ups on incline bench (bent knee), and wrist work (flexing, extending, and rotating)
Friday	Play racquetball (60 minutes)
	Run, swim, or bicycle (30 minutes)
	Static stretch (20–30 minutes)
Saturday	Lift weights (60–90 minutes)
	Include: squats, leg extensions, ankle work, bicep curls, military press, bench press, pull-ups, dips, sit-ups on incline bench (bent knee), and wrist work (flexing, extending, and rotating)
	Practice racquetball skills (45–60 minutes)
Sunday	Off—Rest

Keys for Safety and Conditioning

- Wear eyeguards at all times when playing racquetball.
- Don't swing when your opponent is in your way.
- Keep the court floor dry.
- Wear proper shoes and socks.
- Employ warm-ups that meet your own personal needs.
- Use conditioning exercises to prevent injuries and to increase your racquetball skill abilities.
- Include cardiorespiratory, flexibility, muscular endurance, skills routines, and strength and power in your training program.

CHAPTER 5
Players and Criteria for Determining Your Level of Play

Four major criteria for determining your level of play in racquetball are sex, ability, age, and experience.

Sex

Like most new sports, racquetball was played at the outset predominantly by men, and women players were much less visible than their male counterparts. Women players are now beginning to make major inroads into the world of racquetball. Women players such as Shannon Wright-Hamilton, Lynn Adams, Karen Walton-Trent, Heather McKay, and Jennifer Harding have achieved world-class ranking. The visibility of women's racquetball has been enhanced by the founding of the Women's Professional Racquetball Association (WPRA). More women's tournaments are being held than ever before, and divisions for women have been established in tournaments that were previously all male.

In many tournaments with women's and men's divisions, the women are not subdivided according to level of skill as are the men, but we hope to see this change very soon. In addition, many racquetball clubs are now catering to women players with women's in-house tournaments and challenge courts. Some clubs employ a woman as the club pro.

In racquetball, as in most other male-dominated sports, activities for women have been slowed due to the societal dominance of males in sports. Socially, men have been dominant in racquetball since its beginning; consequently, more men play racquetball than women and are, therefore, much more visible. As more women realize how much fun racquetball is to play and how well skilled they can become, this trend will change, as it has with tennis. Fortunately, mixed doubles allows women and men to compete together on an equal basis, providing more social interaction and showcasing the skills of women players.

Figure 5-1. Heather McKay and Lynn Adams, two top ranked women players (Courtesy Racquetball Illustrated)

Ability

For racquetball tournaments and most other playing conditions, the participants can be rated according to their level of skill and ability. In recreational games, players normally play with a friend of similar ability. In general, racquetball players are divided into novice-beginners, C-players, B-players, A-players, open-players, pro-players, and instructing pros.

Novice and Beginning Players

The novice is a beginner and, therefore, a wide range of skills can be found in this class of player. The novice has little court sense regarding deflection and rebound action of the ball, especially out of the corners. He or she may not understand the importance of center court positioning and usually does not knowingly attempt to hold center court. The beginning player has some knowledge of the rules of racquetball but little insight into the strategies of the game. As a result, many balls are played high, and the player does not consistently bend low. In addition, the novice player lacks the patience to wait on the ball; as a result, overhand shots are prevalent. Because they are unaware of how to stroke the ball with full power, beginner's shots are usually hit with slow to intermediate speed. Novices tend to follow the ball with the body rather than with the eyes, and they seem to spend a lot of time running around the court.

C-Player

The C-player is an advanced novice who has some knowledge of the passing shot, the kill shot, and a few serves. He or she attempts to employ strategy on occasion but is seldom consistent in using strategy. The C-player kills inconsistently, hits fairly good passing shots, is beginning to perfect one good serve, and does not follow the ball with his or her body as often as the novice. Some low shots, as a result of bending the body properly, are evident. The C-player is developing an understanding of strategy and center court importance and can sometimes put these into play. However, patience is still lacking, and the ball is played high too often. The C-player is beginning to understand rebounding and angles in the court; in addition, he or she is learning to hit the ball hard but seldom with control of power shots. The C-player can employ ceiling shots with some effectiveness, and the high-level C-player can kill the ball fairly well on the forehand shot when positioned in center court or front court.

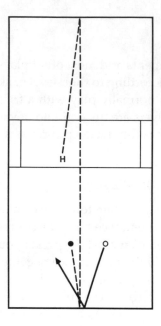

Figure 5-2A. "C" player following ball flight with the body and not the eyes

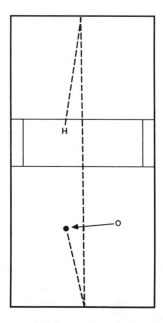

Figure 5-2B. "A" player following ball flight with the eyes and not the body

B-Player

He or she is beginning to look like a racquetball player. The B-player uses a lethal kill shot on the forehand fairly consistently. The passing shot is effective, and the ceiling shot is well played, especially on defense. The B-player understands strategy and uses it about 75 percent of the time although correct use of strategy remains inconsistent. Although the importance of center court is understood, and the B-player attempts to maintain center court position, he or she relinquishes it often. The B-player understands and can react to most angles and rebounds on the court. The backhand is consistent but only occasionally used as an offensive weapon. The B-player keeps the ball lower more consistently than the C-player but still hits some high shots by mistake. The B-player possesses one excellent serve and two or three other less effective serves. Patience is developing at the B-level, and this player hits many shots with power and is consistent with more than half of them.

A-Player

When you reach the A-Division, you are talking about the well-rounded player. The A-player may lack total consistency and may not be able to use all of the minor shots in his or her game as part of an effective offense. But the A-player is very patient and keeps the ball low, and his or her kill shots are lethal on both forehand and backhand strokes. In addition, passing shots are effective from all areas of the court and are a consistent part of the offensive game. Ceiling shots are employed effectively for both offense and defense. Strategy is used effectively most of the time, and short mental lapses occur rarely. Center court position is constantly strived for and maintained whenever possible. The A-player hits the ball with power and authority on all strokes and possesses a wide variety of effective serves. The A-player demonstrates mastery of all basic skills on all strokes (refer to Figure 5-2B).

Open-Player

The open-player is the advanced A-player and displays all of the skills one could ask for in racquetball. All shots can be used for offense, the ball is always hit crisply, and center court position is maintained. Backhands and forehands are equally excellent. Strategy is used continuously and effectively. The open-player is fluid, consistent, and practically error free. In order to win points against the open-player, an opponent needs to hit with perfect placement, otherwise the ball is returned.

Pro-Player

The pro-player is an open-player who possesses the maximum in consistency, experience, hitting power, and precision hitting skills. Although only a handful of individuals are capable of playing at this level—the touring pros—we do have a large number of teaching "pros" at racquetball clubs. These club pro-players may vary in skill from the B-level to the open level. The label "pro" may be more a part of the job title than a description of playing ability. However, a true professional should possess a high A-level of playing ability as well as a thorough knowledge of the game, including both skill and strategy, and should be an effective teacher of all phases of the game. In addition, the pro should have a thorough knowledge of equipment, courts, personalities, and current events in racquetball.

Instructor

Instructors should have the pro-player's knowledge and understanding of the game whether or not they can play at the professional's level. The instructor should be extremely effective in imparting racquetball skills and strategy to students at all levels of play. He or she must master a variety of teaching methods and be thoroughly familiar with the latest racquetball teaching aids, including audiovisual equipment and video tapes, while maintaining good rapport with club members. The excellent instructor should embody the characteristics of any good teacher.

Handicapped Player

Racquetball is so versatile that people young and old, healthy or handicapped can play. Sometimes the rules may need to be slightly altered to accommodate the handicap, such as allowing two bounces, yet racquetball remains a fun game. This section focuses on how racquetball can be played by people with handicaps and by people of different ages.

Racquetball can be played and enjoyed by handicapped individuals whether the handicap is permanent or only temporary. The permanently handicapped player must modify his or her game, shots, and strategies based on the degree of limitation of the handicap. Before beginning to play racquetball, you should check with your physician and, working together, determine what limits should be set on your style of play. Individuals with visual, auditory, and ambulatory handicaps can and do play racquetball. The retarded, the emotionally disturbed, the heart patient, and other individuals with various permanent handicaps can play racquetball if they adjust the game so that it falls within their capabilities and the limits of their handicap. An article in the December 1981 issue of *Racquetball Illustrated* describes Marcia Nave, a young woman who plays racquetball two or three times per week even though she has lost one leg to cancer. She plays without crutches and has the courage to move, balance, and stroke the ball effectively in spite of her handicap.

The temporarily handicapped individual can also play racquetball if the game is adjusted. It is possible that you may not play competitively in tournaments or in recreational competition with a temporary handicap but you may hit in an attempt to keep semiactive. During a supposedly sedentary period, you should receive permission from your physician to participate. This author has played racquetball during two short periods while recovering from surgery, while recuperating from elbow surgery, and three times when a leg was in a cast. He even won a small local tournament while playing with a walking cast. You may need to modify much of what you are doing on the court, but you may be able to be somewhat active.

Age

Age is an important factor in designating racquetball skill level. Let's consider the special characteristics of very young players as well as those of the elderly racquetball enthusiast.

Children

A question the coauthors are often asked is when should children begin playing the game of racquetball? The key is to expose children to the racquetball court and racquetball game early. Begin when they are between 2 and 7 years of age. The important word is *exposure*. A child should see the court, the game, and the equipment and then be allowed to experiment on his or her own. If a child enjoys the new racquetball environment, he or she should be encouraged to continue to hit and play.

Racquetball should be like any other activity in the child's life at this point. The parents should not apply pressure to play racquetball or any other sport. If an activity is fun, children should pursue it at their own pace. You must remember that children from the ages of 2 to 12 years progress through various stages of physical development. These developmental stages will partially determine whether or not a child is ready to handle the complexities of a physical skill such as racquetball. You should also bear in mind that these stages of physical development occur at different times in different children. A developmental stage necessary for learning certain skills in racquetball might occur at age 8 in one child, age 12 in another, and at age 6 in still another child. Parents and/or instructors should not compare their child's skill level, ability, or interest with that of other children of the same age. Interest and skill proficiency are individual matters at this stage of the child's life.

Movement exploration can be very helpful for the young child. Also, exposure to a variety of types of balls, including large and small balls, soft and hard balls, and balls of various colors and textures, is important to the young child. A wide selection of different kinds of balls allows the child to choose what is fun to play with. The same is true with racquets. You should provide smaller, lighter, plastic, colored, bigger, and other different kinds of racquets for the child to experiment with. At early ages, whether preschool or early school age, drilling on forehands, serves, and the backhand should not be done. Allow the child to bounce the ball high and low, to hit it soft, hard, low, high and to different walls. Have the child stand facing forward, sideways, and backwards when trying to hit the ball. Let the child hit the ball after it bounces or experiment with playing the ball in the air before it bounces.

Permit young children's questions and attempt to answer them on their own level. Once interest is shown you can use simple activities such as

Figure 5-3. Let the child have some fun with racquetball!

relays, tag racquetball with yarn balls, multibounce racquetball, and many other fun games. Self-tests such as "How many times can you hit the ball in a minute?" or "How many times can you hit the front wall with the ball in 30 seconds?" can be fun for young children. As the child continues to show interest in racquetball, modified games or lead-up games can be added to the progression of skills. Play one-wall or two-wall games, games with multiple bounces, and games with different balls. You can design many racquetball lead-up games that are fun and beneficial for kids. But remember that each child progresses at his or her own level, from exposure to exploration to low organized skills to modified games. This understanding is very important for the "parent-instructor."

When the child is ready for competition and asks to compete, then the competitive aspects of the game should be introduced. Even at this stage, a child should not be pushed into hours of drills and practice sessions. Young players should play and progress at their own level, not at the level at which the parent-instructor wishes them to play.

If you expose your children to racquetball, listen to and answer their questions, and allow them to have fun with racquetball within safe limits, they will develop a healthy attitude toward the sport. In time, there is a good chance they will want to play racquetball as they grow into adulthood. Remember to let the young players progress at their own pace and to provide appropriate instruction when and if the young player shows an interest in competition.

The Older Player

Who is the older player? It could be someone over 30, over 40, or over 60 years of age. Children have developmental stages of skill levels, and adults have developmental stages of aging. Older players cannot, therefore, be classified categorically by age alone. However, one method of classifying older players is to analyze the older "new" player in comparison with the player who is older but has been playing the game of racquetball for many years.

The first recommendation for the new older player is to have a complete physical, including a stress test, before you step onto the court. If the examination and stress test indicate that you are healthy, you may slowly begin the adventure into the world of racquetball.

Slow and *cautious* are the two cornerstones for the *new* older player. Good long warm-ups and stretching are helpful to increase blood flow to the muscles and to stretch the muscle fibers. You must remember that as the aging process proceeds, circulation slows down, maximum heart rate decreases, and maximum oxygen uptake, probably one of the best indications of cardiorespiratory fitness, decreases. Arthritis is much more prevalent among older players and can create many painful joint problems. Therefore, take your playing slowly and do not overindulge. You should also be aware of the injury factor involved in participating in a new activity. One of the major problems experienced by any aging athlete is the recovery time it takes to get over any injury. As you get older, the rapid, "youthful" recovery from injury does not take place. Therefore, caution should be taken to do everything in your control to prevent injury and avoid the long recovery period. Conditioning, stretching, warming up, good diet, and knowledge of safety factors are excellent methods of helping to prevent injuries.

For the over-35 continuing racquetball player, the game includes a slower paced format, more strategy, and better shot placement. Tournaments have divisions for the 35-and-over (seniors), the 45-and-over (masters), and the 55-and-over (golden) age levels as well as various five-year intervals in between. Racquetball can be played indefinitely as long as the participant adjusts his or her game according to changes in the body due to the aging process. Some older players in their 40s can keep up with players in their 20s, and some players in their 60s can keep pace with players in their 40s. Both men and women can continue to be physically active throughout their lifetimes if they adjust their activity to accommodate the aging process.

A complete physical examination including blood profiles and a stress test is recommended every other year from 30 to 40 years of age and each year after the age of 40.

Experience

Your level of experience will help you decide what type of player you are. For example, whether you have played in tournaments or have had instruction can make major differences in your playing style. In addition, the quality of your opposition and the type and size of the court where you play also have some effect on how well you play. Moreover, the number of years that you have participated should help you to understand strategies, angles of ball bounce, and opponent weaknesses. It is important to try to experience as many different situations as possible—courts, opponents, tournaments, instructors, and play. Experience then begins to mesh with ability, and the longer you play and the more variety you encounter, the greater your levels of skill and strategy become, and the better player you become. There is really no substitute for experience, and this is true for most racquetball players today.

Keys for Determining Your Level of Racquetball Play

- If you are handicapped play racquetball under the direction of your physician.
- Handicapped players need to adapt and modify the game of racquetball to meet their individual needs.
- Employing skill drills rather than playing in game situations is an important modification of racquetball for the temporarily handicapped player.
- Allow children to progress in racquetball at their own pace.
- Allow the child's competitive spirit to emerge on its own.
- Older players should have a complete physical examination and stress test before beginning to play racquetball.
- Beginning older players should play racquetball slowly and cautiously, especially at first, to avoid undue stress and injury.

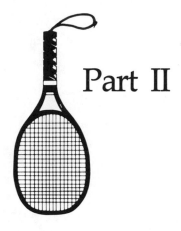

Part II

Skills and Strategies

CHAPTER 6
Forehand and Backhand Shots

As in most racquet sports, the two primary shots or strokes are the forehand shot, hitting from the side of your dominant hand, and the backhand shot, hitting from the side of your nondominant hand. Although these strokes are common in most racquet sports, the mechanics and wrist action differ from sport to sport, particularly in racquetball.

Basic Grips

A number of grips are used to hold the racquet in racquetball. The decision on which grip to employ is based on the individual player's preference and on body position and ball position in the game situation. The basic grips include the *eastern forehand*, the *eastern backhand*, and the *continental*. The grip should be comfortable and provide freedom of movement for the wrist, yet allow the fingers to hold the racquet tightly so that it does not turn in the hand.

For the *eastern forehand* place the nonhitting hand on the throat of the racquet with the racquet head lengthwise, in a vertical position to the floor, and reach down and shake hands with the grip. The butt of the

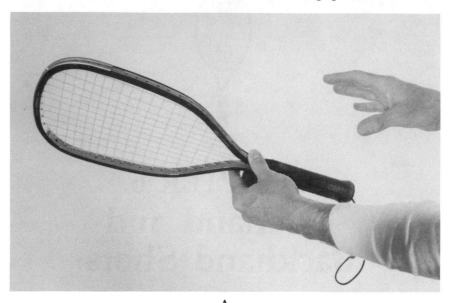

A

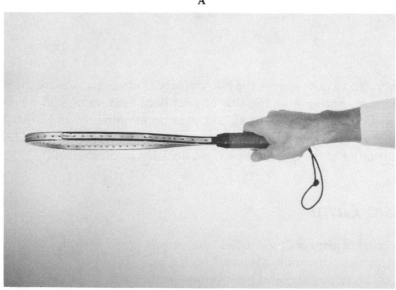

B

Figure 6-1. Assuming the eastern forehand grip

racquet handle is even with the base of your hand, and the *V* formed between the thumb and the index finger runs down through the top flat section of the handle. The fingers are usually together around the handle, although you may prefer to spread the index finger. Do not place the index finger behind the handle as a brace—your finger is not strong

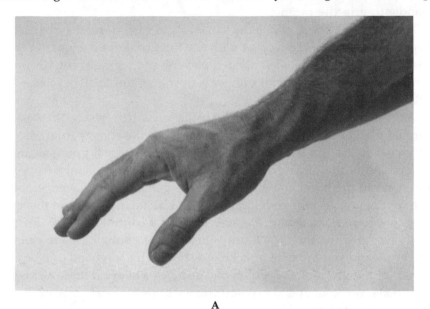

A

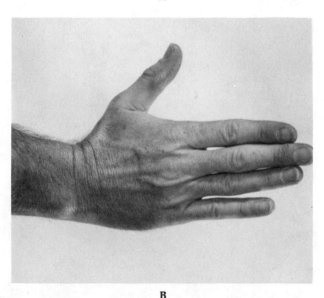

B

Figure 6-2. Two views of the "V" between the thumb and index finger

enough to brace the racquet even though the concept of a brace is good. You also lose control of the grip and get much more racquet rotation with the index finger used as a brace. The forehand grip can also be achieved by placing the hand, palm down, against the racquet face, which is held vertical to the ground, and then sliding the hand down the throat to the handle to grip the racquet.

The *eastern backhand* grip is the same as the eastern forehand grip except that you rotate the racquet with the fingers about one quarter inch to the right (to the left for left handed players) and regrip it. The *V* formed between the thumb and index finger is now over the small beveled edge of the racquet handle.

For the *continental grip,* grasp the handle anywhere *between* the eastern forehand and eastern backhand grips. Because the change from eastern forehand to eastern backhand is slight, the continental grip is actually a variation of the other grips. Although most players change from the forehand to the backhand grip during the game, some players employ the continental grip for both forehands and backhands because this grip does not have to be changed at any time. The continental grip is especially useful when time is a factor—there is not enough time to change the grip—and you must hit a backhand shot with a forehand grip or vice versa. Although using the continental grip helps to avoid these awkward situations, we recommend that you change grips for forehands and backhands whenever possible.

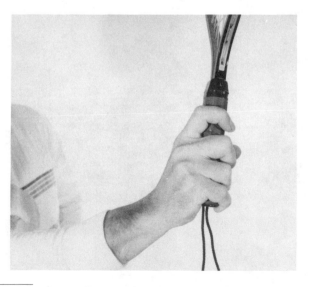

Figure 6-3. The eastern forehand grip with the spread index finger

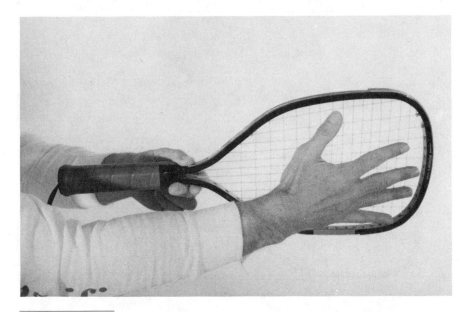

Figure 6-4. Assuming the eastern forehand grip by sliding the hand down the face of the racquet

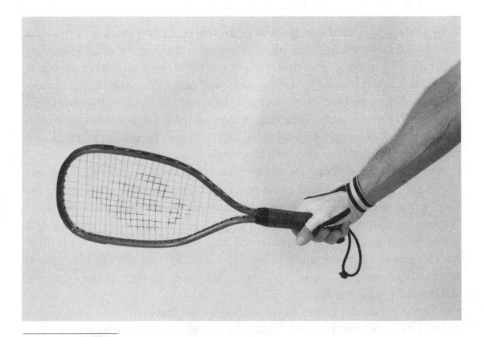

Figure 6-5A. The eastern forehand grip with a glove

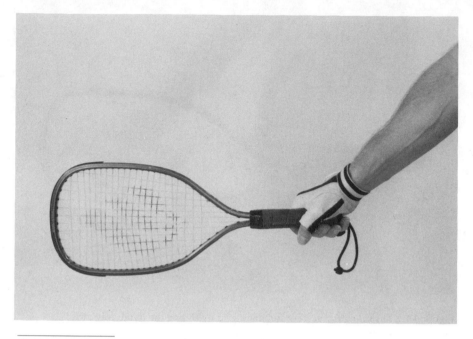

Figure 6-5B. The eastern backhand grip with a glove

Beginners may find it helpful to paint the palm and fingers of the grip hand with contrasting latex paint. Then grip the handle of the racquet, hold it for 15 seconds, and then release the hand. You now have a pattern on your racquet handle to use for the grip. After the paint dries, a backhand pattern can be placed, using a different color, over the forehand pattern. Having a pattern to grip is very helpful for consistently maintaining the correct grip on each hit. Tape can also be placed in *V*s on the handle as patterns for the correct grips.

Some players prefer to use a *two-handed backhand* because it gives them more racquet stability and more power. For the two-handed backhand grip, grasp the handle in the eastern *forehand* position and place the non-hitting hand above it in a forehand grip. The problem with two-handed grips is that you have a shorter reach and less power from your hitting hand because your leverage has been reduced. However, you gain power overall because the second hand is on the racquet—but at the cost of a decrease in your reach.

Some advanced players slightly modify the basic grip by sliding the small finger off the racquet. This allows the ring finger to rest on the knurled section of the handle. This grip increases power because it lengthens the hitting lever (arm and racquet) and it also increases the player's reach. A problem with this adjustment, however, is that a player must

RIGHT – HANDED PLAYER   LEFT – HANDED PLAYER

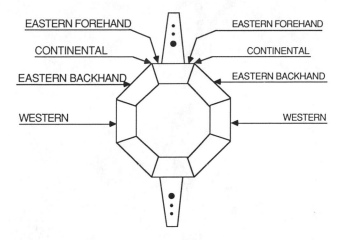

THUMB-INDEX FINGER "V" LOCATION FOR VARIOUS RACQUET GRIPS

Figure 6-6.   A composite for racquet grips. The western grip is no longer used.

have relatively strong fingers and forearms to grip the racquet firmly with only three fingers and the thumb on the handle. If you cannot hold the racquet comfortably with this modified grip, you should use all four fingers on the grip. However, if you can control the racquet with the small finger off the handle, this is an ideal grip to obtain an advantage in power and reach.

Basic Hitting Position

All sports allow for certain variations in the basic fundamentals to accommodate specific situations. Racquetball is no different. Information presented in this section of the book on the basic hitting position can be adjusted to suit a particular situation. We are attempting to describe the ideal position for most shots, the position that allows maximum power, fluidity, and control.

First, getting into the basic hitting position requires that you should *face a side wall*. Whether you are hitting a forehand or a backhand shot will determine which side wall you should face. Facing the side wall is of utmost importance because it is the foundation for the rest of the basic hitting positions. If you have a weak foundation, you can never construct a strong building—and it is the same with your basic racquetball hitting

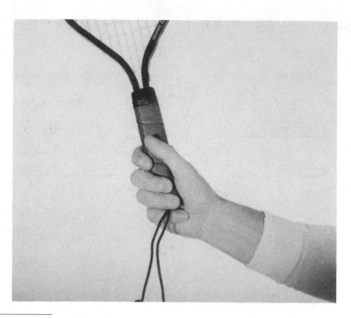

Figure 6-7. An advanced grip with the small finger off the handle

position. Facing the side wall means that your shoulders are parallel to the side wall. Of course, there are times during play when you don't have time to turn your whole body sideways, but even then you need to turn your upper body so that your shoulders are parallel to the side wall.

In the wall-facing position, you should be crouching slightly with knees bent and a slightly flexed abdominal area. Bending and flexing allows you to get lower to the ball and helps you keep the ball lower on the front wall.

The next part of the basic hitting position is the *full backswing* with the racquet cocked well behind your head. Bend the elbow of the hitting arm about 90 degrees in the backswing position. The racquet head is parallel to the front wall. The nonhitting arm is relaxed and pointed back during the backswing, and the nonhitting hand is near the racquet head. This is true for both forehand and backhand shots. When done correctly, the backswing position causes the upper body to rotate so that the shoulders become parallel to the back wall.

From the full backswing position *the hitting arm begins to move forward.* As the hitting arm moves forward, the upper body begins rotating forward and the cocked wrist begins straightening, and as the swing continues forward there is a slight lead with the hitting elbow. If you are hitting a forehand shot, the nonhitting arm comes forward and points to the front wall; this helps pull the upper body around more quickly.

A   B

Figure 6-8. The body is bent and low for the correct body crouch (A); an up-right and high position (B) is incorrect.

If you are hitting a backhand shot, the nonhitting arm follows the hitting arm forward but stays close to the body and helps pull the upper body around more quickly.

As the hitting arm comes forward to strike the ball, the arm is at almost full extension. When you make contact, the ball is opposite and in line with the lead hip. The wrist, which was cocked on the backswing and straightened on the forward swing, rotates and flexes at racquet–ball contact and is bent in toward the body.

As forward arm movement and upper body rotation are occurring, the body weight shifts from the rear foot to the front foot, transferring power into the racquet at impact. Normally the shift of weight takes place by stepping forward with the lead foot. This step is toward the front wall, and the lead foot should be angled toward the front wall at about 45 degrees. It should not be perpendicular or parallel to the front wall.

The last major part of the basic hitting position is the *follow-through* with the racquet. The follow-through should be full and slightly upward. Don't try to stop your follow-through; your body will naturally slow down your arm and stop your follow-through motion.

Throughout the basic hitting sequence, you are watching the ball and in position far enough away from the walls so that you can complete a smooth swing. Remember, you are moving very quickly as you perform

Figure 6-9A. The forehand preparatory phase: high backswing, elbow bent, upper body rotation, knees bent, weight on back foot

Figure 6-9B. The backhand conclusion phase: high backhand follow-through, upper body rotation, weight shift to front foot, proper use of non-hitting arm

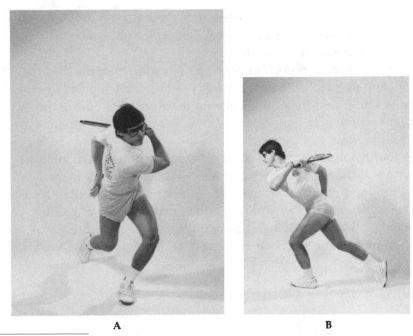

A   B

Figure 6-10. Two views of the forehand follow-through

the sequence of the basic hitting position, from facing sideways to follow-through. As soon as the shot is completed, you must immediately assume the *ready* position to await the next shot. Ideally, each shot you hit should look like every other shot until you contact the ball. If you can achieve consistency with the basic hitting position, you will have an advantage because it will take your opponent a little longer to react to your shot.

Power

The hitter needs to employ many sources of power to achieve maximum ball velocity. First and most important, you must be in the side position, facing the wall, in order to make use of all the power sources. Remember, power beginning in your legs is increased by the other aspects of the swing, but if your body is not in the side position, you cannot achieve maximum force on the ball. Assuming the correct position allows you to utilize both components of racquetball hitting power: overall body strength and the elements of the swing that maximize racquet speed.

The backswing and the follow-through are two essential sources of power. You need a *full backswing*, with a cocked racquet and bent elbow, along with a *full follow-through*. Remember that the follow-through stops naturally because of normal range of motion; do not consciously stop or shorten your natural follow-through.

A third source of power is upper-body rotation from the hip area. The shoulders are parallel to the back wall on the backswing stage of the hitting position, and they are parallel to the front wall during the hitting stage. Rotation of the upper body during this part of the hitting sequence is a major source of power.

A fourth source of power is the wrist rotation-flexion that occurs just before and during racquet–ball impact. Flexion-rotation is the bending and turning of the cocked wrist to achieve maximum hitting force as a result of moving the wrist through the greatest range of motion. Wrist flexion-rotation is exceedingly important, and as you advance in skill, wrist flexion-rotation becomes an ever greater source of hitting power.

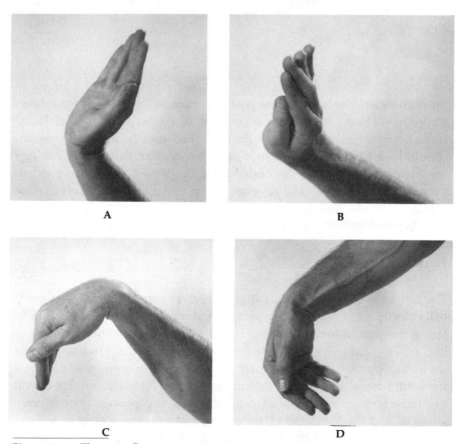

Figure 6-11.   The wrist flexion-rotation sequence

Shifting body weight by transferring the weight from the back leg and foot to the front leg and foot is yet another source of power. You can shift weight while hitting either by taking a step or by changing the point of balance from rear to front.

The sixth source of power is arm action during the swing. On the backswing the hitting arm is bent. As you bring the arm forward through the swing, the elbow leads slightly and then the arm fully extends at racquet–ball impact. The elbow lead and arm extension add power to the shot.

The legs play a role as the seventh source of power. Remember, at the start of the basic hitting position you are crouching with the legs bent, and when the racquet strikes the ball the legs extend. Extending and straightening your legs adds more body force to the shot. Normally, the front leg is partially extended, and the back leg is fully extended.

The eighth power source is the abdominal area, which is slightly flexed in the basic ready position. As the upper body rotates forward during the swing, the abdominal area straightens—an uncoiling action—and this also adds power to the shot.

The ninth and last source of power comes from the nonhitting arm. For both forehand and backhand shots, the nonhitting arm is back near the racquet in the backswing phase of the hit. For the forehand shot, the nonhitting arm comes forward and extends as the upper body rotates. As the nonhitting arm extends, it helps pull the upper body around farther, thus increasing upper-body speed and hitting power. On backhand shots, the nonhitting arm comes forward with the swing but stays close to the body and does not extend forward as in the forehand shot; during the follow-through, the arm stays bent across the chest.

To utilize the sources of power most effectively, all nine components must come together at racquet–ball impact. Failure to do this will diminish your total power supply.

Power Summary Chart

Backswing and follow-through	Full, bent-arm backswing with cocked racquet; full arm extension during follow-through.
Upper-body rotation	On backswing, shoulders rotated parallel to back wall; shoulders rotated forward during swing.
Wrist rotation-flexion	The wrist is cocked before impact; straightens, bends, and turns during impact.

(cont.)

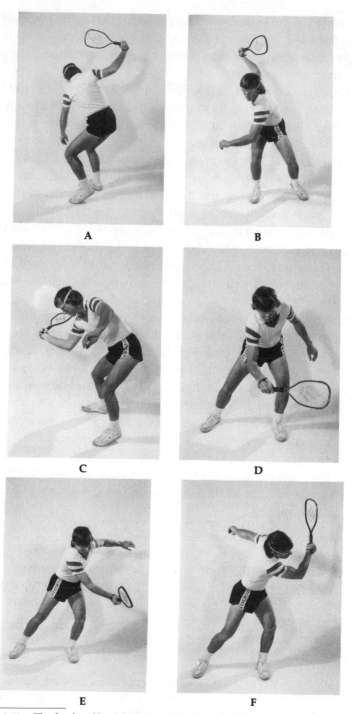

Figure 6-12. The forehand basic hitting position from backswing to follow-through

Power Summary Chart (cont.)

Shift of body weight	The weight shifts from the back leg and foot to the front leg and foot; take a step or shift point of balance from back to front.
Arm swing	The arm is bent during backswing; elbow leads and arm extends during swing and impact.
Leg extension	Both legs are bent in basic ready position; they extend and straighten during racquet–ball impact.
Abdominal area	Abdominal area is flexed in ready position; it straightens and uncoils as the racquet strikes the ball.
Nonhitting arms	On both forehands and backhands, the nonhitting arm adds speed to upper body rotation.

Keys for Grips and Basic Hitting Position

- Use the eastern forehand grip on forehand shots and change to an eastern backhand grip when hitting a backhand shot.
- Be sure that you have the correct grip and that your index finger is wrapped around the handle rather than extended up the back of the handle as a brace.
- Face a side wall when hitting the ball. If you are not facing a side wall, stop yourself and correct your positioning before your next shot.
- Hit from a semicrouched position.
- For hitting forehands the nonhitting arm should extend toward the front wall; on backhands the nonhitting arm should move forward close to the body with the swing.
- Use a full backswing and rotate the upper body so that your shoulders are parallel to the back wall.
- Make sure you are facing a side wall so that you can step forward and shift your weight from your back foot to your front foot as you hit the ball. Shifting your body weight is important.

Drills for Basic Hitting

Grip Drill

Purpose: To practice proper racquet grips and to obtain a feel of racquet–ball impact.

Directions: Stand anywhere in the court, use the correct forehand grip, and bounce the ball on the floor using the forehand face of the racquet. Bounce the ball waist high.

Variations: A. Employ a backhand grip and the backhand face of the racquet to bounce the ball waist high.
B. Use both forehand and backhand grips and bounce the ball up, rather than down, off the correct racquet face. Bounce the ball two to three feet high.

Basic Side Position Drill

Purpose: To practice the proper side-hitting position.

Directions: In a semicrouched position, stand facing the forehand side wall near the center of the court; drop the ball low (about six to twelve inches from the floor), let it bounce, and hit it to the front wall.

Variations: A. Stand facing the backhand side wall and drop and hit the ball to the front wall.
B. Stand facing a side wall near the back of the court and drop and hit the ball to the front wall using both forehand and backhand shots.

CHAPTER 7
Passing and Kill Shots

Two of the most common and effective shots in racquetball are the *passing shot* and the *kill shot*. Unlike specialty shots described in chapter 8, the passing and kill shots are hit with normal forehand or backhand strokes and are intended to end a rally. Your success with these shots depends upon how well you have developed the basic hitting skills described in chapter 6. If you have well-developed hitting position, swinging mechanics, and are patient, you will develop effective passing and kill shots. Simply hitting harder will not develop these skills.

Passing Shots

Of all the shots in racquetball the passing shot is the most versatile and is one of the two best offensive weapons in the game. Unlike the kill shot, where pinpoint accuracy is needed, you can hit a very effective passing shot even though it lacks perfect placement. Also unlike the kill shot, which ends a point without making your opponent run, the passing shot can end a point and it will have your opponent running to attempt to retrieve the ball. The properly employed passing shot, therefore, tends to wear down your opponents because it keeps them moving as they attempt to return the ball. The passing shot is also used to move your opponent out of center court into the backcourt so that you can gain center court advantage.

Shot Strategy

As the name implies, the passing shot is a shot that should go past your opponent. Because the passing shot is an *offensive* weapon, the strategy is either to win a point outright or to force your opponent to hit a weak return. Two factors that determine when you use the passing shot are your position in the court and your opponent's position in the court. Normally, passing shots are hit (1) when you are back and your opponent is forward, (2) when both you and your opponent are on the same side of the court, or (3) when you are on one side of the court and your opponent is on the other side. Passing shots are not usually tried when you are forward in the court although at times you can hit an effective pass from this position.

The passing shot has two elements: the ball goes by your opponent and it takes its second bounce before it ends up in a back corner. Although accuracy is very important, you must hit with enough speed to ensure that the ball goes past your opponent. The passing shot should hit the front wall approximately two to five feet from the floor so that the ball will take a quicker second bounce and will not rebound off the back wall into center court. If a passing shot strikes the front wall higher than this, your opponent usually can hit a return shot. In addition, hit the ball almost parallel to the floor and use enough power on the shot to pass your opponent, but do not pass with too much power on a high passing shot. This may cause the ball to rebound out of the corner or off the back wall toward center court before it takes its second bounce. Remember that the passing shot is an offensive weapon. The three basic passing shots include the crosscourt, the down-the-wall, and the wide-angle shot, and each shot is used in a different situation within the court.

Crosscourt

If you and your opponent are on the same side of the court, hit the crosscourt passing shot. The ball should hit near the center of the front wall and angle back across the court to the far back corner.

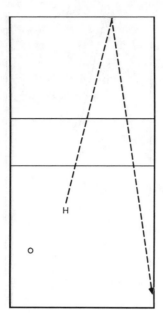

Figure 7-1. The crosscourt pass

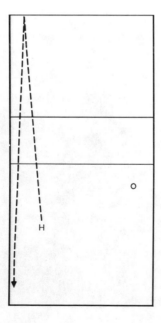

Figure 7-2. The down-the-line pass

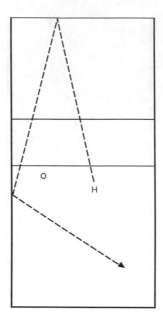

Figure 7-3. The wide-angle pass

Figure 7-4. An ideal backhand power shot situation. Note the stepping action.

Down-The-Wall

If you are on one side of the court and your opponent is on the other side, hit the passing shot directly into the front wall so that the ball rebounds along the wall nearest to you, stays parallel to the wall, and ends in the back corner closest to you. Because the ball travels along the wall during this shot, it is called the down-the-wall passing shot. It may also be called a parallel passing shot or a down-the-line passing shot.

Wide-Angle

The wide-angle passing shot is a regular passing shot hit at a wider than normal angle. This shot can put a little extra distance between the ball and your opponent, and a little extra distance can sometimes make the difference between a successful and an unsuccessful pass. The wide-angle pass is really a modified crosscourt passing shot. Unlike the other two passing shots, however, it is not designed to place the ball in a back corner. When you hit the wide-angle pass you should try to strike the front wall at an angle that makes the ball rebound to the side wall *even with* or *slightly behind* your opponent. The wider angle causes the ball, as it comes off

Figure 7-5. The down-the-wall pass with the opponent back. Not so ideal, but a good shot.

the side wall, to rebound across the court past and away from your opponent. Although you normally try passing shots when your opponent is in front of you, to use the wide-angle pass successfully your opponent must be no farther back than center court. If he or she is behind center court, the ball will rebound off the side wall right to your opponent. Furthermore, accuracy is essential for an effective wide-angle passing shot; if you miscalculate only slightly, the ball will either rebound directly to your opponent or it will go into the back wall and come out as an easy setup. This problem results from hitting the ball too high or too far behind your opponent on the side wall. The target area on the side wall is a two-foot area opposite your opponent; hitting this spot ensures success of the wide-angle shot especially if the ball hits the side wall no more than a few feet from the floor. If you can hit the shot low enough, the ball merely rolls out from the side wall-floor crack. It is important to remember that passing shots are best executed when your opponent is somewhere in the front two-thirds of the court. Concentrate on accuracy rather than speed.

Backhand Shot

Backhand passing shots are essentially the same as forehand passing shots. On the backhand pass, however, lead foot positioning is very important. In a backhand down-the-wall pass, the lead foot steps straight ahead with the toes pointing to the near front corner. With a crosscourt backhand pass, your lead foot points a little more toward the front wall side of the near corner. In addition, you may strike the ball slightly in front of your lead foot on the backhand pass. Although many players are concerned about their backhands and have a tendency to let up on this shot, hitting slightly in front of the lead foot gives you an aggressive shot.

One point of strategy worth noting is that if you and your opponent are right-handed, your forehand crosscourt pass will be very effective because it will end in the backhand corner of your opponent. The same is true of your backhand down-the-wall passing shot. However, your backhand crosscourt pass and your forehand down-the-wall pass will end in your opponent's forehand backcorner. (Of course, the reverse is true if your opponent is left-handed.)

Finally, you should pay attention to the distance the ball travels on passing shots. On the down-the-wall passing shot the ball travels less distance than a crosscourt passing shot hit from the same place. This means that a down-the-wall shot gives your opponent less time to return the ball.

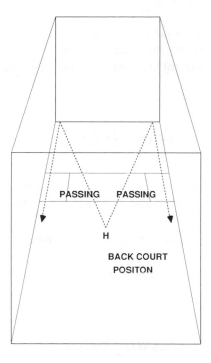

Figure 7-6. The left-handed backhand crosscourt pass shot placement

Figure 7-7. A good time for a down-the-wall pass as Peck plays Hilecher (Courtesy Racquetball Illustrated)

Except for the wide-angle passing shot, the ball should never hit the side wall or rebound out from the back wall. In order to avoid hitting the side wall, change your angle of front-wall contact, hit lower, or hit with a little less force.

Keys for the Passing Shot

- Hit the ball at the correct angle to the front wall so that the ball never hits a side wall on crosscourt and down-the-wall shots.
- Hit the ball low enough and slow enough so that it will not rebound off the back wall.
- Hit the ball away from your opponent; choose your passing shot relative to your and your opponent's positions in the court.
- In wide-angle passing shots, angle the ball against the front wall so that it hits the side wall opposite or behind your opponent.

Drills For The Passing Shot

Paper Bag Drill

Purpose: To practice passing-shot selection in order to keep the ball away from your opponent.

Directions: Place an empty paper grocery bag upright in the court as your opponent. Place the bag in the forecourt or center-court area and position yourself in different locations in the backcourt; drop the ball and hit the passing shot dictated by your position and that of your opponent. Reposition the bag to change your shots.

Drop and Hit Drill

Purpose: To practice hitting passing shots with a rebounding ball.

Directions: Position yourself in various backcourt locations, hit the ball to the front wall so that it rebounds back to you, and attempt to hit various passing shots off the rebound.

Variations: A. Hit the ball away from yourself so that you must move to the ball and hit the passing shot off the rebound.

           B. Have a partner hit the ball to you and practice passing shots off your partner's hit.

Figure 7-8A. Improper pass hitting position, playing the ball too high and not having the body facing a side wall

Figure 7-8B. Proper pass hitting position, playing the ball low and having the body facing a side wall

B. Stand near the back wall, toss the ball gently underhanded and low to the back wall, let it bounce, and hit
various passing shots both backhand and forehand.

Rally Drill

Purpose: To practice hitting passing shots with a rebounding ball.

Directions: Position yourself in various backcourt locations, hit the ball
to the front wall so that it rebounds back to you, and attempt
to hit various passing shots off the rebound.

Variation: A. Hit the ball away from yourself so that you must move to
the ball and hit the passing shot off the rebound.
B. Have a partner hit the ball to you and practice passing
shots off your partner's hit.

Kill Shots

The kill shot is the offensive shot in racquetball that gives players the
most satisfaction. When the kill shot is hit well, it is the most lethal shot
in the game and is normally not returned by your opponent. The satisfaction is derived from winning the point, keeping the ball low, hitting
it hard, and not allowing your opponent a chance to retrieve the ball.

Figure 7-9. The drop and hit drill for the passing shot

Shot Strategy

The key to success in hitting the kill shot is to keep the ball low on the front wall. If you can hit the ball low on the front wall, it will take its second bounce very quickly and be almost impossible for your opponent to return. The perfect kill is a *roll-out*, a ball that hits so low on the front wall that it actually rolls across the floor and is impossible to return.

Hit Low

A number of factors need careful attention in order to keep the ball low on the front wall. One of the most important in successful kills is patience. Patience is needed to wait on the ball so that when your racquet makes contact, the ball is near the floor. Usually, the lower the ball is when you hit it, the lower it will stay on the front wall. To repeat, you must be patient and wait until the ball is close to the floor. Beginners tend to get excited and play the ball too soon and, therefore, find it difficult to consistently keep their kill shots down.

Once you learn patience, the next important requirement for a good kill shot is to get yourself down to the height of the ball. This means that your body must be close to the floor, and to get this low you need to bend at the waist and knees. Bending the knees is the problem for most players, but it can be overcome in the following manner. You are facing a side wall and preparing to hit a kill with either a forehand or a backhand shot. When you bend the legs and waist, remember also to lower your butt. In order to achieve the lowest position with a good base of support, you must put yourself into a lunging type of position, with the lead leg bent under the body and the back leg extended behind the body with a slight bend in the knee. The lunge position is the most efficient way of lowering your center of gravity and thus lowering your body.

Figure 7-10A. Improper kill technique, legs not bent and racquet head dropped

Figure 7-10B. Proper kill technique with bent legs, lunge position, and racquet head up

The next concern for keeping the ball low is the position of the racquet head in relation to the ball on contact. The head should be pointed toward the side wall; it should not be pointed toward the floor. If the head is pointing to the floor, chances are good that the racquet face will be angled back slightly, and this will cause the ball to rise slightly after impact. If the head is pointing to a side wall, the face should remain flat and the ball should stay low and straight after impact.

All basic hitting procedures described in previous chapters apply to hitting the kill successfully. However, a few other points need to be highlighted. Because you need to be watching the ball, your head should be close to the floor when you hit the kill. Lowering your head helps keep

Figure 7-11. Hogan finishing a kill with good form (Courtesy Racquetball Illustrated)

the ball lower on the front wall; when you raise your head, the racquet and your body are sometimes lifted at the same time. In addition, power is a very important component as you become more skilled in making kills. Although accuracy and patience are most important when you are learning the kill shots, remember that the harder you can hit the kill, the quicker it will get to the front wall and the quicker it will bounce twice. To kill effectively from deep in the back court requires that you hit the shot with considerable power; the harder your kill shot, the greater will be your backcourt effectiveness. Of course, accuracy must be achieved first in order to maintain consistent kill shots. But once accuracy is established, you should work on hitting the ball with power. For the best kill shot, play the ball from between an inch from the floor to about ankle high. Timing your swing and racquet–ball contact is also very important for good kill shots.

Hit When in Position

You should hit kill shots when you are in frontcourt or center-court position and when your opponent is deep in the court. Even if you should hit the ball a little too high, the chances of your opponent getting to the ball are slim. If you are back and your opponent is forward, your kill shot must be perfect or it is likely to be returned.

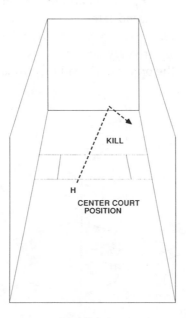

Figure 7-12. A left-handed forehand kill

Hit Level

Remember, if you play a high ball and try to hit it low on the front wall, the ball will probably bounce high off the floor, and your opponent will have too much time to get to the ball. Therefore, do not try for kills when the ball is high.

Another problem caused by hitting kill shots at the wrong level is causing the ball to hit the floor, or skip, before it hits the front wall. Skipping the ball on the kill shot usually results from contacting the ball behind the midline of your body; your racquet face closes and causes the ball to skip. However, a skipped ball can also be caused by hitting even with your midline with a closed racquet face. If your grip is causing the closed face, adjust your grip. Finally, a kill shot can skip because of a lack of power. When hitting the ball this low, if you lack sufficient power to propel the ball quickly, it will hit the floor before hitting the front wall. Check your power supply sources.

Front-Wall Kills

The straight front-wall kill can be hit down-the-wall or crosscourt. Remember, if the down-the-wall or crosscourt kill is a little too high, it becomes a good passing shot, but if it is a little too low, it is a loss of a point or loss of serve. You can also hit overhead kills, but this is a lower percentage shot and will be discussed later.

Kill shots are most effective when you are in center court and your opponent is behind you. They are very good when your opponent hits a short ceiling shot and when the opponent's ball rebounds off the back wall near the center-court area.

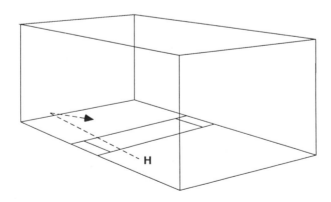

Figure 7-13. The basic straight front-wall kill

Corner Kills

The corner kill can hit front wall–side wall or side wall–front wall. A corner kill that hits the forehand corner of the hitter, side wall first, is called a pinch kill. A reverse pinch is hitting the corner kill to the corner, side-wall first, away from your forehand side. Backhand pinch terminology is the opposite. The splat is another form of a corner kill, and both splats and pinches are discussed in more depth later.

Keys for the Kill Shot

- Hit the ball low on the front wall by bending the knees and the waist.
- Be patient and allow the ball to come close to the floor before you play it. It is much easier to kill a low ball than a high ball.
- Keep your racquet head pointing to a side wall and keep your head down, parallel to the floor.
- Develop accuracy first, speed and power second.

Drills for the Kill Shot

Paper Cup Drill

Purpose: To practice hitting kill shots with a low stationary ball.

Directions: Turn a paper cup upside down within the service zone, place the ball on top of the inverted cup, and hit the ball off the cup. It is important to hit the cup as you hit the ball otherwise

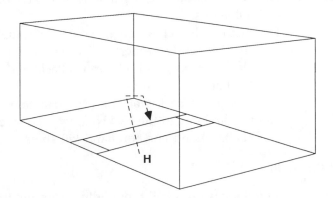

Figure 7-14. The basic corner kill

Figure 7-15. The "tee" or cup drill forcing you to get low for the kill

you will hit up on the ball. This is an excellent drill because the ball is both low and stationary. Hit forehand, backhand, and other variations of the kill.

Variations: A. Use a smaller cup in order to play the ball lower.
B. Move the cup farther back in the court to make the drill more difficult.

Drop and Hit Drill

Purpose: To practice hitting kill shots from the service area with a low setup.

Directions: Stand in the service area facing a side wall, drop the ball low, about six to eight inches from the ground, and hit forehand and backhand straight front-wall kills.

Variations: A. Hit front-wall–side-wall kill shots and side-wall–front-wall kill shots.
B. From within the service area, stand near a side wall and toss the ball gently, underhanded, and low to the side wall, let it bounce, and hit various backhand and forehand kill shots.
C. Move near the back wall, toss the ball gently, underhanded, and low to the backwall, let it bounce, and hit various backhand and forehand kill shots.

Hit and Kill Drill

Purpose: To hit kill shots off a ball rebounding from the front wall.

Directions: Stand in the center court area of the court, hit the ball low and slowly to the front wall, let the ball bounce one or more times, and return the ball to the front wall with a kill shot.

Variation: Position your body to one side of center court and near the back wall and hit and kill.

Low-Ball Kill Drill

Purpose: To force the body low in order to play a very low ball.

Directions: Stand anywhere in the court, drop and hit the ball low on the front wall, allow it to rebound and bounce so that it is within two inches of the floor or lower, and attempt to kill the ball.

Variation: Allow the ball to go by you, hit the back wall, and come forward, and then play it with a kill when it is two inches or lower from the floor.

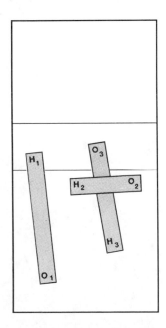

Figure 7-16. The best hitting position for the kill (H-1 hitter) and (O-1 opponent) as compared to other not so ideal positions (H-2 O-2) and least ideal (H-3 O-3)

CHAPTER 8
Back-Wall, Volley, Lob, and Ceiling Shots

Several specialty racquetball shots can be used offensively and defensively when you are caught in particular situations. Although these are specialty shots and require that you have well-developed basic skills, you need not be a top-level player to learn them. Moreover, learning these shots will probably improve your play and allow you to compete with more advanced players. Above all, these are strategic shots, and using them effectively indicates that you have advanced your skill level and that you understand racquetball strategy.

Back-Wall Shots

A back-wall shot is simply playing a ball that has traveled to the back wall and is heading toward the front wall. The back-wall shot is not a

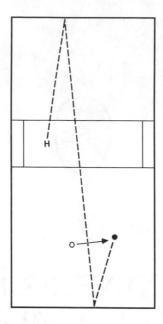

Figure 8-1. A typical back-wall shot

particular type of stroke; rather, it is a strategic way to use other strokes. You can hit forehand or backhand passing, kill, and ceiling shots off the back wall, and any ball played directly off the back wall is considered a back-wall shot. Body position and stroking actions are the same for back-wall shots as for front-wall shots.

One reason for the popularity of the back-wall shot is that after hitting the back wall, the ball is already traveling toward the front wall. You do not have to change the direction of the ball at impact, you have good control, and you can impart more power to the shot.

Speed and Angles

The advanced player considers the back-wall shot an easy shot because the ball is set up for a good return that usually ends a rally with a winning point. For the beginner, however, the back-wall shot is not easy. The ball is difficult to judge because of its speed and various rebounding angles, and beginners generally have two major problems in playing back-wall shots. First, the beginner often plays a high overhand shot on a ball rather than letting it go past to the back wall, and thus loses the opportunity to play an easy back-wall shot. Beginners need patience on all high balls, and they should allow high balls traveling fast enough to go past in order to be able to play the ball off the back wall. Of course, a slow-moving

Figure 8-2. Don't play the ball this high, allow it to go by and then take a back-wall shot

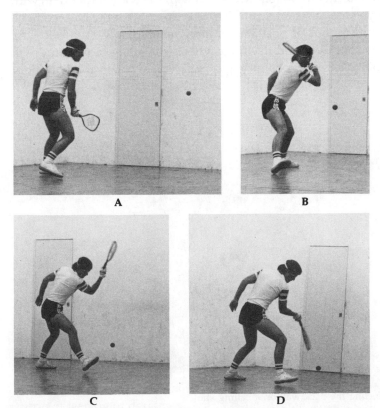

Figure 8-3. Sequence of allowing the ball to go by and then playing a back-wall shot

high ball should be taken before it gets to the back wall because it might not rebound off the back wall, which would put the hitter into a defensive rather than an offensive position.

In addition, beginners should not be overly aggressive on back-wall shots. This tendency can result in playing the wrong high balls and in hitting defensive rather than offensive back-wall shots.

One final point for beginners to remember is to try to avoid running into the back wall when attempting back-wall shots. It can be unsafe as well as embarrassing. If, for example, you are retreating for a back-wall-off-a-ceiling ball, you should reach behind yourself with your nonhitting hand to feel for the wall while you concentrate on watching the ball.

Time and Positioning

A second major problem beginners have is timing and positioning, two problems so closely related that we would like to treat them together. Many beginners attempt to follow the ball with the body rather than with the eyes. If you are constantly running to keep up with the ball, you will probably wind up out of position on many shots. However, following the ball with your eyes and deciding where it is going to rebound will allow you to move to that rebounding spot in time to obtain good position.

Figure 8-4. Feeling the back wall on a ceiling shot

Watch and Move With the Ball

One of the keys to successful back-wall shots is watching the ball. You usually need to move to position yourself to hit a back-wall shot, and never losing sight of the ball while moving or turning your body is essential. When ball contact is made, your head should be down so that you are still watching the ball. Watching the ball helps both in proper positioning and in better timing.

Because most back-wall shots will force you to move backward to meet the ball, body movement speed becomes an important factor in positioning yourself properly. The easiest way to retreat quickly is as follows. Turn to the side where the ball is passing you and step toward the back wall with the foot on the ball side. Then, cross over the lead foot with your other foot and run sideways into position. This is the fastest way of getting into position for back-wall shots. Both back peddling and shuffling to the side are slower movement patterns and give you less time to get into the proper position to hit the back-wall shot. Turning completely around and running will cause you to lose sight of the ball.

For the right-handed player, to hit a backhand back-wall shot, turn your body to the backhand side, step out with the left foot, cross over with the right foot, and run sideways to your position. For the forehand back-wall shot, turn to the forehand side, step out with the right foot, cross over with the left foot, and run sideways to your position. (Left-handed players use the opposite movements.) Always stay in a semicrouched, low position as you move to the ball. Also, starting your backswing almost simultaneously with the body turn for back-wall shots is important for beginners. Getting the racquet back early helps the beginner to avoid rushing the swing and aids in a smoother stroking action.

As with all shots, you must move to the ball, stop and get set, and strike. This means you must learn to judge ball speed and ball angles, and practice is the only way to learn. However, back-wall shots are slightly different because you may need to move back to get the ball or you may stay put or you may have to move forward, as in playing a hard-hit back-wall shot. If you are moving forward, you will be simultaneously moving and hitting toward the front wall, therefore timing becomes a major concern. The benefit of moving forward as you contact the ball is that you hit the ball with more force because of your momentum toward the front wall. But because you are usually moving forward on the hard-hit back-wall shot, understanding the difficulty of correct timing and positioning while attempting to hit on the run is very important.

BB Back-Wall

Sometimes a back-wall shot is hit so hard that it forces you to move to within a few feet of the front wall before you can play the ball. This is called by some pros the BB back-wall shot. What do you do with the ball when you are so close to the front wall? If you do not win the point or the serve, you will be totally out of position in the court and will probably lose the point. You have several options for handling the BB back-wall shot, including a drop shot (see chapter 11), a kill (preferably corner kills over straight kills), and a passing shot. Your opponent's position will dictate which of the shots you should use. If your opponent is deep in the backcourt, then the drop shot or the kill would be appropriate. If he or she is in the center court, the passing shot should be used. Remembering the proper strategy will help you avoid losing points on a BB back-wall.

Ceiling and Corner Back-Wall Shots

Two other back-wall shots require a slightly different hitting technique, the back-wall ceiling and corner balls. When playing a back-wall shot coming from a ceiling ball, remember that the ball is rebounding both down and *away from* the back wall. Normally, you will need to position yourself closer to the back wall for the ceiling-to-back-wall ball because it will not rebound forward nearly as far as a standard back-wall shot. The key factors in the back-wall–off-a-ceiling shot are to get low and to get behind the ball.

With corner shots, remember that a ball might take a thousand or more different angles out of the corners. The only two pointers for back-wall corner shots are, first, be patient and wait for the ball until it gets low, and, second, practice is the only way to learn about corner angles and rebounding. The more you play, the more angles you will learn and the better you will be able to react. (Even after years of practice, however, the best players occasionally misplay a corner back-wall shot.) A good return off a back-wall corner shot is a ceiling shot because it will give you time to get out of a back corner, and into better court position.

Back-Wall–Back-Wall

The last of the back-wall shots is one in which the hitter turns and hits the ball back into the back wall rather than hitting it directly to the front wall. The back-wall–back-wall shot is not desirable because it is mainly defensive. The ball is going up, it is hit in the opposite direction of the front wall, and it must travel a great distance to the front wall—all of which add up to defense alone. This shot is most often used by beginners. Beginners often feel uncomfortable with their backhands, so they turn and hit to the back wall with a forehand, thus eliminating some backhand shots. Or else the back-wall–back-wall shot is used as a last-ditch effort to hit the ball, normally a result of being out of position. Although beginners use the shot more often than intermediate and advanced players, all players must sometimes use back-wall–back-wall shots.

To hit the shot properly you need to be in the side position, as if you were hitting regular back-wall shots, except that now you are oriented toward the back wall instead of the front wall. All other aspects of hitting mechanics are the same as for other strokes. Hitting the ball with great force is important because it must travel farther than a typical back-wall shot. Finally, the back-wall–back-wall shot must be hit with an upward swing. This accomplishes two things: first and most important, hitting upward causes the ball to go up to the ceiling and gives you more time to obtain center court—and second, it prevents the ball from rebounding directly into your body. Remember, the back-wall–back-wall shot is not a desirable shot. It will normally set up your opponent for a kill or pass because you have little control over placement and your opponent has plenty of time to get set for the next return. We suggest using your backhand rather than a back-wall–back-wall shot.

Figure 8-5. Yellen waiting and watching the back-wall ball for a kill against Wagner (Courtesy Racquetball Illustrated)

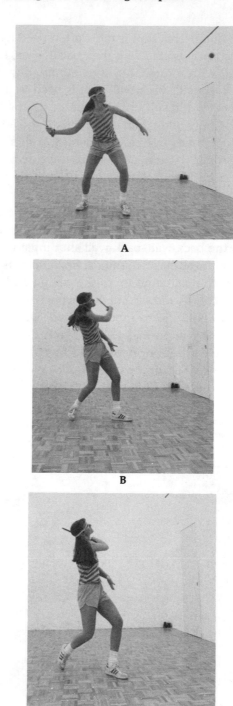

Figure 8-6. Hitting up on the back wall and back-wall shot.

Court Size

The size of the court determines the use of back-wall shots. In regulation courts back-wall shots are not effective when they force you deep in the court to retrieve them, and in oversize courts they are very ineffective. However, in undersize courts the back-wall shot is very effective because, due to the court's short length, the opponent's return of the back-wall shot often ends in the center court area for an easy offensive shot.

Keys for the Back-Wall Shot

- Learn ball speeds and angles through constant practice.
- Never lose eye contact with the ball when playing back-wall shots.
- Be patient and allow high balls to go by you and then play them with a back-wall shot.
- Be patient on your back-wall shot and contact the ball low to the floor.
- Begin your racquet backswing early in order to have more time to stroke the back-wall shot.
- To obtain more force when hitting the ball, play the ball opposite the front hip, not behind the body.
- Hit backhand back-wall shots rather than back-wall–back-wall shots.

Drills for the Back-Wall Shot

Toss and Catch Drill—No Racquet

Purpose: To practice side hitting position, patience, and the arm swing in back-wall shots.

Directions: Stand near the back wall, toss the ball underhand and low to the back wall, allow the ball to bounce, swing your arm as if you were hitting, but catch the ball instead.

Variations: A. Toss the ball as described above but catch the ball before it bounces on the floor.

B. Throw the ball to the front wall, let it bounce and hit the back wall, and swing your arm and catch the ball in the air.

C. Vary the speed and height of all throws in all of these drills.

Toss and Hit Drill

Purpose: To hit backhand and forehand back-wall shots with a controlled setup.

Directions: Stand near the back wall, throw the ball underhand and low to the back wall, allow it to bounce low, and then hit it to the front wall with kill and passing shots.

Variations: A. Bounce the ball to the back wall off the floor and then play the ball in the air off the back wall to the front wall.
B. Throw the ball underhand and low to the back wall and play the ball in the air before it bounces.
C. Toss the ball into back corners and repeat the drills.
D. Throw the ball to the front wall, allow it to bounce on the floor and hit the back wall, and then play it in the air before it bounces using passing, kill, and ceiling shots with both forehands and backhands.

Front-Wall Hit Back-Wall Drill

Purpose: To play balls coming off the front wall and hit them toward the back wall to learn speeds and angles of rebounds in order to obtain good positioning for back-wall shots.

Directions: Stand in the back of the court, hit the ball to the front wall with a passing shot, allow the ball to bounce-hit the back wall, and then play the ball in the air off the back wall.

Variation: Hit higher passing shots and ceiling shots to the front wall, allow the ball to bounce-hit the back wall, and repeat the drill.

Volley

Volleying, or playing the ball in the air before it bounces, is an important and interesting shot. By hitting the ball in the air the pace of the game changes rapidly, adding a new dimension to the game. Beginning players attempt to volley many shots, but the volley is really an intermediate-level shot. Because beginners are often impatient and not used to waiting for the ball, they usually hit the volley at the wrong time and in the wrong manner. This section describes in detail the basics of playing the volley, including court position, strategies, and the mechanics of hitting the shot, but let's begin with a few general observations.

First, the volley is an offensive weapon, not a defensive shot, and it is played most effectively when you are in center court or the frontcourt. Although you can play a volley from the backcourt, it is less effective offensively the farther you move from the front wall. Because you must react quickly to play the volley, you may be hitting from an awkward position. Always try to play the volley low for an underhand or sidearm shot rather than an overhand shot. Play volleys in the forecourt because they are easier to hit when you are close to the front wall, and this strategy gives your opponent less time to react.

If your opponent is scrambling and out of position, playing a volley will normally make his or her situation worse because the volley allows less time to react and increases the pressure. You can play the volley off the front wall or the side wall, and both shots are effective. The side-wall shot gives you more time to react, but you have to cope with new angles. The front-wall volley permits you less reaction time, but you have a straight hit with no angles to worry about.

Face the Side Wall

As with all other racquetball shots, you should be facing a side wall when hitting the volley. Of course, this is often difficult to do because you may have little time to react to the oncoming ball. You should attempt to play the ball to the side of rather than the front of the body. If you do not have time to turn sideways completely, you should rotate your upper body so that your shoulders are parallel to a side wall. This stance is a more open position than the side-facing stance. The weight should be on the balls of the feet. Because of the time factor, you will normally not take a step up as you hit the volley shot.

Figure 8-7A. Contacting the ball low with body facing side wall. Yes!

Figure 8-7B. Contacting ball waist high with only the shoulders rotated to side wall. Yes!

Figure 8-7C. Contacting the ball high with the body facing the front wall. No!

Hit Low

One of the most important aspects of a successful volley is to play the ball low, and the ideal place to hit the ball is below the waist. Above-the-waist volleys are somewhat less effective than volleys played below the waist because of the difficulty of holding the racquet high and hitting with much power or control. In fact, the volley backswing and follow-through generally tend to be somewhat shortened because of the lack of time for pivoting, and the shot is mainly a punch or a block. In any case, remember to hit your volleys below the waist.

Hit Quickly

A few additional maneuvers will also help you hit an effective volley. First, watching your opponent set up for his or her shot is always important but it is particularly critical in the volley because it may give you additional time to maneuver into position to successfully volley. By watching your opponent you can anticipate the next shot, and this allows you to move quickly and to gain a little more time to react. In addition, you should keep your racquet low while waiting to hit the volley shot. Hold your racquet level with the midthigh, which is nearly the perfect height for playing the volley. Because volleying decreases reaction time for both you and your opponent, any advantage you can gain is an important ingredient in making your volley a lethal offensive weapon.

You should also remember that volleying permits you to maintain center-court position (rather than running to the backcourt to play the same ball off the back wall), and maintaining center-court position keeps you in the dominant role in the court. Holding center court also requires less energy than running about to make your shots, and in very long games this can be a decided advantage. Finally, because the volley is a dominating shot, play it aggressively, place it low on the front wall, and use it to put away your opponent.

A Tight Grip

A tight grip on the racquet handle is essential during the volley shot for solid impact on the ball. You will have little time to react, and the ball will be traveling at high speed. Unless your grip is firm, the racquet may turn in your hand, resulting in loss of control and placement. The grip itself may be forehand, backhand, or continental, and the continental grip is quite useful because you need not change it for forehands and backhands. The volley shot keeps your opponent out of center court, helps you maintain offensive pressure, and allows you to vary the tempo of a game—one of the biggest advantages to using the volley. But without a tight, firm grip and solid racquet–ball contact, none of these volley-shot advantages will be yours.

Hit a Variety of Shots

You may use the volley to play kill shots, passing shots, pinch shots, and ceiling shots. Kill shots and passing shots seem to be the easiest shots to master using the volley. The pinch shot takes somewhat more precise timing, and the ceiling shot is very difficult to hit off of a volley. When a ceiling shot is played, it is normally an offensive shot because you use it to maintain center- or frontcourt positioning. Soft midcourt kills and pinch shots are also effective off the volley, especially when your opponent is in the backcourt.

It is worth noting that even if you make a slight mistake in executing the volley, you are still in control of center-court position. Another advantage of the volley is that when you make the shot, you are often between the ball and your opponent, and he or she loses sight of the ball—a legal, visual block.

Finally, if your opponent is driving hard shots at you, don't be intimidated. Try to react as quickly as you can, use the techniques we have been describing, and maintain center court if possible. If you cannot volley a particular ball, let it go by and take it off the back wall. But get back to volleying again as soon as possible; it is one of your best offensive weapons.

Keys for the Volley

- For better control on your volley, stand facing sideways or rotate your shoulders parallel to a side wall.
- The volley should be played below the waist in order to hit effective passing and kill shots.
- Keep a firm grip on the racquet at racquet–ball impact or else the force of the ball will cause the racquet to rotate in your hand and you will lose control of your shot.

Drills for the Volley

Self Toss Drill

Purpose: To practice the proper positioning and hitting techniques for the volley.

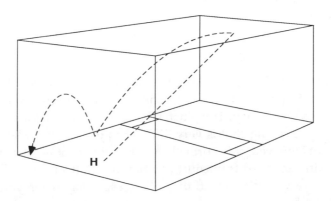

Figure 8-8. Typical ball flight pattern in the lob

Directions: Stand between the service lines in a side position, toss the ball low using an underhand toss, and volley the ball to the front wall with passing and kill shots.

Variations: A. Begin in the ready position and toss and hit different passing and kill shots off your volley.
B. Begin in the ready position and hit volley ceiling shots.
C. Use backhands as well as forehands in all of the drills.

Front Wall Toss and Volley Drill

Purpose: To volley a ball coming directly off the front wall.

Directions: Stand between the service lines facing a side wall, throw the ball underhanded to the front wall so that it rebounds into the air, and volley it to the front wall using both forehands and backhands.

Variations: A. Begin this drill in the ready position, toss the ball to the front wall, and volley the ball.
B. Stand in the service area, throw the ball into a front corner, and play the ball in the air with a volley.

Alternate Bounce and Volley Drill

Purpose: To practice volleying and getting into position in time.

Directions: Stand in center court and hit the ball to the front wall, allow it to bounce, hit it again to the front wall, and then hit a volley shot; continue rally alternating volleys and bounce shots.

Variations: A. Stand in center court and alternate bounce and volley shots into a front corner.
B. Volley the ball to the front wall and continue to rally using only volley shots; do not allow the ball to bounce.
C. Hit continuous volley shots into the corners and the ceiling.

Lob Shot

During the early days of racquetball, the lob shot was used quite often, but it is used very sparingly in today's power racquetball game. The lob shot lost some of its effectiveness in the early 1970s with the introduction of a livelier ball and has now largely been replaced by the ceiling shot. The present emphasis on power racquetball allows few opportunities to slow the ball down enough to hit an effective lob.

However, it can still be a useful shot for certain nonpower players, including some of the senior, women, and young players. The lob is a touch shot using very little power, and control is the key element for success. You should hit the ball gently so that it lands high on the front wall, about three feet from the ceiling. The ball rebounds deep into the backcourt corners—without hitting the ceiling—and remains there. Like the ceiling shot, the lob can be used in a variety of situations both offensively and defensively.

Strategies

Defensively, the lob is an excellent method of returning service, and it can be used offensively to force your opponent out of center court into the back corners of the court. Because the ball takes such a high arch and high bounce, it can be used defensively to give the hitter time to regain center-court position.

The most practical lob shot is hit down-the-wall, or parallel to a side wall. It can be used crosscourt, but this is not very effective because the ball must cross center court and may be picked off by your opponent with a volley. The lob may touch the side wall deep in the court to help slow down the ball so that it stays in the corner rather than rebounding out toward center court. But if the lob hits the side wall anywhere except near a backcourt corner, your opponent will have an easy setup. Some players have enough touch on the lob shot that they can keep the ball consistently in the back corners without ever hitting the side wall.

The slowness of the lob can radically affect the tempo of the game, and the power player may become very frustrated when the game is slowed with lobs and ceiling shots. An opponent's frustration with the slow pace can help the lob-shot player win the game.

Playing the Lob

Today's very lively racquetballs make it very difficult to prevent the ball from hitting the ceiling and from rebounding out from the back wall. Developing the right touch is one of the keys to a successful lob shot. You can play either forehand or backhand lobs although the majority of players use it as a backhand return. The lob shot is hit instead of a power shot—a backhand ceiling shot takes much more power to hit than a backhand lob.

The lob may be hit overhand or underhand depending on your position and the position of the ball in the court. Both strokes require a fluid, slow swing and the proper touch. Side position is not paramount for the lob shot, but good balance and a strong base of support are needed for success. The overhand lob is similar to an overhand throw; racquet–ball contact should occur even with or slightly behind your body. To hit the underhand lob, drop your arm and racquet face and play the ball in front of your body. Use the forehand grip on the forehand side and the backhand grip on the backhand side. Watching the ball until it is struck by your racquet is important and helps to prevent the possibility of mishitting the ball.

Keys for the Lob

- Swing slow and hit the ball with touch and control so that it ends up in a back corner.
- Hit the ball with touch rather than power.
- Use the lob to change the tempo and style of a game.

Drills for the Lob

Bounce and Hit Drill

Purpose: To practice hitting underhand and overhand lobs from deep in the court.

Directions: Stand deep in the court near a corner, bounce the ball low or high, and hit lobs high to the front wall with both backhands and forehands.

Figure 8-9.   Positioning for the backhand underhand lob

Throw and Hit Drill

Purpose: To practice hitting underhand and overhand lobs with a ball rebounding off the front wall.

Directions: Stand deep in the court, throw the ball high to the front wall, allow it to bounce, and play lobs gently to the front wall with both backhands and forehands.

Variation: Stand deep in the court, hit the ball high to the front wall, let it bounce, and return lobs to the front wall.

Ceiling Shot

The ceiling shot was not very effective during the initial years of racquetball, but during the last decade the changes to power play and the introduction of a livelier ball have made the ceiling shot very important. The ceiling shot can be used either offensively or defensively, and it can be hit underhand, overhand, and with both forehand and backhand strokes. The ceiling ball hits the ceiling first, then the front wall, then it bounces on the floor and lands deep in the backcourt, preferably in a back corner.

The ceiling shot can be hit down the line (wallpaper) or crosscourt; it can be hit off another ceiling ball, off a kill or pass, off back-wall shots, service returns, and volleys. In any ceiling shot the ball must not hit a side wall; if it does, the ball will go to center court and give your opponent a setup. The ceiling shot is probably the most versatile shot in the game of racquetball. You will normally use the shot from the backcourt,

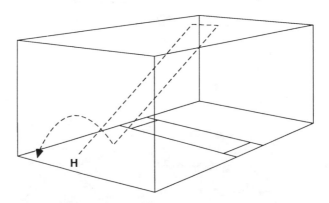

Figure 8-10. Typical ball flight pattern for the ceiling shot

A   **B**

Figure 8-11.   Hitting the ceiling shot is similar to an overhand throwing action

but a reverse ceiling shot can be effectively played from the mid- and fore-court areas. Any serious player must possess a good ceiling shot.

Let's look first at the basic stroke mechanics for successfully executing the ceiling shot. As with other strokes you need to be facing a side wall when you hit the ceiling shot. The side-facing position gives you the power sources needed to hit the ball the great distance from the back of the court to the top to the front to the floor and back again to the rear of the court. You obtain power from stepping into the ball, using a large backswing and follow-through, rotating the upper body, snapping the wrist, extending the leg, and utilizing arm and shoulder power sources. You must understand the power requirements of the ceiling shot and you must incorporate all the elements of proper hitting if you want your ceiling shot to be most effective.

Overhand Ceiling Shot

The overhand ceiling shot is very similar to an overhand throw of a ball or the serve in tennis. Employing all of your power sources, you reach up and contact the ball even with the midline of your body with your arm fully extended. Contacting the ball even with the midline opens the racquet face and propels the ball upward toward the front ceiling. If you hit the ball too far in front of the body midline, the ball will never reach the ceiling—your racquet face is too closed—but instead will travel directly to the front wall. If you make contact too far behind the midline of the

Figure 8-12. The overhand backhand ceiling shot position

body, the ball will hit the ceiling but never reach the front wall—your racquet face is too open.

Playing the ball at the midline of the body should allow the proper racquet-face angle to send the ball to an area on the ceiling one foot to six feet from the front wall. This target may vary depending on your court position when you hit the ball, on the liveliness of the ball, and on a variety of playing situations. But a majority of ceiling balls should strike the ceiling one foot to six feet from the front wall.

The nonhitting arm should be reaching up on the overhand ceiling shot, almost pointing to the ball. This helps to improve your concentration, and the nonhitting arm also acts as a lever to help pull your upper body around faster and give you some extra power. Imagine throwing the racquet into the ball; it will help you achieve a fluid action with the overhand ceiling stroke.

Overhand Backhand Ceiling Shot

The overhand backhand ceiling shot is hit exactly the same as the overhand forehand ceiling shot. Using all of your power sources is critical for this shot because most players have much less natural power on the backhand side of the body than on the forehand side. Playing the ball as high as possible, going up onto the balls of the feet and the toes, helps to cut down the distance the ball travels and thus gives more speed to the shot.

Figure 8-13.   The left-handed underhand ceiling shot form

It is important to remember that on all overhand ceiling shots the ball should travel deep to the back of the court and land in a back corner. The ball should also hug the side wall (wallpaper, down-the-line) or go crosscourt to the opposite back corner. The ball should not rebound out from the back wall but should remain near the back wall. If it comes off the back wall and/or back corner more than a few feet, it becomes an invitation for your opponent to kill; accuracy is therefore as important as power in the ceiling shot.

Underhand Ceiling Shot

All the elements of hitting with power and accuracy discussed for the overhand ceiling shot apply also to the underhand ceiling shot. Of course, the position of contact is different with the underhand ceiling shot, but body position is side-facing, and the swing is identical to passing or kill shots until just before ball contact is made. Lower your racquet head to open the racquet face, snap the wrist (this is not a tennis stroke with a shoulder-action swing), and strike the ball opposite or slightly in front of the front hip. Maintaining an open racquet face to impart upward trajectory to the ball is important. To repeat, you must be using all of your power sources at ball–racquet impact or your shot will lack sufficient strength.

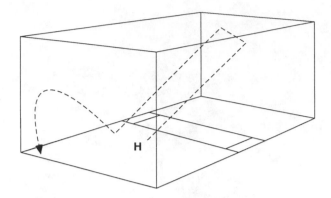

Figure 8-14. The typical ball flight pattern in the reverse ceiling shot

Reverse Ceiling Shot

The reverse ceiling shot is a variation of the ceiling shots we have been discussing, and is the same as the regular ceiling shot with two exceptions: first, the ball is hit to the front wall to an area approximately two to three feet below the ceiling; second, the ball is hit with high upward trajectory so that after hitting the front wall it then hits the ceiling and travels to the back court like a regular ceiling shot. Hitting the front wall before the ceiling—reversing the normal sequence—imparts a great deal of backspin on the ball as it bounces on the floor. The backspin slows down the backward progress of the ball and can create a difficult situation for your opponent, who may expect the ball to be traveling at high speed to the back wall and therefore take the wrong position to play the reverse ceiling ball. Backspin can also make the ball rebound with less force off the back wall, which gives you an effective ceiling shot. However, it may also prevent the ball from reaching the back wall, and this will set your opponent up for a kill.

The reverse ceiling shot is normally hit when you are in the frontcourt, and frontcourt positioning is fairly important in order to achieve the upward trajectory necessary to send the ball high on the front wall and then to the ceiling. From the backcourt it is very difficult to put the proper angle on the ball.

Offensive Use

The ceiling shot requires power, but touch is also important to keep the ball in the backcourt and back corner areas. Let's look at the offensive and defensive reasons for employing the ceiling shot.

The ceiling shot can be used offensively to win a point against an opponent who has difficulty returning high, arching shots. This is a very effective weapon against beginning players. What makes the ceiling shot so effective against beginners? As the ball comes off the back wall or out of the back corners, it is not only coming out but is also traveling downward, and this combination of outward and downward flight is often difficult for beginners to judge. A second offensive use of the ceiling shot is to move your opponent out of center court, and once you have done this you can take center court and utilize offensive strategy. This technique is effective against all players.

Defensive Use

The ceiling shot is defensively important when you are out of position and scrambling to return a ball. It gives you the maximum amount of time to recover and move to good court position while your opponent plays the ball. It is also quite effective for returning serves, especially power serves, and any other shot that you are digging up while scrambling. The ceiling shot is also a good way to return another ceiling shot. Returning a ceiling shot with a ceiling shot often results in lengthy ceiling-shot rallies that continue until one player makes a mistake and the ball is put away by the opponent. In ceiling-shot rallies both players remain in the backcourt until an error is made or a new strategy emerges.

When you are in trouble, the ceiling shot is the best percentage shot; if played well, it gives your opponent very little to hit. The ceiling shot can also be used to change the pace or tempo of your game. For example, if you and your opponent are both hitting hard shots, changing tempo with the ceiling shot can sometimes be very effective in winning a point. A ceiling-ball player can often beat a hard hitter who has not perfected the slower game. A good rule of thumb: If you can't hit an offensive pass or kill shot or you are out of position, go to the ceiling. However, don't use ceiling shots if you can hit a higher percentage shot such as the kill.

The ceiling shot also gives a new dimension to your game, the running dimension. You can run an opponent to exhaustion by intermittently hitting ceiling shots that make your opponent run to play the ball. This is a good strategy if you know you are in better condition than your opponent.

Finally, remember that all ceiling shots travel a great distance, which can cause many errors, and that having total control on a ball that is traveling so far is very difficult compared to a ball hit a shorter distance.

Keys for the Ceiling Shot

- When using ceiling shots, think both offensively and defensively.
- You need accuracy in placing your ceiling shots into a back corner, but power is also important in reaching the target.
- Use the ceiling shot when you are in trouble because it gives you the best chance of recovery.
- Don't use the ceiling shot when a more offensive shot can be played.
- Hit the ceiling shot at the proper angle to the ceiling and front wall so that the ball does not hit a side wall on its way to a back corner.

Drills for the Ceiling Shot

Throw the Ceiling Drill

Purpose: To help the player better understand the flight patterns and power supply needed for overhand ceiling and reverse ceiling shots.

Directions: Stand in the rear of the court and throw the racquetball overhand to the ceiling so that it rebounds into a back corner.

Variation: Stand more forward in the court, throw the ball overhand and upward to the front wall so that it rebounds to the ceiling and then lands in a back corner (reverse ceiling).

Drop and Hit Drill

Purpose: To practice underhand ceiling shots with both the forehand and backhand.

Directions: Stand in the back of the court, drop the ball waist high, and hit underhand ceiling shots.

Variations: A. Toss the ball up high, let it bounce, and hit overhand ceiling shots.
B. Toss the ball high to a side wall, allow it to bounce, and hit either underhand or overhand ceiling shots.
C. Toss the ball high to the back wall, allow it to bounce, and hit either underhand or overhand ceiling shots.
D. Toss the ball high to the front wall, allow it to bounce, and hit either underhand or overhand ceiling shots.

Lob and Ceiling Drill

Purpose: To play a ceiling shot either underhand or overhand off of a high lob shot.

Directions: Stand deep in the court, bounce the ball, hit a slow, high lob to the front wall (it must be an easy hit), allow the ball to bounce, and hit a ceiling shot to the front wall.

Variation: Using the same drill, continue to return the ball back to the front wall with a series of ceiling shots in a rally.

CHAPTER 9
Serves

You are in control of your racquetball destiny when you are serving because the serve is the only shot in racquetball that you initiate and control. You position yourself in the service area, you drop the ball, you decide on the type of serve, and you decide on service placement. No other shot in the game allows you such total control. Moreover, the only time you can score points is when you are serving. In order to score points and win games, you must develop an effective serve.

The Serve Is Offensive

The serve is an offensive weapon; it is not a defensive shot. A positive attitude concerning control and offensiveness when serving largely determines your serving success. However, planning strategy before you serve is crucial for racquetball success. You must choose the serve and service strategies that will keep your opponent off balance. You control delivery and placement of the shot, and your opponent must react. Is the ball moving high or low? Is it hard bouncing or a glancing shot? The decision and the advantage belong to the server.

The server also has an important positional advantage. You stand about 16 or 17 feet from the front wall when you hit the serve, and if you are serving effectively your opponent returns the ball from a position approximately 39 feet from the front wall. This distance factor alone gives the server a tremendous advantage over the receiver. In addition, once you have served, your automatic first move should be to slide into the center-court area; your opponent must not only return service but also attempt to move you out of the center court.

Where to Stand

No two players hit the serve in exactly the same manner, but a number of basic characteristics are common among all successful servers. First, your position in the service area is very important. The best spot is near the center of the service area with your back foot or both feet on the short service line. This position gives you certain advantages. Being near the center of the service area puts you close to center-court position, which

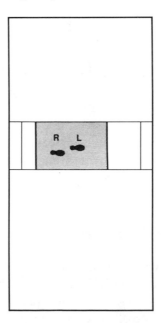

Figure 9-1. Positioning for service (right-handed server)

you want to reach immediately after serving, and allows you to get there in the least amount of time. By positioning yourself at the extreme back edge of the service court, you give yourself enough room to step and slide forward through the serve and still legally remain in the service box. (The rule for service is that you may be on or touch either service line during service, but you may not cross either line into the remainder of the court during service.) You cannot hit a serve with maximum power unless you allow yourself enough room for proper striding, and the short-line position gives you that option.

Ball Delivery

The next important aspect of the serve is delivering the ball to initiate the serving action. Should you drop, toss, or bounce the ball? Making the correct decision is an exceedingly important part of service success, yet the question is overlooked by many players. Whether to drop, toss, or bounce depends on the type of serve you plan to use. In addition, your hand position is important: If your hand is palm down, you will bounce or drop the ball; if it is palm up, you will drop or toss the ball. (The rule book states that you may have one bounce of the ball on each service.)

Let's consider the perfect toss. The ball should have relatively little spin, and the height of the toss and release depends on the type of serve you wish to hit—hard, soft, target area, and so forth. (Beginners should use a high toss to allow more time for their swing.) Racquet–ball contact should occur below the knee. Toss the ball slightly in front of you so that you will make contact near the lead foot as you are striding forward. The ball should bounce almost straight up from the floor with little forward or backward momentum. You should make contact with the ball at the point where it is nearly stationary at the top of its bounce. Hitting the ball at the top of the bounce is critical. If the ball is moving up or down, it presents a moving target that is more difficult to hit and control; at the top of the bounce, however, the ball is nearly stationary and allows you to hit a more effective serve. The toss should be made with the palm up to minimize spin on the ball and to ensure enough time for your swing. Merely dropping the ball without tossing it up gives you less time to react.

Palm Up

The best overall technique is a slight toss with the ball held palm up. This allows maximum control of the ball, a soft release, and ample time to

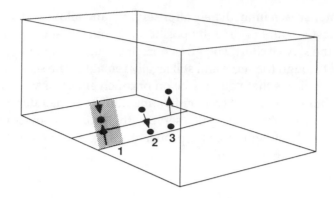

Figure 9-2.   Hit a stationary ball, not a moving ball: Ball 1 has reached its peak and is stationary, whereas ball 2 has already begun dropping and ball 3 is still rising

execute your backswing. Your hand cradles the ball and prevents it from accidentally falling, which sometimes occurs when holding the ball palm down. Hold the ball on your fingers with your thumb on top of the ball and toss it up gently. Remember that the higher the toss, the more time you have to prepare for your shot. However, although a low toss gives you less time to prepare, it also helps you place the ball lower on the front wall. In any case, do not allow the ball to roll off your finger tips because this gives the ball forward movement with backspin and makes effective racquet–ball contact more difficult to achieve.

Palm Down

Use the palm-down technique either to drop or to bounce the ball. The grip is the same as for palm up except that the thumb is facing the floor. The drop from this hand position is fairly effective, and the only problem is that if you are not careful you may drop the ball before you are ready. Dropping or bouncing the ball with your palm down allows you to add more speed during this portion of your serve. The ball travels a shorter distance and/or faster than with the toss, so you—and your opponent— must react more quickly. Of course, you must sacrifice a certain amount of preparation time and control when you use the palm-down drop or bounce. However, the advantage of quickness makes this technique well worth practicing. In fact, practicing a variety of ball delivery techniques for the serve is important. Try the different techniques and keep in mind that the palm-up drop is best for the most accurate delivery.

Figure 9-3A. Palm-up ball delivery for the serve

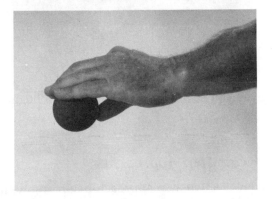

Figure 9-3B. Palm-down ball delivery for the serve

Serving Motion Mechanics

Remember, your basic starting position is near the rear center of the service area with both feet on the short service line. For the right-handed server both feet should be pointing toward the forehand side wall and be lined up with each other, heel to toe, with the left foot closest to the side wall. Beginning so deep in the service area maximizes the available service area size, which is very important for all servers but especially for the tall, long-legged player who might possibly footfault forward during a long stride. This position also helps to give a natural legal camouflage to your serve because your body is spread out as you hit the serve, which makes it more difficult for your opponent to watch the ball. In addition,

Figure 9-4. The heel-toe alignment for the start of the serve

this position gives you several choices on how to begin your stepping approach.

Two-Step and One-Step Approaches

The first technique is a two-step approach beginning with the back foot (right foot for right-handed players). Take a short, jabbing crossover step toward the front wall and then step forward with the left foot in a longer power stride. The second technique is the one-step approach. Start in the same ready-to-serve position and step forward with the front foot in a power stride. The two-step service approach has a couple of power advantages over the one-step method. By beginning with the back foot first, you open your upper body more toward the back wall so that you are building greater upper-body rotation into the service motion. You are also building up more body momentum by taking two steps instead of one step. Both of these elements contribute to a more powerful hit on the serve. But because an extra step is being taken, the skill is more complex to execute and the added power is difficult to control. Numerous variations of these two service approaches are possible, and your foot movements will vary somewhat according to the type of serve you use. In all cases, however, your step is the means of transferring your body weight from the back foot to the front foot in order to obtain power.

Figure 9-5. The two-step service approach

Racquet Swing

Your racquet swing is an important part of a successful serve, especially the backswing. Bring your racquet back behind your body as far as you can while still feeling comfortable. Hold your racquet high and extend your elbow as high as possible. Your wrist should be hyperextended (laid back), and your racquet should be pointing toward the front wall. Your arm should bend naturally at the below. This serving backswing position gives you the maximum possible range of service motion. A variety of service backswings are used by racquetball players. But the backswing mechanics we are describing provide the greatest racquet momentum and thus the greatest force.

Your forward swing should be a natural arm swing from the high backswing position to a low racquet–ball contact position. Your arm should be partially bent and your elbow should slightly lead the racquet handle. Immediately before ball and racquet impact, your arm should be fully extended, and your racquet head should drop down to a 45° angle to the floor. Beginners should keep the racquet head parallel to the floor to avoid opening the racquet face, which results in hitting serves high on the front wall. For advanced players the 45° angle affords maximum power and racquet control and helps to prevent the open racquet face.

You should have a slight natural elbow lead during the swing. This enables you to build more speed into your forearm movement and to impart more speed on the ball. Don't exaggerate this motion, however, because leading excessively can cause both improper hitting technique and elbow injury.

Ball and Racquet Impact

Racquet–ball impact should be made opposite your front foot at the end of your forward stride, slightly in front of the instep. Your wrist action at impact should be the same flexion-rotation as in all power strokes. Your back leg should extend fully, and your upper body should be rotating so that your arm-and-shoulder action contributes maximum force in the serve. Keep your head low and watch the ball. Beginners, especially, should watch the ball until impact is made although advanced players watch the ball only until it is a few inches from the racquet. Advanced players have better hand-eye coordination than beginners, and looking away from the ball earlier gives them a chance to determine more rapidly their receiver's reaction. Your body should be in a low position with a slightly flexed waist throughout the service delivery.

Follow-Through

The follow-through is another very important aspect of service mechanics. It should be natural and should follow your normal range of motion. Do not try to stop the follow-through before it reaches its natural limit.

Figure 9-6. The one-step service approach also depicting the slight elbow lead

Your follow-through can be high or low depending on the type and power of the stroke. As a rule, a high follow-through provides more power than a low follow-through, although it is also used for softer serves such as the lob shot when shot placement demands it. But high or low, a full, natural follow-through is essential for effective serving. You must incorporate all the elements of basic hitting mechanics to serve with power and accuracy—stepping, shifting of body weight, wrist action, leg extension, arm action, shoulder action, and upper body rotation—and the proper follow-through is the culmination of these basic elements.

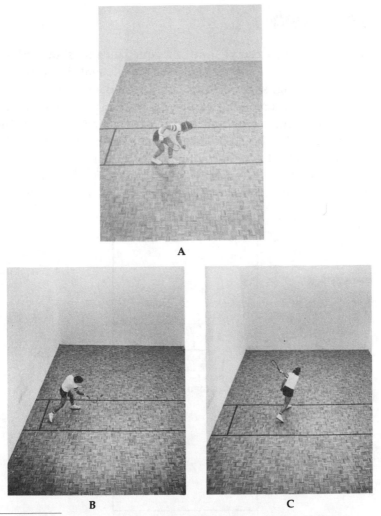

Figure 9-7.   Basic service beginning (A), hitting (B), and follow-through (C) stages. Note the use of the entire service zone from front to back.

The follow-through for the serve is similar to the follow-through for forehand passing and kill shots. Although you may also serve with your backhand, in competition this is not a sound practice. However, for practice games backhand serves give sound practice on backhand mechanics. Practice allows you to concentrate on service mechanics and, more important, to practice the thinking and preparation essential *before every serve* concerning the type of serve you are going to hit and where you are going to place the ball on the front wall.

Power Supply

In order to hit the drive serve, one of racquetball's most powerful shots, with maximum force, you must utilize all the elements in the power supply: high backswing, slight elbow lead, arm and shoulder action, wrist-snap, upper-body rotation, leg extension, stepping, and follow-through. All of them must come together for the drive serve to be most effective.

Your lead shoulder should be down, your wrist hyperextended (cocked back), and the butt of your racquet should be pointed toward the front wall. Your nonhitting arm should be extended after you drop the ball, which helps you obtain good upper-body rotation. Your lead foot should

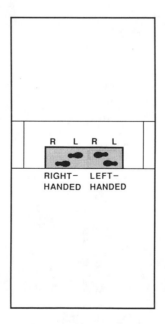

Figure 9-8. The drive serve basic beginning position

be at a 45° angle to the front wall rather than parallel or perpendicular; the 45° angle helps you get maximum upper-body rotation into the serve.

You should drop the ball low and you should contact the ball at knee level or lower approximately opposite the instep of your lead foot. You should begin at the short service line and move forward in the service court as racquet–ball contact is made. Hit most of your drive serves from slightly left of center service court against right-handed opponents and from slightly right of center service court against left-handed opponents. Speed and power are important aspects of the drive serve, and the shorter the distance the ball travels, the greater the speed it will maintain. Therefore, contacting the ball at the front of the service zone and hitting it relatively straight to the front wall makes it travel the shortest distance and gives the receiver the least time to react to the ball.

Variations Using Position, Speed, and Angles

If you do not possess the ability to hit the ball with offensive force, you should consider variations of the drive serve. You can vary the drive serve

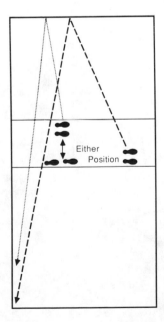

Figure 9-9. The wide deep drive serve compared with the straight forward drive serve. Notice the greater distance the ball travels in the wide drive as compared with the straight forward drive.

by moving to different spots within the service area and by hitting the ball at different speeds. If you move toward the sides of the service area, the drive serve is hit at more of an angle and is very similar to a crosscourt passing shot. This angled or crosscourt drive serve allows your opponent more time to get to the ball because it travels a greater distance and has a slower speed than the basic drive serve. You may also hit the drive serve slower and strive for accuracy by placing the ball at three-quarter or half-speed into the back corners. In addition, you can achieve different angles on your serve by changing the position of racquet–ball contact. For a right-handed server a ball can be angled right by contacting it slightly behind your body midline, and the serve can be angled left by playing the ball slightly in front of your body midline.

Types of Serves

As you read about serves you will see references to drive serves, Z serves, half-lob serves, lob serves, parallel serves, crosscourt serves, power serves, lob Z serves, garbage serves, and many more. Although many types of

Figure 9-10A. Racquet–ball contact forward of body plane—left angle

Figure 9-10B. Racquet–ball contact behind body plane—right angle

Figure 9-10C. Racquet–ball contact opposite front hip—straight service

serves exist, they are all basically derived from three forms: the drive serve, the Z serve, and the lob serve. Possessing a variety of basic serves and service variations is important for keeping your opponent off balance. Over the years, the three basic serves have been modified significantly, and now most servers hit a combination serve that incorporates elements of at least two, and sometimes all three, of the basic serves.

Drive Serve

The drive serve is the most popular serve in racquetball. It is hit hard and low and has a number of variations. The perfect drive serve is hit very hard and barely clears the short service line. You should not hit the ball any deeper than five feet past the short service line. Direct the ball toward a back corner; it either should bounce twice or more before reaching the corner or it should die in a back corner after one bounce. The drive serve is designed to win the point outright or to make your opponent reach and dig for the ball.

You should not hit down or up on the drive serve as you put it into play. Drop the ball at the proper height to hit the ball straight toward the front wall. A downward or upward hit changes the rebounding action

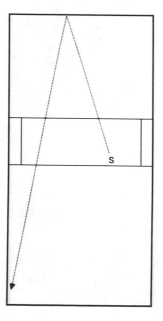

Figure 9-11A. The drive serve

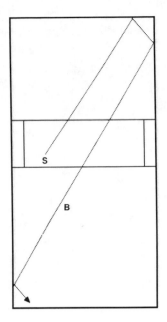

Figure 9-11B. The Z serve

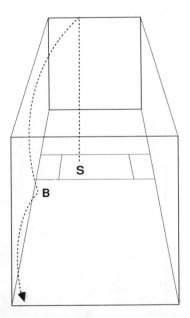

Figure 9-11C. The lob serve

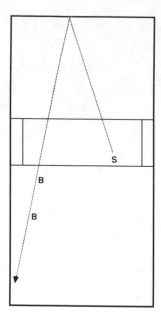

Figure 9-12A. The drive serve with two quick bounces

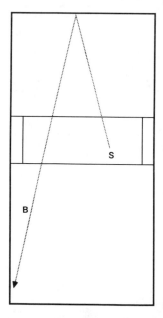

Figure 9-12B. The drive serve with one bounce and then it dies in the corner

of the ball on the first bounce and may give a better opportunity to return service, whereas a ball hit straight to the front wall gives the receiver minimal time to react.

Ball Spin

Most players do not attempt to put any type of spin on drive serves or other types of serves. However, a little natural backspin can make the drive serve more effective because backspin makes the ball rebound quicker off the front wall and stay closer to the floor after it takes its first bounce. On the other hand, topspin is a liability in racquetball. A ball hit with topspin grabs the front wall longer and has a higher initial bounce off the floor, which gives the receiver a better chance of returning the serve.

A flat ball, which has little or no spin, is also very effective for the drive serve. Remember that you must angle the racquet face slightly to impart spin on the ball, and this always involves some loss of power on the shot. However, a flat ball has all the power directly behind the ball, thus giving you maximum speed.

Use of Targets

A practice method that might be very helpful to you in all serves and particularly in the drive serve is to have targets on the front wall with service names on the targets. The targets indicate where the ball should land on the front wall in order to have the ball rebound into the court

Figure 9-13. The use of targets on the wall and in the service area in order to learn proper service angles

at exactly the right place. You may also use Xs in the service area so that you consistently serve to the same target from the same spot in order to get identical ball rebounding angles.

A few other factors concerning the success of the drive serve should be mentioned. The ball should never rebound out of a back corner; if it does, your opponent gets a clear hit on the ball. On the drive serve, the ball should not hit a side wall because this causes the ball to go into center court and sets up the receiver for an offensive shot.

Crotch Serves

Crotch serves, which hit the junction of the side wall and floor, are excellent drive serves because the ball either bounces erratically after hitting the crotch or it rolls out on the floor. The server scores an ace or has a setup on the returned ball. The problem with a crotch serve is that the target area is very small, and consistently hitting the crotch is very difficult. If you hit the serve a little too high, the ball hits the side wall and rebounds to center court and the receiver gets advantageous position. However, sometimes the server can get in a groove and hit a series of successful crotch serves in succession and win many points. Drive the crotch serve mainly to the backhand corner of the receiver because most players are

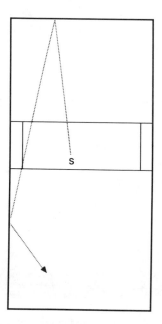

Figure 9-14A. The drive serve rebounding off the side wall to center rear court. No!

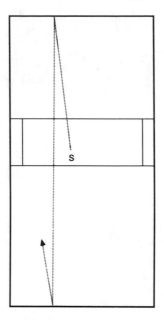

Figure 9-14B. The drive serve rebounding off the back wall to center rear court. No!

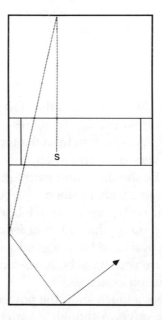

Figure 9-14C. The drive serve rebounding off both the side wall and the back wall to center rear court. No!

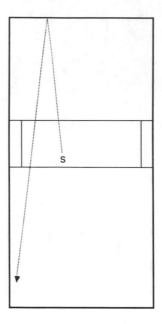

Figure 9-14D. The drive serve to the back corner. Yes!

weak in the backhand. In fact, this is a good strategy for all serves and especially for the hard-hit drive serve.

Lob Serve

The lob serve is totally different from other racquetball serves because touch, rather than power, is the key to success. The lob serve is more of a push or tennislike serving action than the typical racquetball hitting action. You should use very little wrist-snap, your hitting-arm movement should originate from the shoulder, and your hitting arm should remain fairly straight. Use the same body position as in your other serves to take advantage of deception. For the underhand lob serve, drop your racquet head slightly and swing up on the ball in order to give it the necessary upward trajectory. The overhand lob is a good serve, but you cannot deceive the receiver because your basic body position is upright and therefore different from your other serves.

Because the lob serve is a touch shot, the power sources are not as important as in the drive serve. Although a variety of lob serves can be played, the two basic lob serves are the half-lob and the high lob. The basic purpose of the lob serve is to hit the ball fairly high on the front wall, have it bounce behind the short service line, and end up in one of the back corners. Accuracy of ball delivery for the overhand lob can be a problem because you are bouncing or tossing the ball a great distance with your nondominant hand. Spend some time practicing your toss or bounce for lob serves.

Half-Lob Serve

The half-lob is probably the easiest and most practical serve in racquetball. The ball travels a relatively short distance and is hit at a slow speed, and thus it is an easy mechanical skill. You can use the half-lob as a change of pace, as a second serve, and as an offensive first serve that makes your opponent contend with a chest-high return. The five-foot restraining line has helped to make the half-lob an excellent choice of serves. Because the receiver cannot be in or play a ball in the restraining areas, the half-lob cannot easily be picked off on a volley. As with most of your serves, the ball should end up deep in the back corners. The half-lob is most effective in the backhand corner, which causes your opponent to hit a high backhand shot on the service return. A high backhand service return will usually be a ceiling shot because hitting kills and passing shots off of a high backhand service return is not very effective. If your opponent attempts to kill or pass, he or she will probably make an error.

Your body position for the half-lob should be the same as for all other serves. Your service area location should be slightly off center toward your opponent's backhand side. The ball can take one of two paths: You can angle it slightly toward the backhand corner or hit it almost parallel to the backhand side wall. We recommend the parallel half-lob because it hugs the side wall and makes for a difficult return for the receiver. In either case, the ball should not hit the side wall because this puts it into the center-court area. The tendency to hit the side wall is greater with the parallel half-lob than with the slightly angled half-lob.

Hit the ball 8 to 12 feet high on the front wall. It should gently rebound into the restraining area and end up in a back corner. Use relatively little wrist-snap in the half-lob serve. Your wrist should be firm, the stroke should come from your shoulder, and the elbow on the hitting arm should be slightly bent. This type of swing gives you better control on the ball. Remember, the half-lob is a control-touch serve, not a power serve; your swing should be similar to underhand or overhand tennis stroking action. This shoulder action gives you more control on the ball on a touch shot than wrist-snapping action. Because power is not that important in hitting half-lob serves, you need not step into the ball to make use of the other important power sources. However, deception is important, so attempt

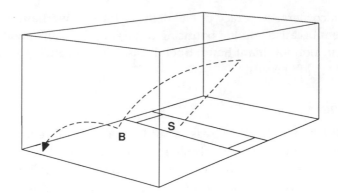

Figure 9-15. The correct landing spots for the half-lob serve. The serve hits 8 to 10 feet high on the front wall, bounces on the floor in the restraining area, and dies in the back corner.

to make your serves look as much like one another as possible, especially the underhanded half-lob serve.

High Lob Serve

Like the half-lob serve, the key factors in successfully using the high lob serve are touch and placement. Hit the high lob serve somewhere around 16 to 18 feet high on the front wall. The ball should rebound in the five-foot restraining zone, or close to it, and end up in one of the back corners. The high lob serve is not quite as easy to hit as the half-lob because the ball travels a greater distance and you have a greater chance for error. The high lob serve makes the service receiver contend with a ball coming almost straight down, and this downward trajectory can cause errors in the service return. On the negative side, the high lob serve goes so high that it gives the receiver too much time to move into position to play the ball.

You can use the high lob serve as a change-of-pace serve or as a high offensive serve to the backhand corner of your opponent. You should be as deceptive as possible on the high lob serve. Your stroking action, which is similar to the half-lob serve, is primarily a shoulder action rather than a wrist action. Your hitting arm is partially bent. Touch and control are the important factors in the high lob serve. The ball should neither rebound out from the back wall nor deflect off the side wall. If either of these situations occurs, you will be giving the receiver a setup. You should stand either along the backhand side wall or slightly to the backhand side of center service court. You can hit the high lob at a slight angle to the front wall or parallel to the side wall. You must be aware that the receiver has

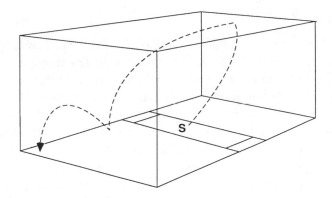

Figure 9-16. The high lob serve

plenty of time to react to a high lob serve. He or she may move forward short of the restraining line and play the high lob in the air as a volley.

Z Serve

The last of the three basic serves is the Z serve, which may be one of the best serves in racquetball because you can make slight errors on the shot and still come out with an effective serve. The other serves do not allow this much margin of error. The Z serve obtains its name from the Z path that the ball follows from the left front of the service area to the left back corner. When properly executed the Z can create some real problems for the receiver in the backhand corner. The stroking pattern is similar to that of the drive serve except that the server is angling the ball into a front corner. There are many variations of the Z serve concerning where the server stands, how hard to hit the ball, how high to hit the ball, and exactly what the ball should do in the back corner.

Placement

Remember that whichever side of the service area you use for the Z serve, the ball should end up in the back corner on that same side. The typical Z serve hits the front wall about five to six feet high and about one foot from the side wall opposite your serving position. After hitting the front wall and the side wall, the ball cuts across court on a diagonal, bounces on the floor within the five-foot restraining area, hits the side wall near your service position, and either angles toward the back wall or comes off the side wall close to and parallel to the back wall.

Power and Angles

Ball speed and front wall angle determine whether the ball ends up parallel to the back wall or angled toward the back wall. The closer to the corner you hit the ball, the more spin the ball will have and the more likely it will rebound parallel to the back wall. Hitting the front wall farther from the corner puts less spin on the ball and sends it toward the back wall at an angle. You must hit the Z serve with enough power. Hitting with too little power also causes the ball to angle toward the back wall rather than coming off the side wall parallel to the back wall.

Let's discuss some of the more common problems associated with the Z serve. A Z serve to the backhand corner hits the backhand side wall more than a few feet from the back wall, and the ball bounces to the middle of the court. This means you are hitting the front wall too close to the side wall and you may be hitting with too much power. Hit the Z serve with a little less power and a little farther from the front corner.

If your Z serve is hitting the back wall before it hits the backhand side wall, you are hitting the front wall too far from the side wall. This allows your opponent a fairly easy return.

The Z serve should hit the floor within the five-foot restraining area behind the short service line. If your serve is landing outside the five-foot

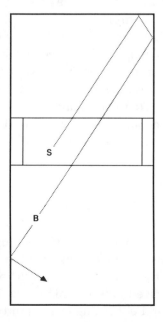

Figure 9-17A. Hitting the front wall too close to the side wall, allowing the ball to go to the center rear court. No!

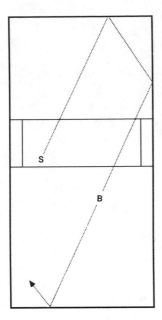

Figure 9-17B. Hitting the front wall too far from the side wall. The ball comes off the back wall rather than the side wall. No!

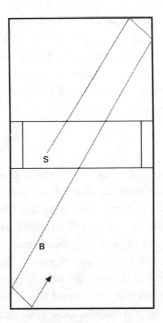

Figure 9-17C. Hitting the ball too hard for its height, causing the ball to come off the back wall. No!

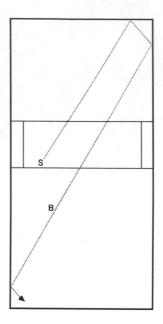

Figure 9-17D.   Hitting the Z serve correctly, with the ball ending in the back corner. Yes!

restraining area, you are probably hitting too hard for the height of the shot, and you can correct the problem by hitting with a little less power. Where the ball hits the floor on the Z serve is very important. The farther behind the five-foot restraining area it lands, the easier it is for the receiver to cut the ball off while it is in the air. Also, many Z serves that hit the floor behind the restraining area come off the back wall too high and result in a setup for the receiver.

Positioning

Disagreement exists concerning service area positioning for hitting the Z serve. Some individuals argue that all serves should be hit from the same spot—to utilize deception—and that the best spot is the center of the service box. This places the server as close as possible to the center court position. However, hitting the Z serve from the center of the service box requires you to hit the ball much closer to the side-wall crotch than when you are to one side of the service box. Using center position makes accuracy a critical factor in the success of the Z serve. If the shot is only slightly off target, you might hit the side wall first. But standing to one side of the service box increases target size, increases the front wall angles of your serve, changes the spin on the ball, and makes the receiver's job more difficult.

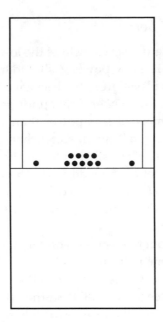

Figure 9-18. The Z serve positions

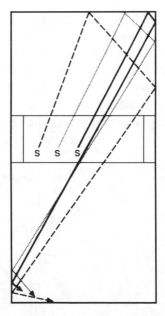

Figure 9-19. The Z server's position changes the angles of the serve, but the ball still ends in the back corner

Variations of the Z Serve

Variations of the standard Z serve include the low-power Z, the high-lob Z, and the garbage Z. The low-power Z should hit about three feet high on the front wall and is played from the backhand side of the service area. Executed properly, the low-power Z rebounds parallel with and close to the back wall. Use somewhat less power than with the standard Z.

You must hit the high-lob Z much softer than either the low-power Z or the standard Z serve. The ball should hit the front wall about 15 to 17 feet high within 2 feet of the side wall. The high-lob Z should take such a high bounce into the backhand corner that the receiver must play the ball directly out of the corner. The receiver should try to volley the lob Z before it bounces.

Hit the garbage Z about ten feet high on the front wall. The ball should follow basically the same pattern of flight as the lob Z. This serve gives your opponent a little less time to react to the ball and imparts slightly different spin and angles on the ball than the other Z serves. Therefore, you can use the garbage Z as an effective change-of-pace serve.

Combination-Variation Serve

As in most sports, the basics of a given skill seem to be modified almost constantly, and racquetball serves are no exception. Many effective serves are not true Zs, lobs, or drives but utilize changes in speed, angle, placement, and height. You can combine or vary any of the three basic serves. In fact, most racquetball players hit serves that are slightly different from

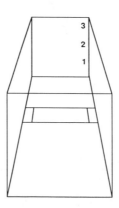

Figure 9-20. Targets for the three basic Z serves: 1—standard Z, 2—garbage Z, and 3—lob Z

the three basic serves. Players often find combinations or variations that give their serves greater consistency and offensive power.

Common variations include three-quarter drive serves, half-drive serves, high side-wall drives, low side-wall drives, crosscourt serves, reverse crosscourt serves, garbage serves, lob drive serves, and wallpaper serves. You can hit underhand serves, sidearm serves, overhand serves, serves from the center service area, and serves from other spots in the service area. You can use soft lobs, soft drives, and soft Zs, or hard lobs, hard drives, and hard Zs. You can hit high or low lobs, drives, and Zs. Of course, we shouldn't forget first serves, second serves, right-handed serves, left-handed serves, backhand serves, and forehand serves.

The important concept in selecting a serve is to find one that you are comfortable with and that helps you win points. Be creative and invent a combination-variation serve to fit your needs.

Second Serves

Everybody misses a first serve now and then. Low drive serves, for example, will often fall short. What should you do on your second serve?

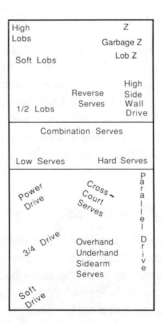

Figure 9-21. The many and varied faces of the serve

You must remember that all of the qualities for successful serving already mentioned must also be used on the second service. Having missed your first serve, you must now hit a successful second serve or you will become the service receiver. Of first importance for your second serve is to get the ball in play. The next consideration is to keep the second serve offensive.

Keep It Simple

A good rule of thumb in second-serve selection is to keep it simple. Use a serve that is basically easy to hit and at the same time an offensive shot. The lob serve meets both of these criteria. Either the high lob or the half-lob are quite good as second serves. The hitting mechanics are comparatively simple, and, if you place the serve correctly your opponent will have only defensive returns. You can also try Z serves, slow drives, garbage serves, and others as a second serve. As with the first serve, you need to use some deception in your second serve in order to keep your opponent off balance.

A good technique of practicing second serves is to hit some of your second serves on first service attempts.

Maintain Concentration

A basic problem many servers have is that they do not concentrate as intently on the second serve as they do on the first serve. But you must concentrate on the second serve, as much if not more than on the first serve, because it is your final chance for the service attempt. Think, concentrate, and try a few unexpected second serves to keep your opponent off balance. Remember not to slack off on your second serve; you are still the server and you should still be on the offensive.

Keys for Service Success

- For most serves, position yourself near the center back of the service area because this places you closest to the center-court area.
- Practice your ball delivery skills because ball delivery technique is critical to the success or failure of your serve.
- Most serves should land in a back corner; this forces the receiver to contend with the side and back walls as well as putting him or her as far from the front wall as possible.

- Accuracy is more important in serving than power, yet ultimately you would like to hit many serves with both accuracy and power.
- Adopt one serve that you like and use it about 70 to 80 percent of the time; pick another serve and use it about 15 to 20 percent of the time; try other serves occasionally for a change of pace.
- Drive serves are hit with maximum controllable force, lob serves are hit with touch and accuracy, and Z serves are hit with force and accuracy.

Drills for Serves

Ball Delivery Drill

Purpose: To practice delivering the ball properly, accurately, and with the right timing.

Directions: Stand slightly left of the center of the service box with your feet on the short service line; practice dropping the ball low consistently for the drive serve; do not hit the ball.

Variations: A. Repeat the drill delivering the ball for lob serves.
B. Repeat the drill delivering the ball for Z serves.

Serving Drill

Purpose: To practice serving drive serves to a left-handed opponent.

Directions: Stand slightly left of the center of the service box with your feet on the short service line, deliver the ball, and hit a drive serve to the backhand corner; hit ten serves in succession.

Variations: A. Repeat the drill by hitting ten lob serves in succession.
B. Repeat the drill by hitting ten Z serves in succession.
C. Alter your starting position to the left, right, or forward; repeat the succession drill with each serve.
D. Vary the drill with different speeds, angles, and heights and hit ten successive serves of each type.
E. Alternate different serves as well as speeds, angles, and heights and hit ten successive serves.

Target Drill

Purpose: To provide points of aim and reference points in the service box.

Directions: Place three-foot by three-foot targets in various strategic aiming spots on the front wall; attempt to hit the target with
your serves so that the serve is effective and offensive.

Variations: A. Place the targets high for lobs, low for drives, and about
four to five feet high and in the corner areas for Zs.

B. Tape reference targets in the service area so that by
always serving from the same spot you improve your service consistency.

CHAPTER 10
Service Strategies and Return of Serves

Service Strategy

Many strategies can be utilized to increase your chances of hitting service winners. The following sections describe some of the most effective strategies.

Exploit Weaknesses

One of your first strategies is to identify your opponent's weakness and to use the serve that best exploits that weakness. If you are not sure which serve to use, try a variety of serves to pinpoint the receiver's weakness.

Concentration

Don't just go into the service box and flail away; you should know exactly what serve you will hit and where it is going before you play the ball.

You must also concentrate on the ball and on the mechanics of your serve. Concentration before serving is exceedingly important. Many players don't concentrate on serves because they think they are in control of the serve, but this is a mistake—you must have total concentration when serving.

Play Percentages

Another service strategy that you should be aware of is to play both high and low percentage shots. Remember that you cannot lose a point when serving; the worst you can do is to lose the serve. You should be aggressive when you serve. Go for the put-away shots *and* play shots that may have a lower percentage chance of success. Cover any balls that you have a chance of hitting because you may win a difficult point. Strategies for returning service are described later in this chapter.

Deception

Deception is a key factor in serving. You try to deceive your opponent by making all your serves look like one another. The majority of your serves should be hit from the same position in the service court, and the mechanics should also look the same. Of course, you can at times move to a new service location or change your mechanics. In fact, sometimes this works to your advantage by broadcasting that another type of serve is coming. If you hit two or three scoring serves from your basic position and with similar mechanics, it may be psychologically favorable to force a new serve on your opponent. The psychological edge is very important to your dominance as the server. In addition, change of service technique also helps you control the flow of play and keep the receiver off balance. Consider serving one or two new serves, returning to your basic serving position and mechanics, and then repeating and varying the sequence.

The importance of deception is that your opponent does not know what serve is coming until after you serve the ball, and learning to serve from the same position with the same skill mechanics is crucial to racquetball success. This may sound confusing because we have just pointed out the advantages of varying your serves and changing positioning within the service court area. But you should be able to do both.

A more subtle kind of deception is possible, which involves letting the receiver know exactly what serve is coming. By doing this you are telling the receiver that you are confident that he or she is not going to be able to handle it. Usually this psychology works best when you know that the receiver cannot handle your serve even when it is obvious which serve is coming. This is, of course, a poor strategy if the receiver can handle your serve.

Another deceptive measure that helps to legally hinder the return is to line up with your left foot in line with the left foot of the receiver when you make racquet–ball contact. This interferes with the receiver's view of the ball as you hit it, and he or she gets a slower start on the return.

Disguised Serve

As you advance to intermediate levels of play, camouflaging your serve becomes very important. Disguising your serve gives the receiver less time to anticipate, and this loss of split seconds can lead to weaker returns and more setups for you.

All of your serves can be disguised in some way; however, the most important serves to disguise are the low drive and low Z serves. Because these are fast serves, any added reaction time for the receiver is definitely advantageous for you. The lob, half-lob, and lob Z serves can also be disguised, but these are slower serves and take longer to reach the receiver, so deception is not as important to you as on the low, hard serves.

To disguise a serve well you need to consider body position, ball position, feet position, shoulder position, racquet position, and screen rules.

Body Position

Remember to follow the rules for the basic hitting position described in chapter 6. For the low, hard serves your body should be in a semi-crouched, low position, and for high, softer serves you can be more upright. But try to make all serves look basically the same until the ball is contacted. In addition, your body itself can help to disguise the ball. Depending upon your position in the service court, the angle at which you hit your serve, and the receiver's position, your body can act somewhat as a legal screen on the ball. You can position yourself to slightly obstruct your opponent's view of the ball.

Feet Position and Stride

Your feet positioning can also help to disguise your serve. *After* the receiver moves into position, line up with your left foot in line with the receiver's left foot. This position helps to legally block your opponent's view of the ball for a split second. The length of your stride into the ball also helps in disguising your various serves. All else being equal, the length of the stride into the ball determines where your racquet contacts the ball in relation to your body alignment. By varying your stride by four to six inches, you can alter your serve without the receiver seeing it.

Shoulder and Racquet Position

Shoulder positioning will change with foot positioning. On certain serves from certain positions within the service area, you can change your service angle by opening or closing the shoulders. The slight change in shoulder positioning forces the ball to the front wall at unexpected angles, thus changing your serve very discreetly. The racquet position relative to your body and the relationship between the racquet head and racquet face and ball contact will also help you change your serve. Dropping the head, angling the face (either more open or more closed), and contacting the ball a little in front of or behind your body provide a variety of ways to change and disguise your serve. Both angles and ball flight patterns are changed by adjusting racquet face or head position.

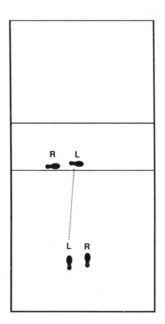

Figure 10-1. Disguising the serve with the server's left foot in line with the receiver's left foot

Ball Delivery

Another important aspect of service disguise is your delivery of the ball. If you deliver the ball close to you, the receiver's view will be obstructed. This is also true of a ball delivered slightly in front of your body. Delivering the ball wide of your body gives the receiver a better view of racquet-ball contact, which allows him or her to more easily anticipate the type of serve that you will hit.

Screen Rules

Disguising your serves is important, but the camouflaging must conform to the rules of the game. The screen serve rule states that a screen ball is one that passes so close to the server as to obstruct the view of the returning side. Most interpreters of the rule use the minimum distance of 18 inches from the body. Any time a ball rebounds in the receiver's area and passes within 18 inches of the server's body, it is considered a screen ball. Do not try to disguise the serve by obstructing the receiver in violation of the screen serve rule. The methods of service disguise described in this chapter are designed to give the receiver less anticipation

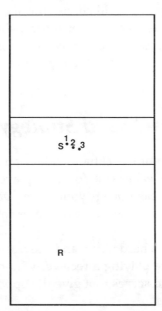

Figure 10-2. The service ball drop in relation to the server's body. The closer the ball (1) the less the receiver can see the ball.

time on your serve, and all of the techniques allow you to play within the racquetball rules.

Serve to the Back Corners

No two servers employ identical strategies and/or skill mechanics when putting the ball into play. However, all servers should strive to hit their serves consistently deep into the back corners of the court. If you can place the serve in the back corners, you can win the point outright with an ace, you can force a weak return from the receiver that you can put away on the ensuing shot, or you can cause the receiver to hit the service return defensively with a ceiling ball. Above all, you do not want your serve to glance off a side wall or to rebound hard off the back wall into the center court area. This changes the receiver from a defensive player to an offensive player, and the dominating effectiveness of your serve is lost.

The server can exercise a good deal of control over both the type of serve played and the receiver's return and rally. You must consider four factors in order to achieve both levels of service control. First, you must decide on the type of serve to use based on your strength and offensive style of play. Second, you should choose the serve that takes advantage of the receiver's weaknesses and defensive capabilities. Third, you must select the appropriate spot in the service area from which to initiate the serve. Fourth, you must consider the type of return you want your opponent to make.

Serve to the Backhand Strategy

Serving to your opponent's backhand side is an important strategy because it is usually the weaker side for most players. Keep the ball deep and in the back corners, camouflage your serves, vary your serves, change pace with your serves, and always take center court position on service relocation.

Hit soft serves against a hard hitter, and use fast shots against the slower paced player. If you are playing a receiver who continually goes to the ceiling, utilize low, hard serves that give the opponent the least amount of time to get set up.

Z Serve to Receiver's Backhand

The most advantageous Z serve is to your opponent's backhand corner. The basic position for the server against right-handed players is the far left of the service box and near the front service line. (If you are playing a left-handed hitter, position yourself to the far right of the service box.) This is the easiest position from which to deliver successful Z serves. One problem, however, is that the position itself may telegraph a Z serve to the receiver. Another problem is that you have placed yourself as far as possible from center court. It will take more time for you to reach center court, and this is detrimental to offensive strategy. But because the Z serve takes a fairly long time to reach the back corner, you should have enough time to take center court.

Relocation After Serving

One of the major strategies in racquetball is to take and hold center court. Service strategy must include a technique for taking center court after delivering the serve. Center court position is the area three to four feet behind the short service line approximately midway between the side walls. But how does one serve and then take center court? The serving stride is forward, away from center court. The key is learning how to change directions.

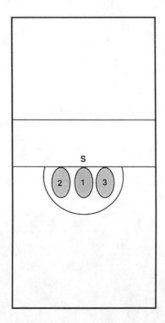

Figure 10-3. Relocate to center court after serving
1—Center-center court
2—Center left-center court
3—Center right-center court

Moving to Center Court

After hitting the serve you must immediately turn your head to the side of the court where you placed your serve to see exactly where your serve goes and to determine how your opponent will play it. As you turn your head, you simultaneously turn your upper body slightly and begin to step or shuffle backwards into center court position. At all times you must have your opponent and the ball in sight. Move as quickly as possible into center court so that you achieve that position before your opponent returns your serve. If you hesitate even a fraction of a second after serving, before you begin turning and moving, you will not have time to take center court and to get set before your opponent returns serve.

Figure 10-4A. Obtaining center court with a stepout

Figure 10-4B. Obtaining center court with a shuffle step

Each player has his or her own variations on the technique to move to center court. But no matter what technique you employ, it is vitally important to obtain center court as quickly as possible while watching your opponent and the ball. The importance of relocating after service is often overlooked by players who take reaching center court for granted. But this technique should be practiced, and because you will hit so many serves to the receiver's backhand, you should concentrate practice on gaining center court from the backhand serving spot in the service area.

Overshading on Relocation

Several circumstances may cause you to slightly shade your drop-back movement toward center court to one side or the other. You may have made an error on your serve, causing the ball to come out to center court, and you must move to one side to allow your opponent an unobstructed return. You may, however, overshade your relocation to center court for offensive reasons. Overshading can cut off some of your opponent's returns. For instance, if you serve into the opponent's backhand corner and you overshade slightly to the backhand side of the court, you can cut off some of the crosscourt passing shot returns by obstructing the angle

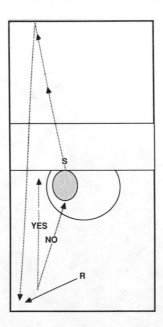

Figure 10-5. Cutting off angles with relocation: By overshading left the server has forced the receiver (R) to hit ceiling or down-the-wall passing shots. Crosscourt passes have been cut off.

with your body, and you force your opponent to hit down-the-wall or to the ceiling.

Be sure to keep your body low, in a semicrouched position, as you move. This enables you to move rapidly and keeps you in the ideal hitting position at all times.

Two major relocation errors can occur. First, the server serves and remains in the service box. This makes you quite vulnerable to any good passing shot even though you are in good position to retrieve kills. If you have an effective offensive serve you will be faced with few kill returns, so remaining in the service area after serving is obviously not the best position.

The other major problem with relocation is running in a small circular path to get to center court. This takes more time than a straight dropback and thus is not very practical. The circle pattern may be used if you are afraid of being hit by the ball or if you need to give your opponent more hitting area. But neither of these reasons is sound if you are serving effectively because the straight drop back will give your opponent ample hitting opportunities without hitting you.

Retreating too deeply into center court may also be a problem. If you retreat too deeply, you are not set for the next return because it takes quite a bit of time to move out of deep center court, and you would be

Figure 10-6. Keep your body in the semicrouched position in serving

very vulnerable to any hard driven passing or kill shots. The deeper retreating position is effective if you know your opponent is going to the ceiling on the return because it helps you play the ceiling shot return.

Return of Serves

Returning serves may well be the most difficult skill in racquetball because the server has so much control—of both the serve and your return options. Serving is a predominantly offensive strategy. Your strategy in returning service centers on neutralizing the server's control and putting the server on the defensive. In the following sections we will tell you, the receiver, how to put yourself into offensive control by returning service.

Body Position

What is the best position for returning service? Wait for the serve in a basic ready position, feet comfortably apart in line with the shoulders for a good base of support. Your weight is forward on the balls of the feet so that you can easily move in any direction. Your knees are slightly bent, your body is slightly flexed at the waist, and your shoulders are parallel to the front wall while you watch the server and the ball. Your arms are partially bent, and your elbows are fairly close to the body. Because most serves will be to your backhand side, hold the racquet with a backhand grip. Hold the racquet even with the midline of the body but be prepared to receive service on your backhand. Hold your racquet between knee- and waist-high for the shortest backswing distance and the quickest return.

Beginners may wish to try the two-handed backhand grip—with the nonhitting hand on the throat above the gripping hand. The nonhitting hand can help to turn the racquet when changing grips, which gives the beginner more control.

Court Position

Your position in the court should be midway between the side walls and anywhere from four to nine feet from the back wall. You should be midway in the court to be able to retrieve balls as easily from your backhand as your forehand side. You may wish to overshade slightly to the backhand side to compensate for the normally weak backhand. But against players of even intermediate skill, the slightest overshading or leaning

| A | B |

Figure 10-7. The receiver's position, front and side views

of the body weight to one side is an open invitation for the server to ace you on the opposite side with a good power-drive serve.

You may vary your distance from the back wall slightly. Normally, four to five feet from the back wall is a good starting position. But if the server is hitting hard drives and continually winning points, move forward up to nine feet from the back wall to cut off the server's angle and give yourself a shorter distance to travel to get the ball. This *up* positioning also creates a psychological edge. You are now taking an *assuming,* or anticipating, position, and sometimes this takes away part of the server's edge.

Be Light on Your Feet

Some receivers like to be moving or bouncing slightly so they can already be in motion in order to move and react quickly to the serve. The physics principle—that a body in motion tends to stay in motion—certainly holds true here, and this is a sound principle and should be employed by service receivers.

Watch the Server

You should be watching the server closely. Pay attention to the server's position in the service area and try to notice cues that telegraph the upcoming serve. The server's position in the service area will often tell you

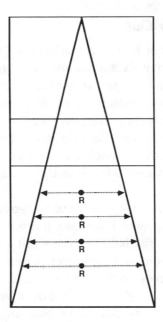

Figure 10-8.   The further the receiver moves back, the more angle he or she must cover, but there is more time in which to do it

what serve to expect. Many players deliver particular serves only from certain locations within the service area. If you can anticipate the upcoming serve by the server's positioning, you can get a jump on the ball and thus reduce the offensiveness of the server. Also, the server may turn his or her body, deliver the ball, and execute preliminary mechanics in such a way that you know which serve to expect. A shorter backswing, angling the body toward a corner, or dropping the ball farther forward can tip you off to which serve might be coming.

Movement Patterns in Service Return

You should be watching the server, concentrating on the ball as it is being served, and reacting as soon as or before the ball is hit. If you wait until the ball hits the front wall or crosses the service line to begin moving, it will more than likely be too late to get into position.

As the server contacts the ball, your first movement is to pivot and step toward the side of the court where you think the serve will land. The pivot, or turn of your body, must be completed simultaneously with the initial stepping action in the desired direction or you will lose too much time.

Cross Over or Step Out

You have two choices of first-step mechanics during your pivot. For a backhand return you may pivot, cross over and step with your right foot, and then contact the ball, or you may pivot, step out first with the left foot, and then cross over with the right foot. Either technique is good and both are quick. In crossing over, the crossover step is one long stride. If you add the initial step-out, it is a short step followed by a long crossover stride. The crossover is quicker if the ball can be played with one step, but if you need extended reach stepping out and crossing over can be advantageous.

Some racquetball players use short shuffle steps to move into the return-of-serve hitting position, which is fine if the serve is slow and you have ample time to move to the ball. But the shuffle step is more time consuming than the step-out and crossover patterns.

Moving to return serves on the forehand side is the same principle as the backhand return except that you cross over with the left foot and step out with the right foot. In all cases the speed, angle, and direction of the serve should determine the angle of your movement pattern, and the faster the serve, the quicker you must move to successfully return the serve.

Move, Be Set, Then Hit

As you move you should stay slightly crouched and attempt to get your racquet back into the backswing as soon as possible. The slightly crouched position keeps you closer to low serves and also allows you to extend your body and legs into the return shot. You should also be concentrating on the ball while you are moving into position for the return of service. The ideal sequence is to move, get set, and then hit the ball. However, you often do not have enough time to do this, and you must play the service return without being able to set up.

Service Return Shots

The three major return-of-service shots are the ceiling shot, the pass, and the kill.

Ceiling Return

The ceiling shot is the best percentage return on any service ball coming to you waist high or higher, and it can also be used effectively on hard

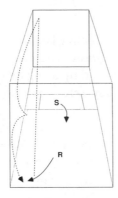

Figure 10-9. Return of service with the ceiling shot

drive serves. The ceiling return gives you a greater margin for error and should also force your opponent out of center court position. Most players prefer to have the ceiling return end up in the back left-hand corner, which causes the opponent to hit a backhand shot. The chances are good that the return of your service return will also be a ceiling shot. As mentioned in chapter 8, although many writers feel the ceiling shot is strictly defensive, we feel that it can be just as offensive as defensive, and in returning service it can be either one. It is defensive if you are digging for the serves, but it can be offensive if you are forcing the server to the defense with your return.

Passing Return

The passing shot can be employed either down-the-wall or crosscourt, and either passing shot should be tried if the serve gives you an easy return. Any time the server gives you a serve that you can hit offensively, you must use the advantage.

Kill Return and Variations

The kill return is very effective off a poorly placed drive serve that is coming at you low and hard. If the drive serve comes out to the center court area, go for the kill.

You can use other variations for service returns including ceiling shots to the right corner, Z-ball returns, volley service returns, and just about any other return shot that either wins a point or forces the server out of center court position.

Volley Return

The volley service return is effective because it gives the server less time to set up in center-court position. You can hit ceilings, kills, or passes off the volley service return, and by using this return you often catch the server off balance. The volley return is also one of the most effective returns against a lob serve. You should volley the lob serve before it forces you into a high backhand shot from the left corner. Some players use what is called a *quick service return*, which is basically similar to other service returns except that you always return the serve as soon as possible in order to give the server less time to get center-court position. The volley service return is an effective quick service return. When using the quick service return, do not allow the serve to go by you. The quick service return surprises the server, but it also gives the receiver less time to react to the ball.

Base your selection of service return on your ability, the type of serve, and the ability of the server. Different returns will be effective for different situations. Learn to hit effective service returns with ceilings, passes, and kills.

Service Return Strategy

As you await the serve you should be thinking offensive return. If the server gives you a plum, go ahead and pick it with a kill or a pass and attempt to win the rally outright. If your opponent's serve is a good serve, then you should employ the ceiling return, which gives you time to get into position and at the same time forces your opponent out of center court.

Keep constant pressure on the server so that he or she feels that if a mistake is made in the serve you will put it away. Don't be foolish and try to score on every service return, but don't sit back and allow plums to go by. Also, hit a variety of service returns to keep the server off balance.

Decide which type of return is best to use against the server before the serve is put into play, but also remember that the type and the precision of the serve will affect your return options. You will need to be able to quickly change your strategy of return depending on the serve itself.

Take advantage of any apparent weaknesses in the server's serves or strategies. Think offensive return first and defensive return second.

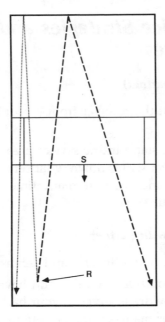

Figure 10-10.   The return service with the parallel and crosscourt passing shots

Keys for Service Strategies and Return of Serves

- Keep your second serve both simple and offensive; it *is* a serve and you should use it offensively.

- By using *very slight* changes in ball delivery and the position of feet, body, shoulder and racquet you can disguise a variety of serves.

- Exploit your opponent's weaknesses, hit to the backhand, hit your serves into the back corners, vary your serves, and concentrate when you are serving.

- Return offensive serves with ceiling and passing shots; return less effective serves with kill shots.

- Position yourself to receive the serve according to the ability and the strategies of both you and the server.

- Be light on your feet when receiving the serve; remember that it is easier to move if you are already in motion.

Drills for Service Strategies and Return of Serves

Disguise Drill (with partner)

Purpose: To prevent the receiver from recognizing your serve until you hit it.

Directions: While you stand in the service area and prepare to serve, your partner writes down what serve is anticipated; repeat ten times and see how many times you successfully disguised your serve.

Return Service Drill (with partner)

Purpose: To practice both offensive and defensive returns of service.

Directions: Position yourself to receive and have your partner hit ten consecutive drive serves to your backhand corner; attempt to return as many as possible offensively and play the rest defensively.

Variations: A. Have your partner hit only lob serves or Z serves and repeat the drill.

B. Have your partner hit all defensive serves and return all serves offensively.

C. Have your partner hit all offensive serves and return all serves defensively.

D. Repeat the drills for your forehand service return.

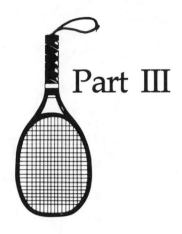

Part III

Advancing Your Skills

CHAPTER 11
Advanced Shots
and Moves

As you progress toward the intermediate and advanced levels of skill, you will begin to add a variety of new weapons to your repertoire of shots. You cannot continue to increase your skill level without mastering these new shots. The following sections introduce and individually analyze the more advanced skills you will need to learn in order to round out your racquetball playing techniques.

Overhead Shots

Thus far we have stressed the importance of patience on most offensive shots, that is, waiting for the ball to get low before playing it. Unlike other shots, however, the overhead is an offensive shot that is played high rather than low. Although it is usually most effective to be patient and to hit a low ball low to the front wall, hitting a high ball low to the front wall can be a valuable option. Overhead passing and kill shots have a low success rate because anytime you attempt to play a ball high and bring it down low on the front wall you have a high chance of error. However, game situations occur when having the overhead shot at your disposal is a definite plus.

Ceilings and Lobs

The racquetball overhead is usually a forehand shot, which is similar in mechanics to the tennis serve or overhead stroke, and it is often effective against a short ceiling shot or a short lob. (Backhand overheads can also be effective but are difficult to execute because most players are weaker on most backhand shots than on similar forehand shots.) Because the overhead is normally played on a high bouncing ball, you usually have time to maneuver into a forehand hitting position. It is effective not only against a short ceiling or short lob shot but also may be used to break up a ceiling–ceiling rally. In either case the overhead pass or kill shot should surprise an unsuspecting opponent. The element of surprise is very important to the success of offensive overheads. Many of your overhead shots will be ceiling shots (see chapter 8). Use the overhead passing or kill shot when your opponent is deep in the court anticipating more ceiling returns and make these shots resemble the overhead ceiling shot— disguise as well as surprise!

A   B

Figure 11-1. The similarities and differences between (A) the ceiling shot and (B) the overhead

The difference between the ceiling overhead and the overhead pass or kill is the position of the racquet on ball contact. For the ceiling shot you contact the ball even with or slightly behind the body. But in the overhead pass or kill you contact the ball slightly in front of the body, which causes your racquet face to close and imparts the needed downward angle on the high-bouncing ball.

Overhead Position

Position yourself sideways so that the upper body can rotate at the waist providing the power needed for these shots. As you begin the shot your weight should be on the back foot. Your arm should be moving in the typical overhand throwing motion used in the overhand ceiling shot. Begin shifting your weight to the front foot as your hitting arm comes forward, and as you contact the ball the weight should be shifted to the front foot, the upper body should rotate, the wrist should rotate and flex, and the legs should extend. Use a full backswing and a natural follow-through. Be sure to play the ball in front of your body in order to take the high ball low to the front wall.

Overhead Passing Shot

The overhead passing shot can be hit crosscourt or down the line, but be sure that the down-the-line shot hugs but does not hit the side wall. If the ball hits the side wall it will rebound into the middle backcourt and give your opponent—who is already in the backcourt awaiting ceiling shots—a setup. Power is very important in the overhead pass because of the great distance the ball must travel on the passing shot.

Overhead Kill Shot

The overhead kill is effective with a little less power than the overhead passing shot because the ball travels less distance and because you would like a short rebound on the kill. Use the front corners for success in the overhead kill. Hitting the corners slows down the shot significantly and causes unexpected rebound angles. This change of speed and direction results from the steep angle of the shot and is critical to the success of the overhead kill. If you miss the corner, the ball may rebound very high to the midcourt area and give your opponent a setup.

Keys for the Overhead Shot

- Use overhead shots sparingly because of the difficulty of successfully hitting the high ball to the low front-wall target.

- Use the overhead as a surprise tactic during ceiling rallies and against other short, high shots.
- Overhead shots are most effective when your opponent remains in the backcourt.
- Speed and accuracy are critical for the success of offensive overhead shots.

Drills for the Overhead Shot

Self Toss Drill

Purpose: To practice setting up overhead passing and kill shots.

Directions: Stand in the back of the court, toss the ball up high, let it bounce, reach up, and play overhead passing and kill shots.

Variations: A. Stand in the back of the court, hit short lobs and/or short ceiling shots to the front wall, let the ball bounce, and play overhead passing and kill shots.

B. Repeat drills but hit only front-corner kills off of the setup.

Ceiling–Ceiling Overhead Drill

Purpose: To hit overheads off of a ceiling–ceiling rally.

Directions: Stand in the back of the court, and rally the ball with ceiling shots; after hitting a series of ceiling shots change pace with an overhead passing or kill shot.

Pinch Shot

The pinch shot is a variation of the kill shot, which hits the side wall before it hits the front wall. The pinch can be hit as a backhand, forehand, splat, volley, or as a reverse pinch. It is most effective when you are in the frontcourt and close to one of the side walls and you play the ball to the closest side wall. Two factors make the pinch a very useful offensive weapon in racquetball. When the ball hits the side wall, the speed of the ball decreases and the ball rebounds slowly out of the corner. Also, because the ball hits the side wall first, it rebounds off the front wall across the court rather than toward the backcourt.

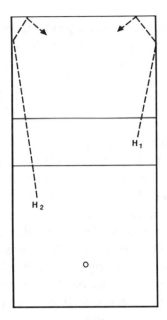

Figure 11-2. The pinch shot hit from the left and from the right

The pinch shot is a good way to change the game's pace. A soft-touch pinch is similar to a drop shot and is effective when your opponent is hugging the back wall.

You can occasionally hit pinches from the backcourt, but you must be really accurate otherwise you may give your opponent a setup in center court. The backcourt pinch should be used sparingly and mainly to catch your opponent off guard.

Hitting Position

Your basic hitting position for the pinch is similar to your position for hitting kill and passing shots (see chapter 7). However, your left foot should be pointed toward the right front corner on forehand pinches, and your right foot should point toward the left front corner on the back-hand pinch. The ball should hit the side wall anywhere from two inches to three feet from the front wall depending on your position in relation to the side wall.

The Opponent Is Behind the Hitter

The pinch is most effective when your opponent is behind you because you can legally screen the ball for an instant, which often helps you win the rally. Hitting the shot with ample power is important. Also, keeping the ball low is critical to prevent a rebound into center court and a setup for your opponent.

Splat

The splat is a pinch shot hit with less angle and more speed. You can play a wide-angle splat by hitting the side wall farther from the front corner than usual. Use the splat when you are less than a few feet from the side wall you wish to hit. This causes a different bounce on the rebounding ball than the usual pinch.

The splat shot stays closer to the front wall than the pinch while angling to the opposite side wall because the ball flattens on one side, and thus the splat sound and the strange angle across the front court. It is exceedingly important for you to play the ball low on the splat shot and on all pinch shots. Bend at your knees as well as at your waist in order to contact the ball low. You can pinch and splat off a poor kill, a passing shot, and even a short ceiling shot.

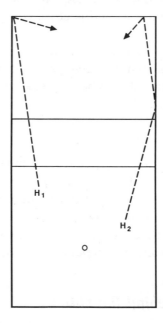

Figure 11-3. The splat from the left (H-1) and the wide-angle splat from the right (H-2)

Reverse Pinch

Most pinch shots are hit into the nearest front corner. But you may also go crosscourt with your pinch, and this is called the reverse pinch. When using this shot, step toward the target corner with your lead foot. The reverse pinch is used more by beginners and intermediate-level players than by advanced players because crosscourt shots in general are preferred by beginning players.

Backhand Pinch

The backhand pinch is somewhat more difficult than the forehand pinch. Remember to utilize all of your power sources when hitting backhand pinches. Some individuals have a tendency to push the pinch rather than hitting through the ball. A key point in avoiding pushing the ball is to think of the side wall as the front wall and to hit the ball to the side wall as if it were a front wall kill. You would not push a front wall kill shot, and this technique may help you hit through the ball properly and execute an effective backhand pinch shot.

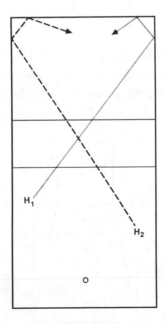

Figure 11-4. The reverse pinch from the left (H-1) and from the right (H-2)

Pinch Volley

Like volley shots in general, the pinch volley is difficult to execute because of decreased reaction time. However, the pinch volley changes the pace of the game, and it will often catch your opponent off guard and allow you to win a point outright. It is, therefore, well worth the effort necessary to master the shot. You need a compact swing on the pinch volley due to lack of time, with a short backswing and short follow-through. A firm grip, upper-body rotation, and watching the ball intensely are all vital for hitting successful pinch volleys. As usual, the pinch volley is most useful when your opponent is either behind or alongside you.

Keys for the Pinch Shot

- Use the pinch when you are in front of your opponent.
- Hit the pinch with power and keep the shot low.
- Don't push the backhand pinch; swing through the shot normally.
- Use the pinch as a change of pace.

Drills for the Pinch Shot

Drop and Pinch Drill

Purpose: To practice hitting pinch shots low to a near front corner.

Directions: Stand near center court but closer to one side wall; drop the ball low and hit pinch shots to the *near* front corner.

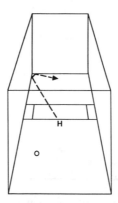

Figure 11-5. The pinch volley is best hit with the hitter (H) in center court and with the opponent (O) behind the hitter

Variations: A. Same drill as above, but drop and hit a reverse pinch to the *far* front corner.
B. Move farther back in the court and drop/toss and hit pinches, reverse pinches, splats, and volley pinches.

Wallpaper Shot

The wallpaper shot is any ball coming off the front or back wall that acts like it is glued to a side wall. The ball is so close to the side wall that it is very difficult to get a racquet on the ball. All of us have had to hit or return a wallpaper shot at some time. If you hit the shot you know that the opponent almost has to play a defensive return, if the ball is returned at all, and if you are attempting to return a wallpaper shot the feeling of frustration sets in. The shot is difficult both because of its closeness to the side wall and because often it will hit the wall and kick out at you unexpectedly. You can't get much racquet on the ball, and the ball may rebound unexpectedly—what do you do?

Do Not Attack

The chances of hitting a good return off a wallpaper shot are probably about one in five; however, some ways of returning the shot are better

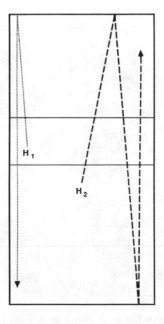

Figure 11-6. The wallpaper shot off (H-1) the front wall and off (H-2) the back wall

than others. First, you cannot attack a wallpaper shot by trying to blast it with all of your power. Even if you get your racquet on the ball and hit it hard, you will probably set your opponent up with a plum. You should think defensively, slow down your swing, and attempt to control the ball. These tactics allow you the best chance of a successful return.

You must also allow yourself enough room between the side wall and your body so that you can swing fluidly. Many players stand too close to the side wall when returning a wallpaper shot, and hitting from an awkward, cramped position makes the return more difficult. Also, if you are too close to the wall and the ball jumps off the side wall, you will have less time to react than if you had positioned yourself farther from the wall.

Hit Ceilings and Wallpapers

Because the wall prevents you from taking a full swing, the ceiling and wallpaper returns are your best percentage shots in returning a wallpaper shot. The hitting technique is more of a scooping action along the wall than a typical hit. Hitting a wallpaper shot return is something like trying to catch a fly along a wall with your hand; you would slide your hand along the wall and scoop up the fly. Use the same technique in racquetball. Use a shorter backswing and shorter follow-through because of the

Figure 11-7. Don't get cramped in your swing for a wallpaper shot

wall. The racquet head may be perpendicular or parallel to the side wall depending on your positioning. The parallel position usually puts more of the racquet face closer to the wall and gives you a better chance of returning the shot.

Figure 11-8A. Wallpaper shot: parallel racquet head

Figure 11-8B. Wallpaper shot: perpendicular racquet head

The shape of your racquet head will also help determine your swing and racquet face position. The largest, flattest surface of your racquet head should be placed along the wall, which may be either the top of the head or the side of the head.

Offensive Wallpaper Return

If you can return a wallpaper shot with a wallpaper shot, you place all of the difficulties we have been describing on your opponent's shoulders. The wallpaper off a wallpaper is good offense but extremely difficult to execute because if the ball hits the side wall it will probably end up as a setup for your opponent. Because this same rule applies to down-the-wall and ceiling shots, you may find that practicing these shots and learning to hit them consistently and accurately will help you play an offensive wallpaper return more effectively.

Keys for the Wallpaper Shot

- Think of scooping, or catching a fly off the side wall, as you return the wallpaper shot.
- Slow down, think defense, don't cramp yourself, and get the largest portion of your racquet face next to the wall when returning a wallpaper shot.

Figure 11-9. A wallpaper shot off the back wall between Hilecher and Hogan (Courtesy Racquetball Illustrated)

Drills for the Wallpaper Shot

Front Wall Toss and Hit Drill

Purpose: To practice hitting a rebounding ball that hugs a side wall.

Directions: Stand near a side wall, toss the ball to the front wall so that it rebounds as a wallpaper ball, and return the wallpaper ball with ceiling shots.

Variations: A. Same drill but return the wallpaper ball with a wallpaper shot.

                  B. Same drill but toss the ball with more force to the front wall, allow it to hit the back wall and wallpaper the side wall; play the back-wall wallpaper shot back to the front wall.

Around-the-Wall Shot

The around-the-wall shot is a crosscourt shot that travels around the court and ends up on the opposite side of the court from where it was originally hit. The around-the-wall shot is a variation of the Z serve; the difference is that the around-the-wall shot hits the side wall before it hits the front wall. Use this shot offensively to change tempo and unbalance your opponent or to break up a ceiling rally. Defensively, the around-the-wall ball gives you time to regain good position because it travels such a long high distance.

Around-the-Wall Ball Path

The around-the-wall shot is normally played when you are in or near one of the back corners. Hit the shot between ten and sixteen feet high on the opposite side wall and three or four feet from the front wall. The angle carries the ball against the front wall, then to the side wall nearest you around service-area deep; the ball then angles crosscourt and first bounces about two thirds of the way crosscourt and ends up near the opposite back corner. The ball is in midair most of the way across the court and is slanting downward. The around-the-wall shot should be hit with medium force.

If you initiate the shot from the forehand side it will end up on the backhand side and vice versa. The ideal placement for the shot is your opponent's backhand back corner.

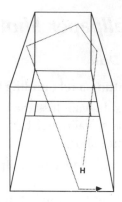

Figure 11-10. The around-the-wall ball

Hit Underhand, Sidearm, or Overhead

The around-the-wall shot can be hit underhand, sidearm, or overhead. The key to success is to hit the ball at moderate speed with the appropriate angle to the side wall target area. Hit the overhand with the stroke mechanics similar to the overhead offensive shot and the overhand ceiling shot.

The three major problems with the around-the-wall shot are hitting the ceiling, hitting too hard, or hitting the incorrect angle to the first side wall. Hitting the ceiling causes the ball to come straight down in the frontcourt and gives your opponent a setup. If you hit the ball too hard it will eventually hit the back wall and come out for a setup for your opponent. Hitting the ball off the first side wall at an incorrect angle will cause the ball to drop short or fly long, depending on the angle.

You will hit around-the-wall shots with both forehands and backhands. Because of the low margin for error, use the shot sparingly. It can be played successfully as a change of pace, as a substitute for a ceiling shot, or as a defensive shot to give you time to gain good court position.

How to Defend the Around-the-Wall

The best defense against the around-the-wall shot is to step into the center backcourt area and to play the ball on a volley. A passing shot is the best strategy in this situation. Beginners sometimes stand flatfooted and watch the ball as it caroms around the walls until it is too late to react. Don't let the ball hypnotize you; decide where the ball is best played and move into that court position and play it.

Keys for the Around-the-Wall Shot

- Use the around-the-wall shot as a change of pace or to break up a ceiling rally.
- Use it to regain good court position.
- Use medium speed and careful placement, but play the shot sparingly.

Drill for the Around-the-Wall Shot

Self Toss and Hit Drill

Purpose: To practice standing in the backcourt and hitting around-the-wall shots.

Directions: Stand in the forehand rear corner of the court, either bounce or toss the ball up, and hit the around-the-wall shot.

Variations: A. Same drill but stand in the backhand corner when you begin the drill.

B. Same drill but vary the speed and height of your around-the-wall balls.

Drop Shot

The drop shot is an effective weapon anywhere on the court; however, the best situation in which to use it is when you are in the frontcourt and your opponent is in the backcourt. It is an offensive shot designed to end the rally or to win the point. If you don't end the point with the drop shot, your opponent probably will on the return. The drop shot is a touch shot; the slightest mistake in its execution will either cause the ball to skip on the floor or hit too hard or high on the front wall and give your opponent a plum.

The hitting mechanics for the drop shot are similar to those for passing and kill shots. If you change your stroking patterns for a drop shot, your opponent may notice the change and be able to anticipate your drop shot. If you should also make any type of error in hitting the ball—too hard or too high on the front wall—the opponent's return will probably be a winner.

Drop shots should be used rarely because of the high chance of error. We suggest using kills or pinches when you are in the frontcourt, and add a drop shot here and there. The drop shot is an effective offensive shot when used at the proper time in the correct manner against the right opponent.

How do you make the drop shot look like a hard driven pass or kill? Let's consider three basic techniques for disguising drop shots. The best technique is to very slightly, unnoticeably, decrease your backswing; as you contact the ball do not use any wrist action, bring your forward arm movement almost to a halt at ball impact, and follow through less than normal. The key to success with this technique is that the mechanics must be deceptive so the drop shot looks like other strokes and that you must hit with the correct touch—not too hard or too soft. Practice is the way to perfect this technique of dropping.

Another method is to slightly change your hitting technique to cut through the ball from a slightly high to low swing. The swing itself has velocity like a pass or kill shot, but as contact is made the force of the racquet is directed more towards the floor than to the front wall. This high-to-low hitting action imparts backspin to the ball and greatly reduces the forward speed of the ball, thus giving you a soft touch on your drop shot. The more you cut through the ball going from high to low, the more force is imparted down and the less force is imparted forward from behind the ball. Once again, deception is important and this technique must also be camouflaged or your opponent will anticipate the drop shot.

Third, perform all mechanics as in the pass and kill but relax your grip on the racquet handle as you contact the ball. The relaxed grip allows the ball to rebound off the racquet face with little power, which results in a soft shot. Relaxing your grip is the most difficult technique to master in hitting drop shots; therefore, it is the least desirable of the three techniques. You may also combine aspects of the three drop-shot techniques and be successful in softly contacting the ball. Remember, the key to the drop shot is deception and touch, and the best time to use it is when you are in the frontcourt and the opponent is in the backcourt.

Play the Drop off a Poorly Hit Return

You may play a drop shot off a pass, a volley, a backwall shot, a kill, or any other poorly hit shot. Hitting off a kill is tricky because the ball is coming extremely fast, and it is sometimes difficult to slow the shot down into a soft drop shot. The best time to hit drop shots is when you do not have to move very far to reach the ball. If you are in motion, the speed of body movement makes the drop shot even more difficult to execute.

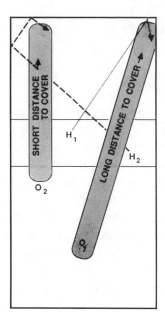

Figure 11-11. The drop shot hit from the service area with the opponent up and with the opponent back

Drop shots are effective against an opponent who has trouble moving forward or who has slow reaction time or who lacks concentration. Drop shots are also excellent against the opponent who stays in the backcourt or who has a tendency to sit back on his or her heels during rallies. If your opponent is slow or tiring, drop shots become quite frustrating for him or her. If the opponent is in center court but does not turn to watch your return, a drop shot can be used quite successfully. This is, however, the only situation in which you want to try the drop shot when your opponent is in front of you.

Drop Shot Placement

The best placement of the drop shot is into the corners with a trajectory similar to a kill or pinch. The use of the corners helps slow the ball down and thus gives a more effective drop shot. It is best to hit drop shots from knee level or below and to keep the ball low on the front wall. You can hit drop shots from a high, even overhead, position, but this makes the drop shot more difficult to execute because the ball going from high to low has a tendency to bounce high after it hits the floor and it gives your opponent too much time to get to the ball. Remember, the drop shot must die in the corners; if it doesn't, your opponent will probably put the ball away.

Back-Wall Drop Shot

Another variation of the drop shot can be used against beginning or intermediate players who hit the ball hard and high. A ball rebounds high and hard off the back wall and travels forward very close to the front wall; the hitter is within a few feet of the front wall, the opponent is in center or back court. The hitter actually slows down the forward momentum of the ball and makes it drop into the corners. This shot is very effective, and if you play on a smaller than regulation court it can be used quite often. The technique is to get your racquet in front of the ball, between the front wall and the ball, to let the ball slide across your racquet face, and at the same time to catch the ball and slow it down. This is not a visible carry or sling. You are moving in the same direction as the ball, so the actual carry is unnoticeable. It is a legal hit in most officials' eyes.

Keys for the Drop Shot

- Use drop shots sporadically when your opponent is in the back court.
- You must be deceptive with your drop shot, or your opponent will have a setup.
- Hit drop shots into the corners because they slow the shot down and accentuate the touch aspect of the shot.

Drills for the Drop Shot

Drop and Hit Drill

Purpose: To hit a slow setup and to slow it down even more so that a drop shot is hit.

Directions: Stand in center court, bend low, drop the ball low, and hit drop shots into the corner.

Variations: A. Stand in the back court and repeat the drill.
B. Same drill but vary your technique of dropping from shortened swing, to cutting, to relaxed grip.

Back-wall Drop Shot Drill

Purpose: To hit a drop shot off a fast-rebounding back-wall ball close to the front wall.

Directions: Stand in center court and hit a high, hard shot to the front wall; let the ball hit the back wall in the air, bounce near center court, and then attempt to drop it into a front corner by slowing down the forward momentum of the ball.

Diving

To dive or not to dive? That is the question. Some racquetball players believe that diving is an integral part of the advanced player's shot repertoire, but other racquetball players say that diving is not needed at any level of play.

The major controversy over diving centers upon injuries. Those who recommend diving say that injury is a part of the game, and those who reject diving declare that it is foolish to intentionally risk injury. You will have to make your own decision whether or not diving should be a part of your racquetball arsenal.

The basic purpose behind diving is to reach a ball that would be otherwise unretrievable. In most cases a dive is solely a defensive shot; however, you can occasionally hit offensively from a dive.

The dive is a last resort in attempting to retrieve a ball. It should never be a normal part of strategy because of the high risk of injury. No other shot or strategy in racquetball has as high an injury rate as diving. The dive should be reserved for special situations.

Figure 11-12. Hogan diving (Courtesy Racquetball Illustrated)

When to Dive

If you choose to dive, reserve the maneuver for crucial points such as tiebreakers or the end of close games. If the score is 17–17, an all out effort in the form of a dive might decide the outcome of the game. Scores of 0–0, 5–2, or even 16–2 would not warrant diving. In addition, if your opponent is not used to diving, the shot can throw a change of pace to a game that may help win the game. The importance of the game should also help you decide whether to dive or not. If it is in the first round of an insignificant tournament, diving is probably not called for; but near the finals of an important tournament the diving tactic might be worthwhile.

In general, keep diving to a minimum and dive only in crucial games and/or points. Apart from the risk of injury, diving takes a great deal of energy, and on many dive returns you are on the floor out of position while your opponent easily puts away your dive return. Also, when you dive and are on the floor in front of or close to your opponent, getting called for an avoidable hinder is a good possibility.

Dive Low

Let's look at the safest techniques to prevent injury while diving and still retrieve the ball. First, begin your dive from a low, semicrouched position. Do not stand erect and initiate your dive. The more momentum you build up going from high to low through a range of motion, the harder you hit the floor and the greater the chance for injury. Start low and dive low; this helps to avoid some injuries.

Preparation

Diving can be divided into preparation, the dive itself, and the recovery phase. Begin the preparation phase in a semicrouched position; take a step or steps as needed depending on how far you have to move to reach the ball; then lean into the dive and powerfully extend your legs and push off the floor. You should be fully extended and relatively parallel and low to the ground.

The Dive

While you are in the air, you should have your racquet out in front of you in a jabbing motion for safety as well as for maximum reach. Having your racquet well in front of you also saves time. You will not usually

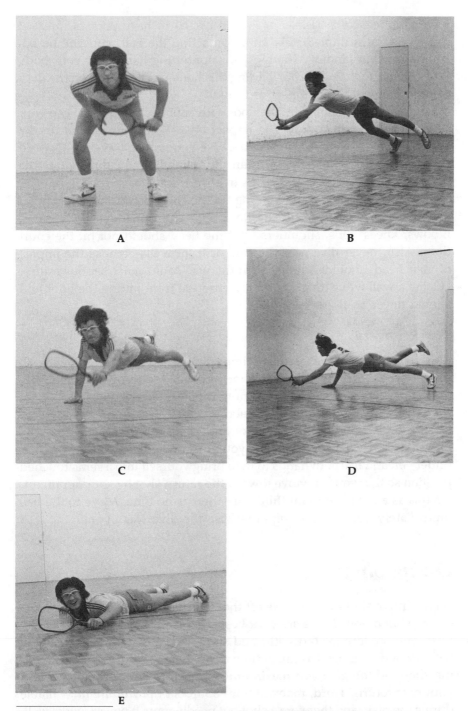

Figure 11-13. The normal forward dive for the left-handed player in sequence

have time to take a backswing, so you need to have your racquet set quickly. Almost immediately after contacting the ball, you will be approaching your landing. Having your nonhitting hand near your body is very important. As you are landing this hand can be placed on the floor to absorb some of the impact of the fall.

In addition, you should hit the floor with your back arched to keep your head and knees away from the impact area. You want to land on the abdominal area of the body, and because you will be traveling forward through the air as you land, you can slide slightly in the direction of the dive. This sliding action also helps to absorb some of the shock impact. Women players must avoid landing on the chest because of the danger of breast injury. Do not hit the floor with any unpadded body parts. Elbows, knees, hips, shoulders, and the head should not hit the court floor. Also, never dive near the side or front walls because the impact of your head, shoulder, or leg with the wall could cause serious injury. Hitting a wall while diving is totally different from hitting the floor and should never be done.

The Recovery

The recovery phase is exceedingly important because your opponent will probably be returning your dive shot. You need to recover immediately in order to have a chance of returning the next shot. You cannot lie on the floor after the dive and think about what a great return you made. So as soon as you have hit the floor and, very important, absorbed the impact properly to prevent injury, you must immediately bring your feet under you and use both hands to help bring yourself into a semicrouched position so that you can move toward the return shot by your opponent. Do this as a reflex, without thinking—there is no time. Move to the ball immediately upon recovering otherwise the dive was in vain.

Diving Shots

What kind of shots are possible off the dive? The basic dive return is the ceiling shot or lob. These are your best choices for a number of reasons. First, you are low to start with, and so it is very easy to get under the ball. Second, you need as much time as possible to recover, and the ceiling shot and lob give you maximum time before your opponent plays your dive return. Third, many of your sources of power are unavailable during the dive, and therefore a shot not needing much power works well.

Figure 11-14. The backward dive

Once in a while you can dive and hit an offensive shot such as a kill, pass, or pinch. This is difficult, but at times you can catch your opponent off guard with this offensive tactic, especially if he or she is anticipating a ceiling shot.

In any case, keep diving to a minimum, in practice sessions as well as in game play. We recommend that diving should be practiced only on a soft, shock absorbing surface such as in foam pits or on extrasoft or thick mats.

Diving occasionally is fine for advanced-level players. If you are diving quite often, however, you need to reconsider your playing strategy. No one's body can take the constant abuse of diving. The less you do, the better off you'll be and the less injury and pain you'll endure.

Keys for the Dive

- Keep diving to a minimum to help avoid body injury.
- Dive low and absorb the landing with a slide and the nonhitting hand and land on a padded body part.
- Don't dive into or near side walls or front walls.
- Recover quickly after you dive.

Drills for the Dive

No drills recommended on the court!

Mat Diving Drill (partner needed)

Purpose: To practice diving on a soft surface to prevent injury.

Directions: Have a partner throw you a low shot; begin in a low position, dive onto the mat, and hit the ball with a ceiling shot and immediately recover.

CHAPTER 12
Court Coverage

The primary factors that differentiate players at different levels are movement patterns and positioning on the court. This chapter is intended to introduce some new ideas on each of these areas under the general title of court coverage.

Movement Patterns

Movement patterns have been specifically discussed for various skills, but at this point a general summary of movement and its specific benefits is needed.

Before the movement begins, you must be in the basic ready position. Feet are about shoulder width apart, weight is forward on the balls of the feet, knees are slightly bent, waist area is slightly bent, and head and eyes are watching the ball and/or the opponent. The racquet is held either at the body midline or slightly to your backhand side. Being light and bouncy on your feet so that you can move quickly is exceedingly important.

Most ready position descriptions show the player facing forward, but in racquetball this is accurate only when you are behind the hitter. If you are in front of the hitter, your head should be turned to watch the hitter. Getting into the proper ready position is important because this affords the best possible mobility patterns. You can move with ease forward, backward, right, left, or diagonally.

Watch Your Opponent

Before moving toward the ball, watch your opponent. Notice where and how the opponent is positioned and, especially, racquet position at ball contact. By carefully watching your opponent get ready to hit the ball you can often determine by body, feet, and racquet position the type of shot to be played even before the ball is hit. Many players telegraph the shot by certain setting up characteristics.

Your opponent may not telegraph his or her strokes, but by watching closely you can react to the ball as soon as it leaves the racquet face rather than when the ball passes you on its way to the front wall. As soon as the ball leaves your opponent's racquet (or sooner), you can be moving to the area where the ball is going because you will know immediately

Figure 12-1. Lynn Adams in the basic ready position, with the head turned to watch Shannon Wright-Hamilton's return (Courtesy Racquetball Illustrated)

Figure 12-2A. Watch your opponent: Can you tell what return is going to be used?

Figure 12-2B. How about now?

whether the ball is going deep or short, left or right. As you move and concentrate on the ball, you will begin to fine tune your awareness of exactly where the ball is going to end up. The closer you and the ball get to each other, the easier it is to decide the *exact* spot where you would like to be in order to take the optimum shot. As you approach the hitting zone, position yourself for the shot. Ideally, you would like to be able to stop, get set, and hit the ball using the correct skill mechanics and power supply sources.

Be Light on Your Feet

Bounciness or lightness on the feet is also very important for your movement success on the court. It is a means of keeping your body moving continuously so that you can easily change your motion direction. Changing the direction of a body in motion is easier than putting a stationary body into motion. Bounciness takes many forms such as shuffling, bouncing, weaving, skipping, sliding, hopping, dancing, or just nondescript moving. But you should be in continual motion and never standing still.

Being in motion enables a player to react more quickly to any of the opponent's shots. The moving player can react more effectively to crotch shots, unexpected wall shots, and strange angle shots. Three factors are critical to ready position movement: first, all movements must be small and controlled; second, your feet must be close to the ground at all times because the farther from the floor you get, the more time it takes to react; and third, you must always be moving on the balls of your feet.

Small, controlled movements are important in order to maintain balance and coordination. If your movements are too large or too quick, you could lose control of your body, lose balance, and thus lose time. If you lose balance you cannot change body direction movements with ease. If you lose control you may be moving too far or too fast in the wrong direction. Losing balance or control takes time to correct and thus you may not be able to get to a ball that you should be able to retrieve. If your feet are too far off the floor, it takes too long to push off the floor to obtain the traction to move your body in the desired direction.

You must remain on the balls of the feet in order to move in all directions. If your weight is distributed evenly on the balls and heels or is only on your heels, you must first get it to the balls of the feet before you can begin moving with control. Transferring the weight to the balls of the feet takes valuable time, and you may not return a shot that you should have been able to return. All of the preliminary movement patterns and skills are designed to help you move quickly so that you can be in the best position to hit the ball with power and control.

Footwork and Positioning

Court covering movement is initiated by moving the feet, and you have a number of choices on how to start your movement. You can step out with the lead foot, jab-step with the lead foot, cross over with the trailing foot, or shuffle step to the side, front, or rear. As mentioned earlier in the return of service section (chapter 10), the step-out and crossover

Figure 12-3A. The step out with the lead foot for a left-handed player's forehand

Figure 12-3B. The crossover step for a right-handed player's backhand

steps are the quickest for covering shots that are far from your starting position. If the ball is fairly close to you, shuffling and the jab-step might work well.

Diagonal Movement Patterns

You may move in any direction, but the most useful patterns are diagonal movements across court both forwards and backwards. Diagonal movements are best because they are the quickest and shortest routes to the ball. Circular paths and angular paths are not as quick as diagonal movements.

Staying low as you move is important. Keep your body bent at both the knees and the waist. You should be in a semicrouched position while moving, just as you were in the initial ready position. The semicrouched position allows you to uncoil into the ball and hit with greater power than if you were standing erect.

Controlling your movement will help you return freak shots and will reduce the number of times you misjudge balls. As you move, try to control the length and speed of your steps. If the ball is far away, take large steps to cover as much ground as possible. As you get closer to the ball shorten your steps to set yourself in an effective hitting position.

Watch the Ball

Watching the ball helps you estimate the movement, speed, and direction of the ball, and these factors determine how and where you should move to cover the shot. Conversely, not concentrating on the ball diminishes the effectiveness of your play.

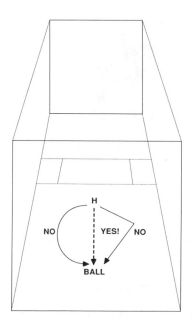

Figure 12-4. The shortest distance to the ball is a straight or diagonal path not a circular or angular path

Your eyes are the instruments that fine-tune your feet. As you become more advanced, you will learn to watch not only the ball but also your opponent's position to help you choose the type and placement of your return shot. But at all stages of play you should concentrate on watching the ball. Many shots must be played on the run, and you will not have time to move, stop, get set, and hit. In these situations, utilizing all the basic skills of hitting becomes more difficult. But if you have been concentrating and watching the ball, you will have the best possible chance of playing even these very difficult chances effectively.

Try to Be Set

Imagine shooting a rifle while you are standing still as opposed to while you are running. Of course, you are likely to shoot much better from the standing position, and the same applies in racquetball. Your shooting is much more accurate and consistent when you can set up properly. If you are running and hitting the ball at the same time, your stroke and shot placement will be less effective. Therefore, trying to get set before you play the shot is exceedingly important.

However, when you do not have time to set up properly, two strategies may be helpful. First, think slow motion and swing with less than full power; hit the ball at half or three-quarter speed. Second, play percentages and use a shot that has the best chance of being successful. These strategies should allow you to hit your best possible shot under very difficult circumstances.

Control Center Court

After playing a shot, your movement patterns should always be in the direction of center court because you can control the game from this position. Center court is located behind the short service line and is a circular area seven to ten feet in diameter. Your movement patterns away from the ball are just as important as your movement patterns toward the ball and reaching center court after your shot is as necessary to successful racquetball as moving into position to hit. All the elements of proper movement toward the ball apply equally to your movement patterns toward center court.

Anticipation

Some players will amaze you with their quickness and ability to return apparently unreachable balls. Quickness in body movement is important,

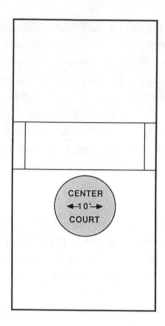

Figure 12-5. Center court—your goal!

but anticipation is also important in successfully returning apparently non-returnable shots.

You can learn to anticipate and thus to improve your ability to retrieve balls, and three key concepts are essential. First, you must analyze your opponent's likes and dislikes. Second, you must remember which shot is used in a particular situation and where the ball will end up. Third, you must learn to watch closely, or read, the ball and your opponent. In the following sections we will discuss these factors in depth.

Analyze Your Opponent

Every player prefers to hit certain shots in certain situations on the court. Once you analyze and learn your opponent's preferences and idiosyncrasies, you can anticipate and play for that shot when that situation occurs. Also, your opponent may be restricted by his or her skill to certain shots in certain situations; if your analysis is correct you will recognize the situation and anticipate the shot. Watching your opponent play other opponents should help your analysis. If this is not possible, observe your opponent's warm up and analyze his or her strengths, weaknesses, and shot preferences. These preferences will appear in the game, and your

Figure 12-6. A high shot to the left handed player's back corner. Anticipate a return of a ceiling shot or lob.

analysis should lead to successful anticipation. If you play an opponent often enough, of course, you will have analyzed him or her already and will be able to apply that information to your current match.

When analyzing an opponent, also look for idiosyncrasies such as improper positioning on certain strokes, odd grips, and other unusual aspects of your opponent's style. These odd habits cause players to hit in unexpected ways that you will be able to anticipate.

Remember Specifics

The second major area of anticipation is remembering, which is different from analysis and takes two forms. First of all you should make mental notes of what your opponent fails to do in a given situation. You are not analyzing specific mechanics, but you are remembering likes and dislikes of your opponent. If you can remember these shots during a game, you can get a jump on the ball.

The second part is remembering where the ball will end up based on its speed, spin, angle, and height. There are thousands of ways for a ball to react in the court. The more you play, the more you learn about the bounce of the ball, and the more rebounds and angles you can recall, the better you will be able to anticipate where the ball is going to end up.

Read the Ball and the Opponent

Effective anticipation requires you to watch the ball and your opponent as he or she sets up and strikes the ball. Watching the opponent can often give you clues about the upcoming shot. Your opponent's point of contact when stroking helps to determine the path of the ball. If contact is even with the front hip, the ball will travel straight. If contact is in front of the body, the ball will travel diagonally left (for a right-handed hitter). If contact is behind the hitter, the ball will travel diagonally right (for a right-handed hitter).

The height of the ball contact is also important. It is easy to play a high ball high and a low ball low, so if your opponent's ball contact is high, look for ceiling shots; if low, look for kills; if waist high, look for passing shots.

Another factor to look for in anticipating is the position of your opponent in the court. If your opponent is deep, most shots will probably be passes and ceilings; if your opponent is forward, look for kills. On any setup or plum, think kill.

Still another factor that helps in anticipation is reading angles and direction as the ball comes off the wall. A ball traveling straight along and close to a side wall will probably be returned straight back to the front wall, and a shot caroming off the side wall has a good chance of being hit back to that side wall.

Reading the opponent also helps anticipation because the way the opponent sets up will often telegraph the shot. If your opponent's feet are pointed directly to a side wall, the shot will probably be a parallel shot. If your opponent's feet are pointed or angled toward the front wall, it will probably be an angled return. If your opponent's hitting shoulder is dropped, look for a lower power shot. If your opponent's hitting shoulder is up, look for a ceiling shot. If your opponent's shoulders are parallel to the front wall, look for a shot with minimum power. Finally, if your opponent is facing the back wall, expect a back-wall–back-wall return.

Watching the ball at all times is also important. You react to the ball's spin, speed, height, power, and angle. If you watch the ball and your opponent's positioning for the stroke, you can react much more quickly than if you face the front wall and react to the ball when it comes into your peripheral vision.

Keys for Court Coverage

- Use the most efficient movement patterns to get to the ball or to get to center court.
- Always watch the ball and your opponent in order to anticipate and react more quickly to the ensuing shot.

Drill for Court Coverage

Turn and Watch Drill (with partner)

Purpose: To learn to watch your opponent and the ball consistently.

Directions: Rally the ball with a partner and practice constantly watching your partner and the ball by looking forward and/or by turning your head to look back.

CHAPTER 13
New–Old Basics and New Ideas

This chapter is designed to be a catchall for new ideas. The first portion of the chapter deals with backhands, quick-draw forehands, half-volleys, Z shots, spin, corner shots, angles, rebounds, splats, and drills. The second part of the chapter contains combination shots, trick shots, shot analysis charts, grunts, and sounds.

New–Old Basics

The term *new-old* basics is used to describe strokes, shots, and techniques that have been used for many years, but of which many people are not aware. These basics will also add some *new* insight for many players. Thus after learning the basic shots, serves, and returns you can now add some additional basics to your game arsenal.

Backhand

The backhand is really an *easier* shot to master than the forehand! Many players, especially beginners, would possibly disagree with this statement, so how can it be true that the backhand is an easier shot than the forehand? Anatomically, as you swing your arm in the forehand, your body is actually in the way of your swing. In the backhand, however, you are swinging away from your body, and it is an easier, smoother shot. The reason backhands are as difficult as they seem is that we do very little in everyday activities to use the backhand side of our bodies. Because of this lack of use, our muscles and our movement patterns on the backhand side are normally weaker than our forehand side. This includes the use of our arms in the swing, the rotation of the upper body in the opposite direction, and the pushing off with the nondominant leg as we hit a backhand.

To improve your backhand you must practice! You may also consider a power backhand and a two-handed backhand. Practicing the backhand is exceedingly important. Beginning and intermediate level players should practice backhands at least twice as much as they do forehands. The extra practice is useful for getting comfortable with the little-used backhand side of the body.

Because the backhand is difficult for so many players, a few other keys for success need to be mentioned. If you are having trouble changing your grip from forehand to backhand, try the continental grip (see chapter 6), which you grasp between the Eastern forehand and the Eastern backhand grips. With the continental grip you keep the same grip for all strokes.

Awareness of your power supplies is very important for a successful backhand. Once again, because of the lack of use of the backhand side of the body backhand shots usually have little power. A few key points might be helpful to the beginner or intermediate-level player. First, periodically check your backswing to make sure that your racquet is well back behind your opposite ear. Having your wrist bent (laid back) is also important. If you need extra power, exaggerate the backswing. Contacting the ball just in front of the lead leg also gives additional power to the backhand.

Some individuals see the backhand like a bullwhip action or the action of snapping a towel. In the backhand all forces should come together at the time of the *snap*—the time of racquet–ball impact. The bullwhip backhand technique is a good idea, but remember your follow-through. Snapping a whip or a towel requires little follow-through, but on the bullwhip backhand a follow-through is absolutely essential.

All of the sources of power (see chapter 6) that we have talked about are important for a successful backhand; employ them all. If you are still uncomfortable, try a two-handed backhand. Use two forehand grips to stabilize the racquet. The two-handed backhand also allows you to keep the same grip with your forehand grip all the time. You never change it; you just add the second hand above the existing forehand grip. The two-handed backhand gives you a shorter reach; however, it aids your stability and gives you some extra power because you have a second hand on the racquet. You lose a little power because your lever arm is shorter and because you cannot bring your racquet through as large a range of motion as you can with a one-handed backhand.

Quick-Draw Forehand

Sometimes a ball comes at you after hitting a crotch, or it takes a freak bounce and you cannot set up properly to hit it with correct mechanics. You need to be able to adjust and, nevertheless, hit an offensive shot, and this shot is termed a quick-draw forehand.

In this quick-action shot the wrist becomes the major source of power because you do not have time to set up. Keep the wrist flexible, almost rubbery; you cannot hit the quick-action shot with a stiff wrist with any power. The swing is modified from the regular forehand swing and is much shorter. Use the bullwhip or towel-snapping backhand action with little follow-through. You will not have time to get your body and feet turned sideways, so you will have to exaggerate upper-body rotation and

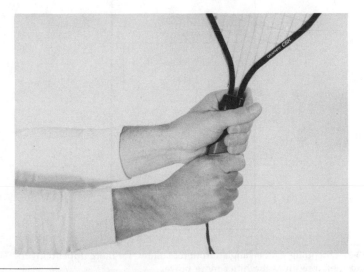

Figure 13-1. The two-handed backhand

shifting of the weight from your heels to your toes to obtain some extra force.

Often when using this quick-action shot, racquet–ball contact occurs behind your ideal hitting position, which creates problems of accuracy and control. Hitting too late may be caused by two factors. First, you may have reacted too late because of the unpredictability of the shot itself. Second, you may have let the ball get past the correct hitting position in order to give yourself a little extra time to react to the ball. These problems can be solved with practice. The quick-draw forehand can be practiced by playing balls with less footwork movement than usual and hitting the ball with a quicker than normal action. Work on and stress the rubbery-flexible wrist action. As you practice quick-draw shots, put yourself in an awkward position when hitting, but try to make the stroke fluid by using extra wrist action.

Your forward stride can also help or hinder your forehand. Many beginners step forward with the lead foot while keeping the toes pointed at the side wall, which limits upper-body rotation. If you angle your foot forward when you step forward, the upper body can rotate farther, thus providing more power in the swing. The increase in upper-body rotation is caused by opening the hips, which allows for greater range of motion.

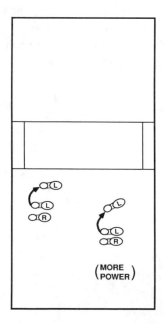

Figure 13-2. Stepping with an angled front foot allows for more upper body rotation and therefore gives the hitter more power

Half-Volley

The half-volley is an option for playing a ball that hits close to your feet. It is not really a volley, but the ball is played almost immediately after it bounces. You play it on the short hop. The half-volley is defensive when it is the only way you can play a ball at your feet and you are only attempting to return it to the front wall. But it can also be used offensively like a volley to catch your opponent off guard and to give him or her less time to react to the ball.

You can hit passing shots, kill shots, and ceiling shots off a half-volley. The best body position is facing a side wall, but you can also play this shot facing the front wall. Getting yourself low is very important for passing and kill half-volleys, but for the ceiling half-volley getting low is not as important. Use any appropriate grip and try to bend at your knees. Keep your back straight and try to keep your racquet head up unless you are going to the ceiling. Lean your weight into the stroke; you will probably not be able to step into the ball because it is already close to your feet. Keeping your head down in order to watch the ball is exceedingly important because if you lift your head, your body will rise, your swing will rise, and the ball will hit high on the front wall. Use a shorter than normal backswing and follow-through because you have so little time to react. You can practice half-volleying by taking balls on the short hop during practice.

Z Shot

The Z shot follows a path similar to the letter Z and is similar to the Z serve. Hit Z shots sparingly because unless you can hit a perfect Z with the ball ending up hugging and running parallel to the back wall, it can set up your opponent. Z shots may be used defensively to give you time to get back in position, or they can be used offensively as a change-of-pace weapon.

It should be hit from the backcourt area to the front wall about 15 to 16 feet high in the corner; the ball hits the side wall quickly and carries diagonally crosscourt, then rebounds off the opposite side wall about three feet to a few inches from the back wall, and then rebounds parallel to the back wall. This makes return shots difficult. The Z shot is quite effective against beginners because they get confused when the ball rebounds off several walls. But against more advanced opponents, the Z shot becomes less effective because they can read the ball's angle and ending points. Unless the Z shot is creeping along the back wall, it will be put away by an advanced player.

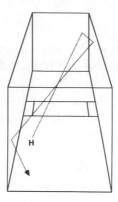

Figure 13-3.   The path of the Z shot

Ball Spin

Ball spin is not nearly as important in racquetball as in other sports. However, understanding the basics of spin and how spin can help in a game situation is important for every player.

First, let's look at how we put spin on the ball. Spin is caused by hitting the ball somewhere off center. Sidespin is caused by hitting the ball on one side of the center, backspin is caused by hitting the bottom of the ball, and topspin is caused by hitting the top part of the ball. Hitting between these areas can cause combination spins. But remember that any spin added to the ball is often lost after the ball contacts a wall or two. The final spin on the racquetball is a result of the speed of the ball, the angle of the ball, the angle of the ball bounce, the height of the ball, and the angle of the racquet head at contact. Ball spin is a somewhat complicated feature of racquetball.

Because every player has a unique swing, and thus will put different types and amounts of spin on the ball, spin should be looked at by every player according to his or her own skill mechanics. To begin, notice that hitting different parts of the ball surface allows you to vary the spin you are imparting (see Fig. 13-4).

Now take a practice shot and then repeat the shot using a variety of different spins. Observe how each type of spin affects the rebounding action off the front wall, the floor bounce, and where the ball eventually ends. Keep your court position and the speed of the shot the same while you experiment with different kinds of spin. After this exercise, try varying your hitting speed, slightly changing your hitting position, and using several different levels of racquet–ball contact.

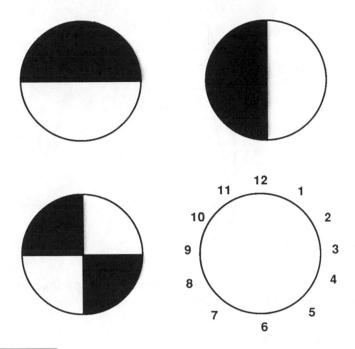

Figure 13-4. You can divide the ball a number of ways in order to develop hitting areas on the ball, so as to impart spin on your shots

Using ball spin can be an important way to help your game, but you need to understand how your style of play and ball spin affect each other. In order to understand this interaction you need to practice spins and to find out which type of spin works best for you in a given situation.

Splats

The splat is really a very hard elongated pinch shot. The ball is contacted very close to a side wall and is hit into the side wall near where you originally contacted the ball. The ball usually has a large amount of spin on it which causes it to be unpredictable when it comes off the front wall.

The ball is hit similar to a parallel passing shot but it glances off the side wall and becomes a type of pinch. The glancing off the side wall imparts excessive spin to the ball which can cause the ball to react like a perfect pinch, streak down through the center of the court or spin off the front wall in a cross-court pass. In any case the splat receives its name from the distinct sound it makes when it hits into the front wall. It makes a ''splat'' sound and then comes off the front wall in a strange manner. The splat is a power shot and if not accurately placed it many times can come off the front wall and set-up your opponent. The splat can be hit

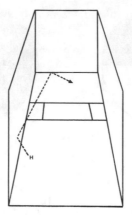

Figure 13-5. A typical splat

either underhand or overhead and should be used sparingly since there is a good chance of the ball coming out to center court.

Corner Balls and Shots

Let's now consider the importance of placing your shots in the back corners. What we mean by the back corner is a cube three feet by three feet by three feet. First, hitting your ceiling shots, passing shots, lobs, and serves into the back corners is exceedingly important. The offensive advantage is that it makes your opponent hit the ball the longest distance to the front wall, thus allowing the greatest chance for error. Second, if your shot stays in the corner cube, the opponent must contend with both

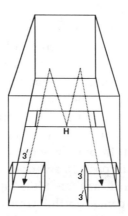

Figure 13-6. The corner cube areas are two of the "gold mines" of the court

the back and side wall in taking his or her swing. Third, a ball hitting in the corner can take odd bounces and angles, which can further frustrate the returner. So the corners are excellent areas of the court in which to hit the ball. Not only are the backhand corner and the center court the two most important areas of the court, but hitting to the corners also enables you to take and hold center-court position.

Even if your shot to the corner is less than perfect, the ball may still be difficult to return. It might come straight out of the corner hugging the side wall or it might come out running parallel to and hugging the back wall. But given these possible difficulties, what are the best techniques for returning a ball out of the corners? Most of the time a good corner shot will force you to be defensive, and a good option is the ceiling shot. When the ball goes into the corner, be patient, decide where it is going to end up, and position yourself for the best possible return. This is a good example of the necessity of watching the ball; moving to where you think it will end up and deciding where to position yourself will depend on your ability to remember rebound angles. If you do not know the angles, you must practice hitting balls into the corner. Attempt to understand and remember the angles as you return practice shots out of the corner.

Once in a while it is to your advantage to play a ball while it is moving through the back corner rather than waiting until it begins to come out. If you think that the ball is going to rebound hugging a wall, it might be a more difficult shot to wait on the ball than to play it in the corner.

Your footwork is important in playing corner shots. If you are overly anxious you will be jammed into the corner. Be patient and play corner balls with backhands on the backhand side of the body. Don't try to play them with forehands by running around your backhand. Take controlled steps and employ cross-over and step-out approaches in order to reach the ball. Remember that if you have to contend with the backwall and sidewall, you may have to slightly alter your ideal hitting position in order to bring the ball out of the corner with a good return.

Angles

Tens of thousands of angles are possible as a ball bounces off the floor, ceiling, walls, and corners of the court, and we cannot teach you all of these angles. You must play points, rally the ball, and begin to learn for yourself exactly how different shots rebound. Angles also change when you play a new opponent because every player has a unique style of play, which affects the ball's angles.

If a ball is hit hard, the angle at which it rebounds will usually be less than the angle of the same shot hit with less power. More power means sharper angles, and less power means wider angles. Also, in most cases the sharper the angle of a ball into a corner, the more quickly it rebounds through the corner.

Rebounds

Racquetball is a game of ball rebounds. You should decide where you think the ball will end up and move to that position rather than trying to run after, or follow, the ball. This strategy helps you to reach the appropriate hitting position and to spend less energy and time getting there. The higher the ball is hit onto the front wall, the higher it will rebound into the air and travel into the backcourt.

Any time a ball hits a crotch during a rally it will take unpredictable bounces, and you should prepare yourself to react accordingly.

Drills

Practice is important, and one of the most important ways to practice is the use of drills. Two factors are important in practice drills. One is that you can work from simple drills to complex drills, and the other is that you can benefit from repetition.

Because of the ease of keeping a ball in play after only a few times on the court, many beginners do not spend time practicing skills and using drills. Like any sport, racquetball requires practice in game situations and in skill drills, and both are important components to successful racquetball.

Simple to Complex

Throughout this text drills have been stressed. We would now like to discuss more about progressing from simple to complex drills. Let's look at a drill to practice forehand kills. The easiest place to hit forehand kills successfully is close to the front wall, so we start our drill in the service area. Next, it is easier to hit a kill low to the front wall if we contact the ball near the floor, so we need a low ball in our drill. It is also easier to hit a stationary ball or a ball with only one direction of force. How can you hit a stationary ball for kill practice? Use a tee. A small paper cup will do. Hitting the ball off the cup keeps the drill simple. Staying in the service area also keeps it simple. The actual swing and hit should be partial speed, maybe half- or three-quarter speed, for control purposes. To make this drill more difficult you can drop the ball low, move farther from the front wall, and hit harder. You can make it more difficult by having the ball moving not only up but forwards or backwards as well. You can also make it more difficult by changing the speed, angle, and height of the ball before contact is made. It is important to drill from the simple to the complex. It is like working from the basic foundation of a building (simple) to the total structure (complex) of the building.

Repetition

The repetition factor in practice drills is of major importance. Drills allow you to get maximum benefits from practicing over a given period of time because of their repetitive form. Also, repetition is excellent for perfecting your skills. The recurring patterns used in drills can help speed up the learning sequences in skill acquisition.

One of the problems is that practice drills can be boring because of their repetition. To avoid boredom think creatively and modify your drills. For example, in the kill drill previously mentioned, you could attach targets to the front wall such as jar lids, paper, balloons, cups, and so forth, and you could raise and lower the tee. Adding some diversity to drills can spice up your practice sessions. Drilling is paramount to successful racquetball playing, so take time each week for drilling sessions as well as playing time.

New Ideas

Every sport has people who are innovators, exhibitionists, or simply eccentrics, and yet add positive, new twists to the game. Presented in this section are some new ideas about unconventional shots, methods of charting game play, and *reading* racquetball games by watching and listening for telltale clues to how the ball is played.

Combination Shots

Shots that combine two or more basic techniques are called combination shots. Every racquetball player hits a shot that cannot be classified as standard, and yet this unorthodox shot can be played for a winner. You can combine shots, for example, by trying overheads on what are usually underhand shots, or hitting shots in the forecourt that are normally hit from the backcourt, or driving shots with power that are customarily returned with control. You should also consider shots that are hit at strange angles and with odd spins, and don't forget the oddball shot that may use too many or two few walls to accomplish its purpose.

When employed in the right situation, combination shots will place your opponent on the defense, increase your time to regain good court position, or win a point or service for you. Some shots described in previous chapters are actually combination shots; the splat, the reverse ceiling, the Z shot, and the back wall–back wall shot all meet the definition. Try to hit an overhead pinch or reverse pinch in the backcourt or in center court, with power or with touch, or try hitting a backcourt drop reverse pinch. These shots have all been hit at one time or another but have never been discussed or written about at length. Combination shots are fun, practical, and they can be creative. In a strange rally situation or an unfamiliar court position, step forward and try your own combination shot to continue the rally or to win a point.

Trick Shots

Most trick shots are awkward, last-ditch shots, but you can hit winners with them—demoralizing winners. They can be played by combining movements and skills when you are caught in an unfavorable position, and by practicing trick shots you can increase your percentage of winners. Remember, trick shots should be used only when you are caught out of position. Using them for any other reason is not very practical.

Trick shots are combination shots employed to return an apparently nonreturnable ball, which may be nonreturnable because of your poor positioning or because of a great shot by your opponent. Sometimes trick shots are used because you get handcuffed by a freak ball or crotch ball that was totally unexpected.

Many trick shots are possible, just as many combination shots are, but a few trick shots are employed more often than others. The between-the-legs kill, pass, ceiling, or pinch are common trick shots. It should be noted that trick shots can be defensive or offensive. If you can hit a good between-the-legs kill, you not only score a point but your opponent may also become dejected. It is depressing for your opponent to hit an excellent shot that should not be returned, and not only is it returned with a trick shot but it is also a winner.

Between-the-legs shot.　Let's take a look at the between-the-legs shot. This shot is usually employed when you have mispositioned yourself or when the ball takes a freaky bounce off the back wall or side wall. Let's say that a back-wall shot is coming right at you and that you are inadvertently facing the back wall. You allow the ball to drop down between your legs, and then you hit a forehand flick-shot through the legs to the side of the front wall. A flicking action is used because you have no time or space for a windup and follow-through. Also, this shot can be modified by lifting one leg so that a larger opening is available through which to hit the ball.

Forehand backhand.   Another fairly common trick shot is a forehand backhand. This shot is executed when you are attempting to play a ball on your backhand side that has gone deep into the court, and you are moving toward the backwall. The ball takes a strange bounce, and all you can do is hit the ball as you are facing the back wall with the forehand face of your racquet on the backhand side of the body. It is usually an underhand shot.

Behind-the-back shot.   A third trick shot that is seen sporadically is the behind-the-back shot. Once again, it is usually employed when you are out of position. It is usually executed from the normal backhand side when you are facing the back wall, and you contact the ball with the forehand face or backhand face of the racquet. This is also a flick-shot because of difficult body positioning.

Shot Analysis Chart

A shot analysis chart is a means of recording where you hit shots, the type of shots, and their success in a match. It will give you a good indication of where you performed well and where you had the most difficulty, and you can use this information to improve your point output. You can design your own chart for other skills such as overheads, pinches, lobs, and drop shots. In any case, use this chart to record the total number of shots you hit, your percentage of forehands, and your percentage of winners. It can be very helpful in improving your game. For example, if you find that you were successful on only 25 percent of your backhand kill attempts and that you were successful on 85 percent of your forehand passing shots, you will know that you have to work hard on backhand kills in practice but spend much less time on forehand passing shots.

You must have a coach or friend record your shots for you, and because the ball travels so fast in racquetball it is possible that not all shots will be marked. Two recorders can do a more thorough job, with each recorder having responsibilities only for certain shots. If two recorders are impractical, one person recording as many shots as possible will still

Figure 13-7. A series of trick shots used only when caught out of position and only when no other shot will work: (A) behind-the-back; (B) forward, between-the-legs; (C) backward; (D) wall, between-the-legs-backward trick shot; (E) climbing the sidewall for a ''high'' backhand.

give you a fairly accurate analysis of your game. See page 230 for a sample shot analysis chart.

The Grunt

The grunt is a sound that we hear in many situations of maximum exertion. For example, if you have to move a large heavy object by pushing it, you may well grunt while completing the task. Grunting is the result of applying maximum force. Physiologically, it is the effect of the diaphragm forcibly expelling some residual air from the lungs. The diaphragm is an internal muscular structure beneath the lungs, which contracts and expands under a variety of different situations. We sometimes grunt when we are hit in the abdominal area by an object, such as a ball; the diaphragm contracts and forces our residual air out of our lungs.

In racquetball the grunt is a sign of near maximum body exertion and/or extension. This level of exertion is important in achieving maximum force on your hits and maximum hustle around the court. For example, if you are hitting power drive serves, you should be grunting on every serve because the serve requires maximum force to be effective.

If you are not grunting on hard-hit or hard-to-retrieve shots, you are probably not maximizing your efforts. Notice if you are grunting on your supposedly maximum-effort shots. Grunting just for the sake of grunting, of course, is not really helpful for skill improvement. However, learning to maximize your efforts so that a grunt is heard indicates that you are going all out for the shot, and this is an important aid in winning points.

Sounds

Listening to the sounds in the court can help improve your game. Other than grunts, the sounds that are important to a player are the sound of feet, the sound of racquet–ball contact, and the sound of ball–wall contact. You should be able to use these sounds to your advantage to help you anticipate and react more quickly in a given situation.

For example, if you hear your opponent's feet close behind you while you are in center court, you know that your opponent is moving forward, and you should play a ceiling shot or a passing shot rather than attempting a kill. Also, the sound of a ball coming off a racquet with a cracking sound tells you that the ball has been hit hard. Some individuals have

ANALYSIS OF RACQUETBALL SHOTS

MATCH _____   DATE _____   COURT _____

PLAYER _____   GAME #1   2   3   WIN — LOSS _____

	First Serve	Second Serve	Return of Serve – Down the Line		Passing Shots – Cross Court		Passing Shots – Down the Middle		Volleys – Kills		Volleys – Passing		Ceilings – Parallel		Ceilings – Angle		Kills – Corner		Kills – Straight		Backwall Shots – Passing		Backwall Shots – Kills	
			F	B	F	B	F	B	F	B	F	B	F	B	F	B	F	B	F	B	F	B	F	B
Number of Shots																								
Number of Successful Shots																								
Number of Winners (Points)																								
Number of Placements (Complete Ace)																								
Number of Points Lost																								

different ball–racquet contact sounds for their kills, passes, and pinches. If you can attune yourself to the differences, you can use the sound to anticipate and reach an otherwise unplayable ball.

Another sound you need to pay attention to is the sound of ball–wall contact. The sound of a crosscourt passing shot may be quite different from that of a pinch, and these differences should enable you to react

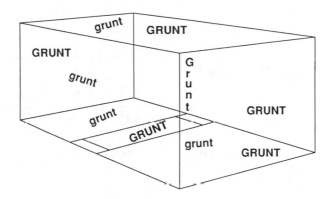

Figure 13-8. Grunts should be heard all over the court especially on power shots

quickly to the ball. The lack of sound and partial sounds are also important. The lack of sound indicates a touch shot, and partial sound may indicate a spinning ball or a mis-hit shot. Recognizing the meaning of these sounds—or lack of sound—should also help your reaction.

You should also know that balls from different manufacturers make different sounds. You need to get used to the sound of the ball you are using, and this idea carries over to court structure, floor structure, racquet brands, and various string tensions. If you are playing on a court for the first time, hit for a while to get used to the sound. The same is true of new balls, new racquets, or new strings. A newly strung racquet gives not only a different hit but also a different sound that you need to get used to.

Background sounds are also important to your racquetball success. This is unwanted sound from adjacent courts, balconies, hallways or, the external building. The noise may be from voices, ball hits, yells, scrapes, or automobiles. You must learn to block out these sounds as you play. They are distractions you must learn to ignore because they can cause a momentary lapse in concentration and thus possibly a loss of a point or rally. Sounds within the court are to be listened to and used to your advantage; external sounds are to be blocked out.

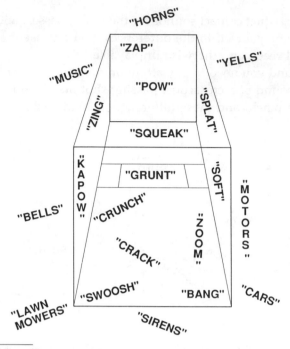

Figure 13-9. Sounds both in and out of the court are important in racquetball

Keys for New-Old Basics and New Ideas

- Practice difficult rather than easy shots.
- Drills help to speed up skill acquisition, but you must also play points; both practice methods enhance the learning of racquetball skills.
- Trick shots should be practiced but used sparingly in game situations because of their degree of difficulty.
- Use court sounds to your advantage but block out background noise.

CHAPTER 14
Basic Errors and
How to Correct Them

Throughout the text attention has been given to fundamental concerns within a specific area of racquetball. The purpose of this chapter is to consolidate into one unit the most basic errors found among racquetball players, to illustrate these errors, and to offer specific suggestions for correcting them.

Top Ten Errors

1. *Playing the ball too high.* Playing the ball too high often results from impatience and hitting the ball too soon. This problem causes awkward swings because too little time is available to the hitter. Playing the ball high also keeps the ball high on the front wall.

Figure 14-1. Playing the ball too high

Wait for the ball to get low, hit the ball sidearm or underhand but not overhand. When practicing, let the ball bounce a number of times before you swing rather than just once. This will give you ample time to get set and will also allow the ball to be bouncing low when you swing.

2. *Hitting without power.* Improper body position and not using all of the power supply sources can cause a lack of power.

Make sure you are facing a side wall on all shots. If you are facing the front wall, you cannot employ all of your power supplies. You should check for a high backswing, good follow-through, stepping into the ball, upper body rotation, and wrist rotation-flexion. The legs should extend into the shot, and both the shoulder and the elbow should help as the ball is contacted. All of these forces must be concentrated at racquet–ball impact, and the correct point of contact is approximately opposite the lead foot.

3. *Bending improperly.* Without properly bending, you will have great difficulty keeping your shots low. Bending only at the waist does not allow you to achieve a low enough body position.

You must bend not only at the waist but also at the knees. The combination of waist flexion and knee flexion allows you to get very low. But you achieve the lowest positioning while bending by also lunging, which gives a good base of support, lowers your center of gravity, and allows you to extend your legs into the shot easily.

Figure 14-2. Getting down low

4. *Hitting balls to midcourt.*   Hitting balls at the improper angle or too hard can cause this error, which gives the opponent an easy opportunity for an offensive rather than defensive return. Concentrate on hitting the balls into the back corners.

If your shot is going to midcourt off the side walls, adjust your shot angle to the front wall. If the ball is going to midcourt off the back wall, hit the ball lower to the front wall or hit with a little less

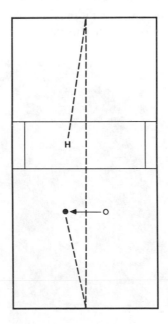

Figure 14-3. Hitting the ball to center court

power. If the ball is going to midcourt off the front wall, change
your shot angle to the front wall and hit the ball lower on the front
wall.

5. *Not maintaining center-court position.*   This causes you to lose the control and tempo of the game and makes you a defensive player rather
than an offensive player. But to play effectively you need to be
constantly moving toward center court.

   On returns you should attempt either to win the point or to
maneuver your opponent out of center court so that you can move
into center court. Remember, center court is the circle seven to ten
feet in diameter directly behind the short service area. You must
hit the correct shot at the right time in order to move your opponent. Use ceilings, lobs, and passing shots when your opponent
is forward. Use kills, pinches, and drops when your opponent is
back.

6. *Following the ball with the body.*   If you are constantly running around
the court chasing down balls, you will be awkward, tired, and unable to have time to get set for your shot. You must learn to judge
where the ball will end up and then move to that position.

   Watch the ball at all times. When it leaves your opponent's racquet, watch the ball and decide where it is going to end up and
move to that position to hit the ball.

Figure 14-4. The eyes have it! Yellen playing Wagner (Courtesy Racquetball
Illustrated)

7. *Not playing the angles correctly.* Failing to understand rebound angles will prevent you from hitting many shots successfully. You must learn how a ball is going to rebound both off the walls and off your racquet face.

   To understand wall angles, you must practice with different speeds and differently angled shots and watch where the ball goes. Because thousands of wall angles are possible, a great deal of practice is required. Use both drills and practice games.

   The racquet face angle should be flat. If the face is too open, the ball will go high. If the face is too closed, the ball will go low. The same is true if you play a ball sidearm or underhand. When the face is angled back, the ball will go off to your right, and if the face is angled forward, the ball will angle off to your left (for the right-handed hitter). For maximum ball control and accuracy, practice keeping the racquet face flat.

8. *Hitting with power but with no accuracy.* A beginning player who is a hard hitter can win many games by overpowering his or her opponents. But power without accuracy is quite ineffective against a more highly skilled player who has patience, waits for the ball to setup, and then returns it for a winner.

   You may need to sacrifice some of your power to improve your accuracy, but you should not radically change your swing or abandon the power sources of proper hitting mechanics. For example, don't stop your follow-through or shorten your backswing. Instead, try slowing down while maintaining good stroke mechanics. See if your accuracy improves while practicing hitting at three-quarter or even half-speed.

9. *Running around your backhand.* Some players think, "Do anything but avoid the backhand at all costs because it is my weakness." If you are hitting too many back-wall–back-wall shots it is because you are attempting *not* to use your backhand.

   Remember that the backhand is an anatomically easy stroke to hit; the problem is we don't use it enough. Therefore, think backhand on every possible shot to get as much practice as possible. This will help you become more familiar with and more comfortable using the backhand. Take balls out of the backhand corner with backhand shots, try serving with your backhand, and try making all hits with backhands when practicing.

10. *Missing the ball.* This is caused by awkward play and the result of the many problems already mentioned.

Figure 14-5. A good side position hit, with good eye contact with the ball, by Lynn Adams (Courtesy Racquetball Illustrated)

Use the side-facing basic hitting position, anticipate where the ball will end up, and stress accuracy rather than speed. Be patient, learn court geometry, and follow the ball with your eyes and not your body.

Keys for Basic Errors and How to Correct Them

- Think and practice your skills both in drill and game situations; make use of shot analysis charts and video taping.
- After playing a match study the parts of this book (or other racquetball books) that address the specific areas in which you had the problems during your match.

CHAPTER 15
Playing Strategies
and Tournament Play

Strategies have been briefly mentioned throughout the text, but this chapter will take an in-depth look at various strategies and how you might best use them. Remember that many strategies change and become more or less important as racquetball skill levels change. However, a few basic strategies apply to all players, and these are discussed first.

Strategies for All

Whether you are an advanced, intermediate, or beginning player, the following strategies will help you improve your play. These strategies focus on the basic principles of racquetball play and will also help you develop insight into the game. In fact, chapter 17 ("More with Marty") reinforces these basic strategies as the basis of effective tournament play.

Hit to Your Opponent's Weakness

Hitting the ball to your opponent's weakness is one of the most important basic strategies in the game of racquetball. The weakness of the majority of players is usually the backhand.

Hit Away from Your Opponent

A second major strategy is to hit the ball away from your opponent. For example, hit pinch shots, kills, and drop shots when your opponent is in the backcourt and passing shots, lobs, and ceiling shots when your opponent is in center court. You should also hit to the right side of the court if your opponent is in the left side of the court and vice versa.

Control Center Court

A third major strategy for all players is to control center court, the circle seven to ten feet in diameter just behind the short service line. This position affords you an equal chance to reach all portions of the court and gives you offensive rather than defensive shot selection.

Shoot For the Corners

A fourth strategy for players at all levels is to hit most shots into the back corners, in particular the backhand corner. Because the corners are the farthest from the front wall, your opponent must return the ball over the greatest distance, and this gives him or her the greatest opportunity for error. Also, the two walls (in the corners) make swinging the racquet very difficult, so hitting into a corner should impede your opponent's swing. In addition, unusual and unexpected rebound angles occur out of the corners—yet another offensive advantage. These strange angles and rebounds make life more challenging for your opponent on the court.

Be Patient and Play the Ball Low

A final strategy of major importance to all players is to be patient and to play the ball low rather than rushing and playing the ball high. This is much easier for the intermediate and advanced level player to do than for the beginner. Yet all players need to strive to be patient and to play the ball low. The lower you play the ball, the lower it will hit the front wall and the more difficult it will be for your opponent to return.

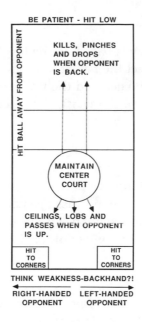

Figure 15-1. Strategies summed up!

All of the strategies are summed up in Figure 15-1. Remember, these are basic strategies for all levels of play.

Shot Selection Strategies

The remaining strategies in this chapter are based on your skill ability or the skill ability of your opponent or both. Knowing your own and your opponent's relative levels of skill is an essential part of racquetball strategy. Your strategies in any given situation will be based to a large extent on your abilities at that time and/or your opponent's abilities. It is also important to understand that strategies can change from match to match, game to game, or even point to point depending on the abilities of the players.

Aggressive Shot Selection

The aggressive strategy includes three steps. Step one is to employ the kill, the most offensive shot in the game, whenever possible. If you cannot hit the kill, the second step is to go for the next most offensive shot, the pass. Step three: If you cannot kill or pass, be defensive and hit the ceiling ball. Thoughtful use of offense is the key to this strategy.

Ball Height Strategy

A second general strategy is based on the height of the ball at racquet-ball contact. If you contact the ball at knee level or lower, you kill. If it is contacted between the knee and the waist, you hit a passing shot. If the ball is contacted above the waist, you need to go to the ceiling.

The Two-Shot Strategy

A third strategy employed by the top pros is the kill-and-ceiling two-shot strategy. You kill everything except the chest-high or higher ball, which you take to the ceiling. You hit no passing shots, around-the-walls, lobs, drops, and so forth. Almost every ball is killed unless it is too high. This strategy, of course, is not very useful for the beginner.

Court Position Strategy

A fourth strategy addresses your position and your opponent's relative position on the court. This strategy states that if your opponent is be-tween you and the front wall and you have a setup below waist high, you should pass. If your opponent is behind you and you have a setup, you should kill.

Serving Strategy

A last strategy for shot selection is based on whether you are serving or not. If you are serving, you should be on offense at all times and take risks on employing offensive shots. In other words, hit kills when serv-ing. However, when you are receiving, hit passes rather than kills and ceilings rather than passes. You should not take risks when receiving. (See Shot Strategy chart on page 243.)

Each of these five strategies can be used in any given situation and modi-fied to fit your needs as a player. You can take elements from each one and create your own strategy of play for your own game—one that fits your needs, your style of play, and your level of play.

Play Your Game

"Play your game" sounds simple and it would be if you did not have an opponent who was trying to play his or her game. Your strategy may collide with your opponent's strategy because of the differences in your

Shot Strategy

(1) Aggressive Strategy	(2) Ball Height	(3) Two-Shot	(4) Court Position	(5) Serving
S Kills first	Below knee— kill	Kill or ceiling	Opponent between you and front wall—pass	When serving take risks—kill
K Passing	kill			
I second	Knee to waist—		Opponent behind you —kill	When receiving no risks—pass and ceiling
L Ceiling third	pass			
L	Above waist—			
S	ceiling			

respective styles of play. You may not be able to impose your strategy—play your game—and thus prevent your opponent from executing his or her strategy. But this does not mean you should abandon your overall strategy. You must learn to be somewhat flexible when parts of your game are not working, and you should be able to subtly adjust these parts. For example, if all of your pinches are coming out high, don't give up on kills but try straight, front kills rather than pinches. You are not changing your total strategy, but you are making slight adjustments within your overall strategy. Making modifications within your strategy is much more effective than modifying your entire strategy. This is an important distinction to remember.

Scouting and Knowing Your Opponent

You need not, of course, scout an opponent you have played regularly. However, if you are playing someone you have never played before, you should scout him or her. Look at court speed. Is the player fast or slow moving on the court? Is the opponent tall, short, left-handed, right-handed? Does he or she have good reflexes? Is the new opponent a shooter or a passer? Is the opponent a control player or a power player? Can the opponent switch gears and change styles of play without deteriorating? Does the player always hit the same shots in the same situation? Does the player telegraph shots? Does your new opponent lose concentration? How does the opponent react under the stress of losing and winning? You should take advantage of your opponent's weaknesses and play away from his or her strengths, and scouting is an excellent way to learn what you're up against before the match begins.

In general, try to disrupt your opponent's playing style without disrupting your own. If you are playing a power player, slow the game down. Hit slow, soft, high shots, ceilings, and around-the-wall shots. Hit high, soft serves—Zs, lobs, half-lobs, and half-speed serves—against the power player. If your opponent is a control player, speed up the game's pace and hit hard, low shots. Shoot and pinch. Service should be power serves and hard Zs with a great deal of speed on the ball. Hit shots as hard as you can without sacrificing accuracy.

But you should not forget to play your game whenever possible. If you can play a winning power game (your game) over a power player, do so. The same is true if you and your opponent are control players. Play your game and use strength against strength or strength against weakness—and scouting helps you identify the opponent's weaknesses. You will play best employing your best strategies and skills. Modify your style only if it is not winning for you. If your style of play is being devastated you can do no worse by changing tactics, and you just might change the game around.

Playing the Left-Handed Opponent

If you are right-handed and your opponent is left-handed, you should be aware of this before you step in the court so that you can switch your mental set to play a lefty. Waiting until you get part way through a game may be too late to make the needed adjustments.

Left-handed players have some distinct advantages over right-handed players. First, left-handed hitters are in the minority of players, but the majority of their opponents are right-handed. Thus they are very familiar with right-handed players, but right-handed players are not as used to left-handed players.

A second point to remember is that the elements of play of a left-hander are opposite to what a right-handed player does. For example, the ball has a different spin on it and takes reverse angles out of the corners. These factors must be carefully thought through in order for the right-handed player to adjust properly.

Lastly, because all players design their strategy to play right-handers, the left-handed player playing a right-handed player does not have to alter his or her own style of play. However, right-handed players have to totally change their strategy and style when playing a left-handed player.

If you're a righty playing a lefty think opposites and be sure you have your left strategy ready before you step in the court. Of course, if you're a left-handed player, you can exploit all of these advantages to keep the right-handed hitter off balance.

The Mental Game

Often the physical skills of two players are equal, and yet one player consistently comes out the winner. The reason for this dominance is the mental aspect of the game. In this section various mental and emotional aspects of the game will be discussed. Racquetball is a game of flows of points, and it is important to keep these flows going for you rather than against you.

Set Positive, Specific Goals

The importance of the motivational goals you use both before and during play cannot be overemphasized. You must set specific goals and they must be positive. If you don't, you really have no game plan, which is like taking a car trip to a new place without having any directions. Furthermore, they must be focused on your behavior, *not* your opponent's behavior.

A positive, specific goal might be phrased, "I am going to hit 80 percent of my kill shots perfectly." Don't use a negative approach such as, "I will hit only 20 percent of my kills poorly." Think positive about every situation. Avoid general, nonspecific goal statements such as, "I will play well." This is too broad. Tell yourself, "I will hit 95 percent of my ceiling shots to the backhand corner."

Concentrate

Concentration means focusing your attention completely on the game you are playing as it is being played. Failing to concentrate turns the flow of points to your opponent. To play racquetball effectively you must be paying attention to a number of factors: watching the ball and your opponent, hitting with proper mechanics, gaining and holding center court, playing your game rather than the opponent's game, playing offensively rather than defensively, and so on. If you are worrying about your last game or your next game or if off court distractions gain the upper hand, the quality of your play will suffer. But if you can concentrate on the match in progress, you will play at your highest level of skill and the final score will reflect that fact.

Play One Point at a Time

Play each point as it comes. Don't be concerned with the midgame or the endgame until you get there, and don't worry about the previous point or the next point—concentrate on the point you're playing as you play it. Moreover, play each point enthusiastically. This makes you feel better about yourself and may cause your opponent to lose concentration. Furthermore, mix up your shots to keep your opponent off balance; this tactic is helpful regardless of your overall strategy. Remember, be positive, set specific goals, concentrate, and play each point as it comes. You may be excused for getting physically fatigued, but there is no excuse for mental fatigue (see next section) or lack of concentration.

Time-Out

Time-outs are strategically important from a number of different perspectives. First, if you think you need one, take it when you need it. Don't wait and risk getting fatigued. Use your time-outs early in the game as well as late, although it is usually a good idea to save at least one time-out for the last part of a game.

Time-outs should be used if you are physically exhausted and you need a rest or if you are slightly hurt. Also, if you have lost concentration and mental control of the game, call a time-out. Finally, you should call time-out to stop a flow of points being run by your opponent. This is important in today's shorter 15-point and 11-point games. Many players think that if your opponent runs off four points in a row, a time-out should be called whether you are ahead or behind. You don't want your opponent to sneak through the game and win or catch up to you.

When your opponent calls time out, stay psyched up and spend the time concentrating on your game. In other words, use your opponent's time out for your own benefit. Keep hitting the ball if that helps you when your opponent walks off the court.

When you are receiving service, you are entitled to a ten-second mini-time-out if you need a little time to get it together. Raising your racquet tells the server and referee you need your ten seconds. Also, when time is called because the ball breaks, equipment needs repair, or sweat gets on the floor, maintain your concentration and don't let these unforeseen incidents annoy or distract you.

Playing Tournaments

Tournaments are a different ball game from everyday playing with your friends. You must adjust physically and mentally and shift gears when heading into tournament play. The remainder of this chapter contains a variety of suggestions and information to help you prepare for and to play better in tournaments at every level of competition—local club tournament as well as state, regional, and national level tournaments.

Win or lose, tournaments can be a lot of fun. Be a good sport, learn from your mistakes, play to win, accept it when you lose, and remember that racquetball is improving your health both mentally and physically and may help you live a longer, happier life.

Probably the most important characteristic of racquetball players is the desire to win, and today's tournament players are faced with fierce competition at all levels of play. The desire to win can cause some intensely stressful situations that even the most seasoned player has trouble coping with. We believe that competitiveness takes some of the fun out of the game for the person who plays purely for enjoyment and fitness, but it is also the driving force behind the popular success racquetball has attained in such a short time.

Tournament racquetball players are a many-sided group of athletes. It is very difficult to describe a clear-cut style of tournament playing because under certain situations a well-rounded player will exhibit almost every style of play. This ability to adapt is what makes the best players come out on top. In general, however, there are power players and control players. If you can master both styles of play you are well on your way to reaching your maximum racquetball potential.

The Power Player

The basic characteristic of power players is aggressiveness. Their shots are low and hard, they rarely use the ceiling, and their game is very fast

AARA STATE RACQUETBALL CHAMPIONSHIPS
OFFICIAL ENTRY FORM

MEN'S EVENTS	WOMEN'S EVENTS
☐ OPEN	☐ OPEN
☐ A	☐ A
☐ B	☐ B
☐ C Advanced — have won a C, D, OR Novice match.	☐ C Advanced — have won a C, D, OR Novice match.
☐ C Intermediate — never won a C, D OR Novice match.	☐ C Intermediate — never won a C, D OR Novice matc
☐ SENIOR (35+)	☐ SENIOR (35+)
☐ SENIOR C — never won a B level or higher match	☐ SENIOR C — never won a B level or higher match
☐ MASTERS (45+)	☐ MASTERS (45+)
☐ GOLDEN MASTERS (55+)	☐ GOLDEN MASTERS (55+)
☐ JUNIOR (18 & under)	☐ JUNIOR (18 & under)
☐ JUNIOR (16 & under)	☐ JUNIOR (16 & under)
☐ JUNIOR (14 & under)	☐ JUNIOR (14 & under)
☐ JUNIOR (12 & under)	☐ JUNIOR (12 & under)
☐ JUNIOR (10 & under)	☐ JUNIOR (10 & under)
☐ OPEN DOUBLES	☐ OPEN DOUBLES
☐ A DOUBLES	☐ A DOUBLES
☐ B DOUBLES	☐ B DOUBLES
☐ SENIOR DOUBLES	☐ SENIOR DOUBLES
☐ JUNIOR DOUBLES (18 & under)	☐ JUNIOR DOUBLES (18 & under)

NAME _____

ADDRESS _____

CITY _____

STATE _____ ZIP _____

PHONE (day) _____

PHONE (night) _____

BIRTHDATE _____ AGE _____

SEX ____ MALE ____ FEMALE

PARTNER'S NAME _____

SHIRT SIZE ____ S ____ M ____ L ____ XL

AMOUNT ENCLOSED

1st Event ($10.00 junior) .... $ 20.00
2nd Event .... _____
3rd Event .... _____
Referee waiver fee—(# of
    events times $3.00) .... _____
AARA membership of $6.00 .... _____

Total Enclosed $_____

SPECIAL NOTES

1. ALL DOUBLES play will begin on Friday. Doubles divisions will be determined by highest level player.
2. AARA strongly recommends eye protection, JUNIORS ARE REQUIRED TO WEAR EYE PROTECTION.

WAIVER CLAUSE: I hereby, for myself, my heirs, executors and administrators, waive and release any and all rights and claims for damage I may have against the AARA, R/H Club and their respective sponsors for any and all injuries suffered by me in connection with any participation in the AARA State Racquetball Championships.

_____   _____
Signature   Signature of Parent or Guardian if under 19 years of age

Figure 15-2. The basic tournament entry–announcement form

AARA STATE RACQUETBALL CHAMPIONSHIPS

— General Information —

LOCATION
Racquetball and Health Club

TOURNAMENT BALL
PENN—Ultra blue will be the official ball.

ENTRY FEES
Entry Fees will be as follows:

First event	— $20.00 ($10.00 if junior)
Second event	— $10.00
Third event	— $10.00

If entering three events, one event must be a doubles event.
ALL DOUBLES play to begin on Friday, February 24 at 2:00 PM.

ALL ENTRIES MUST BE RECEIVED BY 5:00 PM FRIDAY, February 17
Draw and seedings will be done at 8:00 am on Saturday, February 18

ELIGIBILITY — AARA sanctioned. All participants must be members of AARA. Memberships available on this entry blank or at the tournament registration desk for $6.00. Participants are to be of amateur status as prescribed by AARA rule book, page 25.

PLAY — All matches will be 2 games to 15 points with a 11-point tie-breaker. Consolation rounds will be held in all singles events. AARA rules will apply.

REFEREES — A SPECIAL RULES CLINIC AND REFEREE CERTIFICATION PROGRAM will be conducted at this tournament. The rules clinic will be at 1:00 on Friday, February 24th, followed by the referee certification test at 2:00 pm. All referees will be paid $3.00/match in the tournament. In the event that there is a shortage of available paid or certified referees, then the loser of each match has the option to referee and earn his/her referee waiver fee first, before the winner(s) of each match would be required to referee the next available match. It will be the responsibility of each match winner to determine if his/her referee duties are fulfilled, either by the loser of his/her match or another paid referee. Failure to do so may result in forfeiture of his/her match.

STARTING TIMES — Players must contact R/H Club for his/her starting time. Requests for special starting times will be honored, if possible. However, refunds will not be given if such time is unavailable. All players must be able to play at anytime during the days of the tournament. Starting times will be available after 12:00 noon on Monday, February 20. Any player failing to show for his/her match within five (5) minutes of the scheduled starting time shall forfeit the match.

CLASSIFICATION AND CANCELLATION — The Tournament Directors may reclassify, deny or redraw any entrant in the interest of fair competition. Any event with fewer than 4 entries may be combined or reclassified.

HOSPITALITY — Hospitality is provided by AARA, R/H Club, and sponsors throughout the tournament.

FACILITIES — 14 courts (1 glass side wall with spectator viewing, 4 partial glass back walls, all with gallery), locker rooms, co-ed jacuzzi, nautilus, indoor jogging track.

AWARDS — Plaques to first place, second place and consolation winner. Each participant receives a 50/50 polyester/cotton fashion-look tournament shirt.

paced. Knowing what they are going to do is easy, but stopping the power player can be very difficult, especially when he or she is hot. Power players frustrate their opponents with quick reflexes and seemingly impossible shots. Of course, this style of play has disadvantages. Power players are more susceptible to injury and must be in excellent physical condition or they will tire out long before the finals of a tournament. It is also difficult for power players to come from behind when they are not playing well.

The Control Player

Control players, on the other hand, have no basic characteristics. You can never be sure what they are going to do. They use a variety of shots and seldom make mistakes. A control player conserves energy and frustrates the opponent with time-outs, lob serves, ceiling shots, and a low-key style of play that sometimes bores spectators but is very effective against the opposition. Technically speaking, the control player shows a wider range of talent, but the determination and explosiveness of a power player can offset this dimension and produce some very exciting matches.

Preparing for the Tournament

Your preparation for any physical endeavor should start many months before the event takes place. Tournament success depends on both how skilled you are as a player and how long you can maintain your skill. Many excellent players simply run out of gas before they reach the finals because they have not reached their peak physically. In addition to many hours of racquetball, sprinting, jogging, aerobics, and weight-lifting are necessary to condition yourself for a tournament.

Mental Preparation

Mental preparation is also very important and is closely linked to physical preparation. It is a lot easier to plan and execute your strategy if you know you are in shape and physically prepared to do whatever needs to be done throughout the tournament.

Mental preparation before a tournament is fairly complex because your strategy depends on many variables.

- *Type of ball* to be used—some are fast and some are slow.
- *Type of wall panels*—some are faster than others, some allow more spin on the ball.

- *Glass walls*—some players have a vision problem.

These factors vary from tournament to tournament and facility to facility, and they must be taken into account during your preparation. When you know what to expect, you can adapt your strengths and weaknesses to the situation. You should analyze your game realistically, determine your advantages and disadvantages in terms of the tournament variables, and develop a unique game plan for yourself.

Adequate physical and mental preparation should help make you confident in your ability and ready to deal with the pressures of the crucial first game, which is when you get rid of the butterflies, see what kind of shape you are in, and try to execute the strategy you have planned.

Warming Up

You should spend a lot of time warming up before the first match. You need to make sure that all of your muscles are loose because with the excitement, tension, and added adrenalin it is very easy to pull a muscle if you are not completely ready to play. In most tournaments, when you lose you are finished, and to lose the first round is not only embarrassing but expensive as well. Do everything you can to win and make it to your second match. Once you survive this ordeal, it will be easier to prepare for the matches that follow. Find out who else you will be playing and get a little rest before the next match.

Scout Your Opponent

Some players do not like to watch the next opponent play. They think that if they play their best, they will find weaknesses in their opponent's ability during the first game and be better able to adapt than if they start the game with a preconceived notion of what to do. No two players are alike, and their strengths and weaknesses must be determined on a one-to-one basis. Using time-outs wisely is the best way to adjust your game or to stop your opponent's momentum.

The Calls

You also need to prepare for the fact that because racquetball is such a fast game some questionable calls will invariably occur. You are going to win some and lose some, and maintaining your concentration through these moments is crucial. An experienced player can use any display of emotion against you, and some players use emotional outbursts intentionally to try to ruin the opponent's concentration.

The Tournament Structure

Racquetball tournaments are a lot of fun and they should be! You pay anywhere from a $20 to $40 registration fee to exhibit your skills, so what exactly do you get? Upon arrival you are asked to check in, and at that time you are given a bag of goodies. Depending on the amount of your registration fee, this bag may contain the following: T-shirt, shorts, eyeguard, wrist and headbands, socks, rule book, door-prize tickets, and an assortment of coupons and discount cards from area sponsors for food and equipment.

During some tournaments meals are included for players. All tournaments offer Gatorade, fruits, and, yes, even beer to participants, of which only the less serious players should partake. The tournament usually sponsors a big party and dinner on Saturday night for the players, which also occasionally changes the outcome of Sunday's matches.

Certain other practices are common in tournaments. Most tournaments are held on weekends. Early round play begins on Friday afternoon or evening, and play continues through Sunday. Quarter-final matches are Sunday morning, semifinals are played at noon, and finals commence about 4:00 P.M. After your match, you usually will referee the next match on your court unless the tournament is large.

Divisions

Depending on the type of tournament and court availability, consolation rounds may be held for first-round losers. This means that you get a chance to play at least twice even if you lose your first match. The number and type of events in tournaments vary depending on the number of entrants and court availability. Most tournaments offer open or A divisions, B and C divisions, and a doubles division or two for both men and women. The larger the tournament, the more events will be available. Most amateur tournaments are sponsored by a business as well as the host racquetball facility. Also, most tournaments are sanctioned by the American Amateur Racquetball Association. In order to compete, you must pay an entry fee for each event and be a member of the AARA or state ARA. The tournament draw sheets are usually displayed in the main lobby area, and your starting time can usually be obtained a day or two before the tournament by calling the host club.

Facilities

Normally, the host facility will open other parts of the club to all tournament participants. You may be able to lift weights, run or swim indoors, enjoy hot tubs and steam rooms, and relax in the club bar. If the tournament is too large for one facility, different divisions may be played at different sites. For instance, the B and C divisions might be played at the local YMCA, and the open and A divisions might be played at the host racquetball club.

Prizes

Most tournaments offer trophies to first and second place finishers in each division. Many tournaments are now offering cash or other valuable prizes for first place in the men's and women's open division. Television sets and up to $1,000.00 are common prizes.

Referees

Do not be alienated by the term *referee*. You must remember that an official in a tournament match is a person first and an official second. The referee is one of three officials found at tournament matches. The tournament director and linespeople are the other officials. The responsibilities of officials are explained in appendix A of this book (see Racquetball Rules, Section III, *Officiating and Play Regulations*).

The referee may be a person hired strictly to officiate for the tournament. If the tournament is large enough referees may be paid $3.00 to $5.00 a match. If referees are to be paid, the host facility may offer a short referee clinic prior to the beginning of the tournament. Usually, however, the referee will be a player from the tournament. The duties of the referee are also found in Section III of the Racquetball Rules, so specific responsibilities will not be included here. But we will offer some general thoughts about officiating that are important to both the player and the referee.

Know the Rules

If you referee you need to know all of the rules so that when a call is made or is questioned, you can correctly cite the appropriate rule. Incorrect calls frustrate the players and rattle the referee, so you should try to keep incorrect calls to a minimum. Learn the rules and be consistent with your calls. If you interpret a rule closely or loosely call it that way throughout the match.

Control the Match

The referee must be in control of the match, the players, and sometimes the gallery. You must be decisive as well as correct on your calls. You may allow a player to question a call, but you should be able to quickly and clearly explain the reason for the call. If you know that either or both players harass the officials, take charge, explain to them that you will not allow any abuse on the court, and plan your strategies before you begin refereeing. Arrive at the court early and be organized. Know your responsibilities concerning the players, equipment, scoring, and starting the match on time. As the referee you will also be the scorekeeper. Keep score accurately. You should have a pretournament meeting with the tournament director to learn about local hinder calls and other idiosyncracies of the host club that might affect rule interpretations. If a pretournament meeting was not held, you will need to talk to a local club player and find out the local rules before you officiate.

Linespeople

It would also be to your advantage as a referee to appoint two linespeople you can count on to know the rules and to make decisive calls. When rules are questioned the three of you will need to confer and make the final decision according to the official rules.

Like players, some linespeople and referees are better than others, and you should remember that fact when you question a call. When officiating, do the best that you can.

Keys for Strategies and Playing Tournaments

- Keep the ball away from your opponent, hit the ball to his or her backhand, control center court, and be patient.
- Tournament play is much different from everyday play; be sure to prepare both physically and mentally when you enter a tournament.
- You will probably have to referee during a tournament; make sure that you know the official and local rules, that you take charge, and that you are consistent and organized as an official.

CHAPTER 16
Doubles and Court Games

Doubles

Like doubles in tennis, doubles in racquetball has begun to grow in popularity, and a variety of factors have helped the doubles game to catch on. First, having four people on the court is more friendly and interactive than the game of singles. Doubles is not as physically demanding as singles because you only cover a part of the court rather than the whole court. In doubles the new challenge is to more precisely place your shots; the openings for placing winners are fewer because two opponents are covering the court.

If you have a weak backhand, finding a partner with a good backhand to play that side of the court may enable you to be successful in doubles. Some players prefer doubles because they find it faster and more thought-provoking than singles—you must think more to gain the smaller advantages in doubles. The game can be faster because the ball can be cut off by a partner, and that gives everyone less time to hit and react. Also, with cost per hour divided four ways and with limited court space available, doubles can be more practical than singles.

Doubles safety is worth a special mention here. With the addition of two more bodies and racquets in the court, the increased pace of the game, and more shots in a given period of time, safety must be a paramount concern. Most doubles players learn to shorten their swings in both backswing and follow-through. Players new to doubles must be very careful about their swings. Another major safety factor is to stay out of the way of the three other players and avoid getting hit by the ball. Having a plan of operation for your doubles strategy before entering the court is another method of helping to cut down injuries in racquetball doubles.

Doubles Formations

The two basic formations used when playing doubles are the side-by-side and the I or front-and-back. These formations may be modified or combined. The formation will determine the playing strategy.

Side-by-Side

The side-by-side formation divides the court down the middle from front to back and each player is responsible for half of the court. To use this formation effectively the players should be about equal in court coverage and shot ability because each covers 50 percent of the court. If both partners are right-handed, the one with the stronger backhand should play the left side of the court. If partners are left-handed and right-handed, the left-handed player should play the left side of the court.

If players of different ability are partners, side-by-side can be slightly modified. The stronger player handles the left two-thirds of the back court, and left half of the front court. The other partner is responsible for the right half of the front court and the right one-third of the back court. This variation can be further modified depending on the differences in both coverage and hitting abilities of the partners.

The right side player may hit as few as 20 percent of the team's shots in a game, especially if the backcourt is divided by one-third to two-thirds. Normally, the left-side player decides who takes the shot and gives the short commands such as *yours* or *mine*. The left-side player is the leader, and the verbal commands are short because there is so little time to react in doubles.

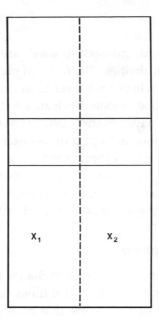

Figure 16-1. The side-by-side formation

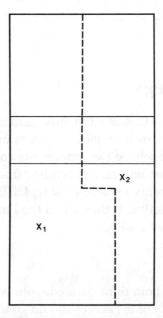

Figure 16-2. Modified side-by-side formation with X-1 being the stronger player

I Formation

The I formation, or front-and-back, is used rarely because the partners must have specific skill abilities. The forward player needs to be quicker, more aggressive, and a better retriever than the back player. The back player must be a great deep shooter with an accomplished, well-controlled ceiling game. The up player controls center court while the back player maneuvers from side-to-side to pick up well-placed passing and ceiling shots. A modification of the I formation is to stagger slightly from side-to-side while keeping the same basic I formation coverage. Another modification is for the front player to move more forward and to the right to cover the right front quarter of the court only.

Combination Formation

Sometimes your formation strategy must change from point to point. You are playing basically side-by-side, but at times you must switch to front-and-back. The important factors are that both partners know that the switch has been made and that at the earliest opportunity you will switch back to your usual formation. Combination formations are usually dictated by a certain game situation that forces one or both partners out of their usual formation.

Doubles Strategy

The skills in doubles are basically the same as in singles, but doubles play requires some changes in strategies. All shots must be precisely placed in doubles because you have two opponents covering the court rather than one. Shot selection will vary depending upon your opponents' formation. If your opponents are side-by-side, kill shots, pinches, and ceiling shots are very effective. If they are in the I formation, passing shots and pinches work very well.

Service

If your opponents are both right-handed, your service strategy is similar to singles. The majority of the serves should go to your opponents' backhand corner. However, if you are playing against left-handed and right-handed opposition, you will probably have two backhands in the middle of the court, and your serves should be directed to the back middle of the court to force a backhand return.

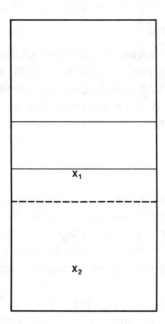

Figure 16-3. The I formation

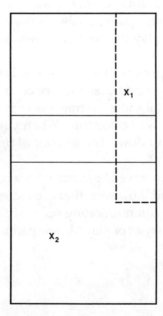

Figure 16-4. The modified I formation

Center Court Control

Controlling center court is a must in doubles. Center court gives you better court coverage; you are closer to the front wall, and your shots should be more accurate. Holding center court also allows you to be in front of your opponents. Thus you can see the ball more easily, and you do not have to hit around your opponents.

Communication

Communication between partners is another exceedingly important factor in winning doubles. Communication must begin prior to the match. Discuss your verbal cues, your coverage patterns, the use of time-outs, the types of serves, and your offensive and defensive shot selections. You should also be deciding what your opponents' strategies will be against your team.

Don't allow your team to play your opponents' game. If you find this happening, call a time-out and get back into your game plan. If one of your opponents is hot and not missing, don't be intimidated. Work on the other partner. If your court coverage is not working, modify or completely change the coverage pattern. Always position yourself in the most advantageous place to play the next shot even if your partner has just returned the ball.

Try to isolate your opponents' weaknesses and attack the weaker player or the weak spot in their formation. Concentrate on hitting passes, pinches, and ceilings. Kill shots are fine, but they need to be almost perfect roll-outs to get by two opponents. When you can, play the ball on the volley in order to cut down the amount of time your opponent has to return the ball.

It is very important to have a partner who works well with you and vice versa. You may find, however, that even after you play together for a while you are still not communicating successfully. This may be caused by having incompatible styles of play. A new partner for each of you might be to your advantage.

Practice and Praise

For good doubles play it is important to practice together with your partner as often as possible per week. Work on your problems from previous matches and work on your strong points. Make sure that during your matches you let your partner know how well he or she is playing both overall and on a particular shot. This helps your partner's confidence and may provide a psychological advantage over your opponents.

Mixed Doubles

Most of what we have been discussing about doubles applies to mixed doubles; however, some differences apply. First of all, your partner should be of about equal ability to you so that neither of you gets frustrated at the skill level of the other. This is a doubles game, and the more highly skilled partner should not be taking shots away from a less skilled partner.

Side-by-side play in mixed doubles seems to work best. Women players should be thinking that every ball is coming their way and they should be ready for this situation. The real keys for mixed doubles success are trust your partner, learn to work as a team, compliment each other, be compatible physically, and think doubles.

Cutthroat

A new game called cutthroat allows three players to compete against one another. This game basically pits the server as a team against two receivers as a team. Hits must be alternated from team to team as in regulation doubles.

When the server loses service he or she rotates either clockwise or counter-clockwise and becomes the partner of one of the previous opponents. The other opponent rotates to serve and plays as a team against the other two-member team. This sequence of rotation continues until the game is concluded. The server is always playing against the other two players. Each player keeps his or her own score, and the game ends when a server reaches game point.

The strategies employed in cutthroat are a combination of singles and doubles techniques. As a member of the doubles team you employ singles strategy when playing against the server; as a member of the singles team you employ doubles strategy when serving. Take advantage of weaknesses in either case. Center court control is paramount to successful cutthroat play. An important point to remember is that you are constantly shifting gears from doubles strategies to singles strategies.

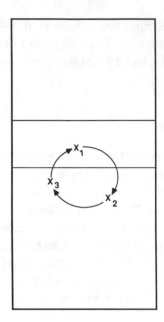

Figure 16-5.   Rotation for cutthroat

Court Games

The sport of racquetball is versatile. Although throughout this book we have discussed four-wall indoor play, racquetball can be played outdoors and/or on three-wall, one-wall, or even two-wall courts. Racquetball is also played on courts smaller and larger than regulation size.

Three-Wall Racquetball

Three-wall racquetball has a front wall and two partial side walls extending back from the front wall anywhere from one to two feet to about 25 feet. With no ceiling or back wall, the ceiling shot and back-wall play are gone. The ball is played a little higher than in four-wall courts. The lob is used quite often, which gives you the maximum time to regain your position in the court. Because there is no back wall, many shots must be played on the volley in order to cut them off. More side-to-side movement is used in three-wall play and less up-and-back movement than in four-wall play.

One-Wall Racquetball

This is similar to the three-wall game but now the pinch shot and all side wall shots are eliminated. Passing shots that are angled work very well because they drive your opponent out of the lined court to retrieve the ball. It is often impossible to run the ball down, and even if you are successful you are so far off the court that your opponent can hit an easy winner on the ensuing shot. The long rallies of four-wall play are not found in three-wall and one-wall racquetball.

Two-Wall Racquetball and Modified Courts

Two-wall racquetball is played in a space with a front and back wall or a front wall and one side wall. The wall situation will determine the playing strategies and limits. Courts of modified size are found for one-, two-, and three-wall games of racquetball. Modified courts that are smaller or larger than regulation are also found in four-wall racquetball. In small four-wall courts the power player with controlled kills is almost unbeatable—the court is just not long enough for you to force this player out of kill range. Volley shots and ceiling shots are not as effective in small courts, but the back-wall shot becomes the most important shot in the game. If the service zone is placed in front of its regulation distance from the front wall, the power server has a distinct advantage because the power serve travels less distance and becomes even more lethal.

In larger-than-regulation courts the ceiling shot, passing shots, and lob serves are very important shots, and the kill and power shots are relegated to the back seat. Some of these odd-size courts were originally squash courts.

Each nonregulation court has its own basic strategies and playing patterns. If you are visiting one, all we can do is wish you good luck.

Keys for Doubles, Court Games, and Courts

- Communication and compatibility of partners both on and off the court are paramount in the success of a doubles team.
- Apply strategy appropriate for the type of game and the type of court.

Figure 16-6. Heather McKay playing Shannon Wright-Hamilton. (Courtesy Racquetball Illustrated)

CHAPTER 17
More With Marty

Court Tactics

I know what you're thinking. Sure, anyone who can serve the ball 140 miles per hour and play eight hours a day can say racquetball strategy is simple. But what about the average guy on the court? Have faith, strategy is simple for you too. The basic rule for you is to shoot when you control center court and move your opponent out of center court when he or she is there and you're not. Hit up and down the alleys and attack your opponent's weaknesses.

The game seems complicated only when you have to worry about your imperfect shot execution while trying to capitalize on your opponent's weaknesses. You may think I am going to complicate things by going through a long list of tactics (methods), but basically these things are only an extension of the basic strategy. I don't always use these tactics, but I have seen them used or have used them in the past. You usually learn by watching other players or reflecting on past losses. Sometimes they

Figure 17-1.   Heather McKay and Sarah Green in action (Courtesy Racquetball Illustrated)

work, and sometimes they don't. But they're good to know. Who knows? One of these gems could be the key to turning around an entire match.

Scouting

To put tactics into the proper light, we really need to see how they fit into the whole picture. A match should begin at least four hours before the referee says "play ball." I don't scout players anymore because they're the same players I meet at every tournament, but you should because you probably play different players each tournament.

There's no sense in working more than you have to. If a player can't return a Z serve, you should know about it before the match starts, not at the end of the match. Ideally, you should watch the match that will determine whom you will play next. Some of the general things you should evaluate are foot speed (is he or she a speedster or a sloth?), reflexes, height (tall or short), shot style (shooter or passer), playing philosophy (power or control), patience (short or long), resilience to failure, and endurance. For each of these player categories there is a standard avenue of attack. Some other points to note are the following: What are his or her responses to different serves (ceiling, pass, or kill)? What are his or her favorite serves? How effective are they? Does he or she telegraph serves? Watch the service motion to pick up keys that can be used as an early warning of intention.

If you can't scout your opponent, see if you can get a trusted friend to scout for you. Even if you can watch your opponent play, it's sometimes good to get a second opinion.

The Base Plan

Now that the scouting report is in, it's time to draw up the grand plan. The grand plan, of course, is intended only as a base from which to start. The worst approach is to go onto a court not knowing what you're going to do and praying that you'll get a great idea during the match. A good opponent will blow you out before you know it. The second worst approach is to go into a match with a game plan chiseled into stone, which you won't change for anything. You should start with a well-defined plan of attack based on your scouting report so that you have a sense of purpose and direction. During the beginning phase of the match (the first five points), test out this plan, see if those weaknesses that you spotted are still there. As the match progresses, constantly reevaluate the plan and adapt according to the situation. This is the hard part because you have to make a judgment about your abilities and your opponent's abilities. You hope that the plan will be effective as the match progresses.

Preparation

After the plan is drawn up, you are two steps away from being ready to play. The next step is to set up for the match. I know it may sound extreme, but Steve Strandemo (and other control players) used to make sure he had a dozen slow balls with him just in case the tournament supplied fast balls. Of course, this often leads to a funny situation when the control player brings in his dozen dead balls and the power player brings in his dozen superballs; then there are 24 balls bouncing around the court during warm-up. What I'm trying to get at is that you don't want to worry about equipment shortage or malfunction during the course of a match. Check out your equipment and make sure you have extra racquets, shirts, gloves, and towels before the match begins.

Now that you are exhausted from watching, planning, and organizing, it's finally time to warm up. Begin by doing some stretching exercises. As the blood begins to flow into your muscles, do some jumping jacks or jog a quarter mile to warm your body up to playing temperature. Finally, get on the court to begin the stroke warm-up. You should begin by warming up the basic strokes with an emphasis on good weight transfer and wrist snap. As I've said before, these are critical parts of any stroke and have to be working properly before you move on to increasing the speed and range of your basic shots. Spend the final few minutes hitting your shots at full speed. By this time, your bread-and-butter shots should be down pat. With the game plan in your head, you should now be ready for the match to begin. But what is in this game plan and how will you carry it out? Here are some guidelines with which most players start.

Service Tactics

Obviously, any weakness in the service return should be attacked, but what if there is no clear answer? Here are some basics: Use low, hard drive serves against very tall or slow players. The idea is that a tall player will have more trouble reaching down. Move the serve side to side against a slow or poorly conditioned player. This tactic should wear your opponent down quickly, and you will start getting a bundle of weak returns. Use a high lob or high Z serve against a short or impatient player. Make the short player jump up to return the serve or stretch up into an unaccustomed position. Eventually, you'll wear him or her down because he or she will be using weak muscles. Tempt the impatient player to go for a low-percentage kill shot. More than likely, the ball will pop up for a setup. Another way to tempt the impatient player is to hit low lob (junk) serves in which you vary the height and speed. Hit three or four shoulder-high slow lobs. Then quickly hit a three-foot-high, medium-speed junk serve into the side wall. The ploy sometimes works after a series of drive serves. The unsuspecting, impatient player will probably leave the ball up after going for a kill using the same stroke he or she uses against a slower, lower junk serve. The Z serve works wonders against big klutzes and players with poor footwork.

There are two key points to remember about the service return. The first point is know your limits. I know that my best shot is to kill any drive serve to my backhand down the line, but it probably is not the best choice for you unless you have a good backhand. The second point is that the motion of your opponent's wrist is the key to reading the serve. The wrist cannot lie. Where the wrist goes, so goes the serve. Forget all the feet shuffling, hip wriggling, and arm pumping your opponent throws at you during the serve. If the wrist snaps early, the serve is going cross-court; if it snaps late, the serve is going down the line. If the wrist snaps very early, it's going to be a Z serve and if it snaps very late, the serve is going to be a Z in the other direction. Watching the wrist-snap is also a good way to focus your concentration during the match. If you can't remember which way the wrist snapped on the last serve, you're probably daydreaming.

Several service return tactics can keep you on the offensive. On slower serves such as lobs or junks that are shallow, move up and half-volley the serve for a kill, pass, or ceiling shot. By half-volley I mean hit the ball after the bounce as the ball is rising from the floor. You do not have to stay behind the five-foot line after the ball has hit the floor. Coming up on the ball can surprise your opponent and get you a quick point. It can also be very intimidating if he or she hasn't seen the shot. I've seen many a junk serve expert give up the junk after someone cut the serve off and drilled the ball into the corner for a winner before the server even knew what happened. As you approach the ball, if you find out you can't kill the ball, there's plenty of time to hit the ball into the ceiling. The half-volley ceiling ball is also effective. Because the server is usually relaxed and the half-volley ceiling ball travels much faster to the back court than a normal ceiling ball, he or she will have to rush the shot.

What if the server is hitting a good, deep lob? An effective return is to volley or take the ball out of the air and drive the ball either down the line or crosscourt. Again, if you're late or early, you can still punch the ball up to the ceiling for an effective return. Of course, in this case you cannot contact the ball until it passes the five-foot line.

Breaking the Rhythm

The point of all these tactics is to make your opponent uncomfortable and break his or her rhythm. Rhythm-breaking tactics can also be used during a rally.

As you see, court position is an important element of court tactics. When you set up behind your opponent at mid- or three-quarter court, the typical response is to shoot or drive the ball down the right wall. But when you are close to your opponent and behind him, he or she really can't see what you are doing. He or she normally leans to the right in anticipation of the shot down the line but feels like a fool realizing the ball has gone in a different direction. The shot is easy to hit because the wall will impart a natural spin that will bring the ball down very fast.

You can refine your tactics by varying the pace of each shot. Hit three hard shots and then a medium speed change-up. One of my favorite change-up combinations is to hit a hard, sharp, pinch shot that squirts out of the corner because it contacts the side wall only a few inches from the front wall. All you hear is a plunk as the ball hits the side and front walls almost simultaneously. I combine this with a wide, medium-speed pinch that contacts the side wall about two or three feet from the front wall. If my opponent sees the pinch coming, he or she remains frozen in disbelief because the ball is moving so slow compared to my normal pinch. The feet can't decide to move while the eyes are watching the shot develop.

Along with all of these tactics, you must balance your offensive intensity, which is akin to a controlled rage, with patience. Try to force your game style onto your opponent. If you are more versatile than your opponent, choose a game style that clashes with his or hers. For example, occasionally slow the power player down and use power against the slow, deliberate player. Let your opponent know that you are going to make the game uncomfortable for him or her every minute of the match.

Miscellaneous

Now we come to some must topics for rounding out your court tactics education. Some players have made the time-out an art form. They use it to control the whole tempo of a match. The master of the time-out was Charlie Brumfield. In the old days, he could get players to literally froth at the mouth just by taking very long 60-second time-outs during which he would tell the gallery his life story.

The time-out should be used primarily to stop your opponent's momentum. It should never be used when you are on a hot streak. You can use time-outs to pace yourself, but you're really better off to get in better condition. If you are scoring one point after another without much resistance, you should increase the tempo of the game. Take just enough time to get ready to hit a drive serve. Don't waste a lot of time talking to the gallery at this time. You want to score as many points as you can before your opponent finds out that he or she should call a time-out.

If you win a long rally, quickly get to the service box and get set to serve. This tends to unnerve your opponent. If you need to rest, do it in the ready service position so that your opponent is forced to wait for your serve or call a time-out. If you respond automatically in this situation, your opponent will never discover that you're hurting just as much as he or she is.

The most unpleasant topic is how to deal with the cheater. What's a person to do when the other player picks up double bounces and shoves you all over the court while the referee just smiles? It really depends on how important winning is to you. For some people, a shrug of the shoulders is appropriate. But I believe in the law of the West. If the referee can't control the game, get a new referee. If that doesn't help, it's time for two eyes for each eye and two teeth for each tooth. The key is that you tell your opponent the ground rules that go into effect if the situation persists. You have to gain control of the situation. This also means that if you still get cheated, you accept the situation as is and don't get emotionally involved. Every point should be played with emotional detachment.

Strategy: It's Simpler Than You Think

A friend of mine once said that there are two kinds of people: those who look for complexity in life and those who look for simplicity in life. The same observation holds for racquetball strategies: those who ramble for hours on end about the intricacies of racquetball strategy and those who think strategy can be summed up on one short paragraph. I believe that racquetball strategy at the top tournament levels is, indeed, very simple. Racquetball strategy at the lower levels is much more complex because there are so many more unknowns and so many avenues of attack.

Racquetball strategy is trivial if you completely outclass your opposition because you can do almost anything and still win. A sound plan is important only when your opposition either is a potential threat or is clearly better than you are. That is, he or she has physical, mental, and psychological traits that are as good as or better than what you have. It is only then that a strategy or plan becomes important. Only then will the choice of shots and serves have meaning. Only then will the choice of the game pace need to be made.

But the basic strategy is still simple. It can be summed up by the following rules. Shoot when you control the center of the court; otherwise, don't shoot. When you get hopelessly behind, go for broke. When you're way out ahead, keep the pressure on the opposition. It doesn't make any difference whether you are a power player or a control player, a loser more often than a winner. The details of racquetball strategy (e.g., where to hit the ball) are simple. The difficulty is in deciding what tactics (methods) to employ in carrying out the plan and then assessing the success of a plan during the course of a match.

When you control the center-court position, go for a kill. You know you are in control of center court when (1) you are in center-court position and your opponent is behind you, or (2) you are behind your opponent but he or she is off to the side of the court.

In situation one, the best shot to take is a near-side pinch. The pinch shot should be hit almost straight into the juncture of the front and side walls, low and hard, so that there is very little time for your opponent to recover from backcourt. Even if you miss the shot, the chances are that the ball will come off the side walls funny because of the tremendous spin on the ball. Sometimes the shot is called a splat ball because of the sound of the ball doubling the walls. In situation two, when your opponent gets trapped near a side wall, the best shot is to kill down the far side wall. In both cases, the selected shot makes the opponent run the farthest distance to retrieve the ball. If he or she gets to the ball, the shot will be weak. In the long run, the accumulated mileage will eventually take some speed and accuracy from his or her shots. In either case, I use the *three-one rule;* that is, I hit three regular shots and then one complementary shot just to keep my opponent honest.

If you don't control center court (you are on the run or in backcourt), then you should not go for a kill because you'll probably leave the ball up or catch the side wall with your shot. Then your opponent has an assortment of options while you are trapped helplessly in the backcourt. You're better off hitting a shot that moves the opponent out of center court. Steve Keeley has a good rule of thumb for this situation: Think pass first, then ceiling. There's only one exception to the rule: When you're on the run and there's a choice between hitting a half-hearted lob or going for the bottom board because the effort required to extend the rally is probably not worth the effort. It's better to put the whole point on the line by taking a chance on the shot than to chase the ball for what is probably a losing situation anyway.

When I hit a pass shot, I normally hit to the backhand; that is, down the line on the backhand side and crosscourt on the forehand side. That's because most players' backhands are much weaker than their forehands. In my case, hitting to a right hander's backhand moves the ball to the side of the court that is my strength. I use the three-one rule again to keep my opponent honest. Note that I very seldom hit a pinch from the backcourt because it's almost suicide if you mis-hit the shot. In one situation, I go for a pinch because if I set up deep in the left back corner and my opponent isn't standing in the center of the court, the shot is a sure winner for me.

This strategy assumes that the score is relatively close. When you fall way behind, you have to go for broke and pray that you'll get hot. It's too late to think about percentages if you are hopelessly behind because you need to score lots of points fast. If you get a big lead, you still need to maintain pressure. Many a time I've seen a player blow an 18 to 4 lead because he or she started to play safe. A big lead is a dangerous situation because there's a tendency to let up, and once you let up, you can lose all your momentum. Once your momentum is gone, it's hard to get it back. When you get a big lead, you should try to open up the lead. Take a few medium-percentage shots. If you miss them, it's no big deal. If you hit them, your opponent will feel even greater pressure and try to hit all shots perfectly to catch up with you.

That's basic racquetball strategy in a nutshell. But as I said in the beginning, if you are much stronger or much weaker than your opponent, you have to adopt a different strategy. If you are weaker than your opponent, you can start off with the basic strategy to see if on a particular day you can get hot. But in most cases, you'll quickly end up adopting the come-from-behind strategy anyway. If you are stronger than your opponent you can afford to take more risks and go for more kills. The whole problem is determining your ability relative to your opponent's ability. It's a tough problem because the relationship changes from day to day and sometimes from minute to minute.

In determining your relative skills, you should understand your scoring zones. Scoring zones are those areas of the court where you can hit kill shots with about a 90 percent success rate. If you compare your scoring zones with your opponent's, you'll get a good feel for your relative skills. On defensive shots, you should strive to move the ball into your most productive scoring zones. For example, my best scoring zone is any place on my backhand side. Because my backhand is better than anyone else's backhand and because I have no equal in physical strength, I'll go for a kill shot from deep left court even when my opponent is in center court. The velocity and accuracy of my backhand makes the shot worthwhile for me.

On the pro tour, I know every player's strengths and weaknesses. Unlike amateur tournaments where you often don't know your opponent, I play the same people all the time. So my decision process is fairly simple. The only questionable element is how I'm feeling on a particular day. In addition, because I'm stronger, faster, more patient, and more accurate than any other player on the tour, I have a wider range of options.

When I play an aggressive player (someone who uses the come-from-behind strategy right out of the starting blocks and throughout the whole race), I try to keep him moving and behind me. I use a lot of drives left and right and wait for him to shoot. I know that in the long run, he'll leave more shots up than he keeps down. Most of these players can't rally for more than three or four shots before they have to go for a kill, even when they're out of position. In this situation, patience pays off in the end.

When I play a control player, I try to be more aggressive and take the first shot because he gives me ample opportunities to shoot the ball. By doing this, I put pressure on him and eventually make him feel he has to hit better and better shots just to keep up. In the end, I break his will to continue rallying.

A control player finally breaks out of his mold and enters my domain, the serve-and-shoot strategy. Then, it's all over because he's playing my game. Of course, most players, whether of the power or control philosophy, cannot shoot on the run, so I try to keep them moving as much as possible. My strategy is to start them on the run with a drive serve. I try to keep them running until the ball moves into one of my scoring zones. Then I go for the kill.

My game is really very simple. It's based on a simple strategy with a small set of uncomplicated shots, nothing fancy but very effective. You may have noticed that I didn't mention the now-popular overhead shot in this entire discussion. I never use it because it doesn't gain anything for me; it's too easy to defend against and too easy to mis-hit. You're better off sticking to basic shots like kill shots down the line and pinch shots and enlarging your scoring zones from frontcourt toward backcourt. Work on developing some bread-and-butter shots that are automatic point producers. Your whole game should revolve around moving the ball around until you get a shot in one of your scoring zones.

In the end, though, one day you'll run into the only player who is perfectly matched with your skills. That's when you'll get the true test of what you're worth. In that situation, when your head, heart, patience, stamina, skills, and organization are tested to their limits, you can't be trying to unravel a complicated racquetball strategy. A simple strategy is all that's needed.

As I said in the beginning, at the top levels of play the strategy is very simple because there are very few weaknesses to pick on and very few inches of give in anyone. But as we descend to other levels of play, the weaknesses offer greater opportunities to be attacked. That is when tactics are vital.

Championship Service Strategy

Unquestionably, the serve is the most important shot in racquetball. As the philosophers of racquetball always preach, the serve sets the tempo for the ensuing rally. There is no other shot where you have complete control of the future. So, it is obvious that a player should use a serve to his or her greatest advantage.

The service strategy is surprisingly simple in the power racquetball game: Hit a hard drive serve to the backhand. Assuming you are playing a right-handed opponent, your bread-and-butter serve should be the low, hard drive serve angled into the left, rear corner. The second bounce should hit the floor near the side wall directly opposite the receiver's position. The objective is to hit the serve low enough so that the second bounce hits before the ball reaches the back wall but close enough to the side wall so that the receiver has to reach a long way. The idea is to hit the serve hard enough so that your opponent can't pounce on it and hit an offensive return.

The angle of the drive serve also adds a degree of difficulty to the return. By angling the ball right to left across the body, the ball will move away from the backhand. Thus, there is a very limited region in which the receiver can effectively return the ball. And if a ball is moving at a high speed, your odds of a weak return are even greater.

But trying to hit the serve into the left, rear corner allows maximum room for error. The worst situation is when a serve comes off the back wall. This is a plum for your opponent. Another serve to avoid is one that catches the side wall high. Contrary to popular belief, aiming for the side wall is basically a poor strategy. Any ball hitting a side wall slows down considerably. It then becomes a virtual setup unless the ball jams the receiver or takes a bad bounce.

I recommend my three-one rule. This rule says that for every three drive serves I hit to the left, rear corner, I hit one different strong serve. I may use (1) a drive down the right wall to the right, rear corner; (2) a hard Z serve to the forehand; (3) a jam serve to the left. All three serves are hit with the same motion as the drive serve to the left, rear corner. If the receiver is leaning to the left, the surprise serve will earn a bundle of aces or setups on the return.

The drive down the right wall is hit like the drive to the left except that the contact point is a little farther back. The serve should run down the right wall without catching it. Ideally, the second bounce should hit before the ball gets to the back wall. But even if the serve does hit the back wall, if it is along the side wall you can still get a weak return because of the surprise element. The secret is in making the drive to the left a fearsome serve that must be reckoned with in every service situation. Later in the match, the serve to the right can be effective because fatigue will have dulled the receiver's reaction time: The legs will be moving to the left while the eyeballs are moving to the right.

The hard Z to the right should be hit three or four feet high on the front wall with the intention of catching the right side wall in the rear after the first bounce, or it can be hit about six inches high with the intention of just clearing the service line and taking its second bounce near the right wall about 10 or 15 feet in front of the back wall. The low Z complements the drive serve to the left because not only does it move the receiver in an opposite lateral direction from the drive left, but it also moves him or her in an anterior direction. Of course, if you mis-hit the low Z, it's a virtual plum.

The jam serve is hit so that it catches the side wall near the floor. You will have to experiment to find the best spot on the side wall because the position of the receiver, the liveliness of the ball, and the bite of the side wall all contribute to the final trajectory of the serve. The result must be a fast serve that comes into the receiver's body. You hope that the receiver is anticipating a drive left and has started to turn to the left. Upon discovering this poor judgment, the receiver has to spend some time back-pedaling to adjust to the incoming serve. If the ball doesn't lose much speed off the side wall, the receiver will be jammed.

Some pros use the drive serve to the right because they think they can partially (though legally) screen the serve. But I don't like or depend on that strategy. In most cases, pro players can read the serve. It's almost cheating. And I think more restrictive service rules will eventually take that serve away.

The proper place to start the serve is from about one step to the right of center in the service zone. The step off-center is required to get the proper angle. Starting in the center reduces the needed angle.

Starting off-center opens you up to a strong return down the left wall. However, I have found that the benefits of this off-center starting position far outweigh the potential losses. Most likely, the service motion will carry you almost into the center of the court. A single step will get you to the left side of the court and another step will get you to the side wall, so you will not be as far out of position as you might think. However, if you are the kind of server who serves and stands, there is the danger that you'll be burned almost every time by even a mediocre return.

After every serve, I look for and expect an offensive opportunity. I look for an attempted kill or pass down the left wall. If the return turns out to be a ceiling ball, I still have time to recover and return the ceiling ball with another ceiling ball. The drive serve left is moving far enough away from the backhand so that a pass to the right is almost nonexistent or at best weak. The most frequent weak return I get from the drive left is one that catches the left side wall and comes out toward the center of the court. When this happens, the receiver is trapped in the backcourt. Then I pinch the shot into the left corner. Even if the receiver can recover and get to the pinch, he'll have to run a long distance. Then, he will be lucky if he can even hit a decent shot. The long-term effect of all this running is fatigue and frustration, which leads to more errors.

There's no secret to executing the serve. It's a normal forehand power stroke. The contact point is slightly in front of the right hip and about five inches off the ground. Take a full pendulum swing and hit it almost flat with lots of wrist-snap. Most racquetball players tell you to aim for a spot on the front wall. But have you ever tried to watch the front wall and the ball at the same time? Nonsense!

Experiment with different contact points and weight-shift directions until the serve ends up where you want it. Then, repeat the shot until it's second nature. But not only must the serve end up where you want it; it should also feel smooth and effortless. If not, keep experimenting. This *feel* method of practice will do a lot more for you than counting the number of times that you hit a spot on the front wall.

You should devote many hours to practicing the drive serve and its complementary serves. To get that one–two punch effect of the drive serve strategy, you need to make the service motion natural, effortless, and seemingly identical for all the hard serves. At the beginning of the season, I spend many hours practicing the drive serve combinations in hopes of regaining the magic usually lost over the summer months of less concentrated playing. Unfortunately, the magic of the combinations is easily lost because of the critical role that timing and deception play in hitting a good serve-combination. But even without the array of complementary serves, the drive serve to the left still can bring many moments of what looks like offensive brilliance. There have been many times when I have gone into the tie breaker with nothing to depend on but the drive serve. History shows that, in those moments, I have more often than not come out winning by eight or more points just because I spent the hours necessary to hit an effective drive serve for a longer duration than any other player on the tour.

Once the serve is working, you should vary the delivery speed. Variance in delivery speed will throw the receiver's timing off because he or she won't be able to time the return. Receivers tend to start leaning at the same point in a server's delivery. So if you vary the delivery speed, the anticipated weight transfer of the receiver is thrown out of tune. This situation also leads to loss of confidence and balance and subsequently loss of performance.

If you have a bionic arm, you can hit the drive serve using the three-one rule for a whole tournament. Unfortunately, no one is that strong, not even me. So you have to pace yourself. There's nothing worse than being so tired that the drive serve becomes a setup and the rest of your game deteriorates along with the serve. This means hitting some junk, lob, and soft Z serves occasionally so that you can conserve enough energy for an entire tournament. A nice side benefit is that soft serves throw off a lot of players especially when he or she has seen five or six hard serves in a row and has adjusted to reacting to a drive serve.

Unlike the hard serves, spin can aid in hitting the soft serves. Use some underspin (although not overly exaggerated) when hitting a junk or soft Z. The underspin allows you to hit the serve deeper without losing control of the serve. The result: fewer balls coming off the back wall. Use some overspin or topspin when hitting junk or high lob serves. The topspin lets you hit the serve more shallowly on the first bounce but carries high and deep enough so that the ball is much higher than normal once it reaches the receiver. Thus the junk serve can be hit effectively with either top- or underspin.

Some players preach that you should continually vary your serves to keep the receiver off balance. But I believe that once a serve is working, you should stay with the winning game plan. If a player has a weakness, that weakness will only get weaker with time. The weakness may not show up right away, but as a match gets older, those weaknesses will invariably show up. The drive serve is just the ticket for revealing those weaknesses. The power game revolves around the drive serve. Master the drive serve, and you've got about 25 percent of the game in the bag.

How to Beat Marty Hogan

It's clear that the ranks of power-game zealots are swelling. Look at the top tournament finishers and you'll see more and more power-game followers. So how are you going to stay in the race? How are you going to beat the power player?

What Is the Power Game?

In order to win, you'll have to know what you're up against. What is the power game? As the founder and head disciple of the serve-and-shoot style of play, the name Marty Hogan has become synonymous with the phrase *power game*. But in truth, the words power game are misleading because the image that these words suggest is undisciplined, unthinking ball blasting. Nothing could be further from the truth. A better term for my style is *power-based* racquetball. But since very few people use that phrase, I'll drop the *based*.

One of my friends said that creativity is the ability to recognize new relationships between old ideas. I created power racquetball at the St.

Louis JCCA (Jewish Community Centers Association) during a time when the rest of the world was following the pied piper of the control game. But this is the first point I want to make: The world is always changing, everything's relative, and you have to keep adapting and looking for new relationships, new ideas. That's the thrill of racquetball. Maybe you'll even find the next new game style.

But make no mistake; when I first started playing, I didn't go up into the mountains, meditate for ten days, and come back with power racquetball. I didn't start with a grand plan. I discovered it through long hours of experimentation. I started as a ball blaster, but my game has evolved and matured. Those opponents who don't understand how far my game has progressed will never beat me.

Power racquetball in simple terms is a strategy that uses power as the primary element in winning points, games, and matches. This is in contrast to a control strategy in which power is secondary to accuracy and shot selection. The difference is one of emphasis and not one of elements. Your chance of winning diminishes if you don't understand the relationship of the elements and instead overemphasize one element at the expense of the other elements.

The elements of winning racquetball fall into two classes, tangible and intangible. Intangible elements are desire, heart, organization, perception, creativity, inner strength, and so forth. That's all because you can't teach those elements. You either have them or you don't. The tangible elements are power, accuracy (control), endurance, court coverage, and shot selection.

The premises of power racquetball:

- Each shot can be less accurate because a mis-hit can still be missed by the opposition.
- Shot selection is less critical because the opposition can't effectively counter a ball moving at high speed.
- Less court space needs to be covered because the ball speed limits most contact points to the back court.
- Rallies are short.

In oversimplified terms, hit the ball hard enough and you'll have to worry less about everything else. So the central question that the power player has to answer is, How hard is hard enough?

That's power racquetball in a nutshell. But let me emphasize that the central question is relative to the opposition. And that's why no one can continually overemphasize one element and still win.

Classical Methods

There is no debate on how to win a point: Kill the ball before the opposition does. Even the control player adheres to this rule. For example, Steve Keeley used to always say, "Shoot, then pass, and if you really have to, go to the ceiling." The ongoing debate is over how to get into a situation where the risk of shooting the ball makes the choice worthwhile.

When a control player plays a power player, he's hoping that the power player will:

* Get arm fatigue before the end of the match.
* Get frustrated by a slow pace and high balls.
* Have a long cold spell.
* Take bad shots.

That's why a control player goes to the ceiling, moves the ball side to side, uses slow, high serves, and likes to play with a dead ball.

This archaic strategy still works at the local level. It's a work of art to see a control player slowly pick apart a power player and reduce him to a beaten, frustrated ball blaster. The control player uses time-outs, the wet floor ploy, and the "Would you say the score again?" trick along with pinpoint passing shots to reduce the effectiveness of the power player. Then, when the time is right, he turns up the knob on his shooting machine and the points start rolling in.

At first glance, the control strategy looks foolproof because there's no pressure to be always on. Just do your road work and wait for the opposition to give you the game. If your execution is off, win by attrition.

But the game has changed. The basic assumptions of the classic control game are weak at the local level of play and flat out wrong at the top levels of play. The power player at the top now is so accurate, quick, and strong that the classic control game has evolved into control with power in reserve. Everyone at the top has to be able to blow the ball by the opposition when the situation dictates. It may be a work of art when a control player picks apart a power player, but it's awesome when a power player blows out a control player.

So in order to beat the power player, the control player has to predict how successful his classic control strategy will be. The prediction depends in part on the degree to which the power player has developed the five tangible elements of winning racquetball relative to those of the control player. It also depends on the situation (e.g., is the ball slow or fast?). If the control player's prediction comes out negative, there's only one answer left for him: serve and shoot, and pray for a lucky day.

Figure 17-2. Jerry Hilecher in action (Courtesy Racquetball Illustrated)

Beating Marty Hogan

The preceding discussion is just a framework for beating the power game. To beat me, you have to beat a person who hits the ball at least 20 percent harder, is more accurate, can hit an offensive shot from anywhere on the court on a dead run, and is stronger than any other player. In short, I have the most awesome arsenal of shots anyone has ever seen, and I will scratch and claw for every point if I have to.

And beating me once doesn't mean you've found a long-sought-after secret. It's been said that the test of a person is how he handles a loss. I'm going to lose some matches, but each time I'll come back stronger and more determined to win. I'll adapt. I'll do what it takes to win.

Look at the record and you'll see that there's only one type of player who has even come close to consistently threatening me. He's the player who can stand toe-to-toe with me, slug it out, and get up again when he gets knocked down.

Right now there's only one way to beat the power game at the top levels of play and only one way to beat Marty Hogan: fight fire with fire. I'll give you a bit of advice. Learn the power game. It's going to be around long after Marty Hogan.

How to Play the Power Game
With a Slower Ball

There is a group of doubters that says I would be out on a corner selling tacos instead of making a living playing racquetball if the ball was slowed down to a speed like it was in the old days. Those critics are either out of touch with reality or doing some wishful thinking. The record shows that I have rarely lost a tournament with a slower ball. The plain truth is that the Marty Hogan power game works as well with a slow ball as it does with a fast ball. But you do have to make some adjustments. It's those adjustments that I want to describe here.

Good Old Days

In the early 1970s, there was really only one tournament ball, and, yes, the ball seemed so *sloooow*. Most players couldn't hit a ceiling ball that would come off the back wall. Games were long ceiling-ball rallies that would end when someone hit a short ceiling shot and the other player killed the ball.

But when I started playing serious tournament racquetball in the mid-70s, the ball speed increased tremendously, and, I will admit, so did my game. Power racquetball and Marty Hogan came along at the right time because the faster ball was perfect for my serve-and-shoot style.

But as racquetball grew, ball manufacturers popped up everywhere, and players lined up behind their favorite ball. Today, most of the balls are converging toward the perfect speed for levels of play.

But believe it or not, the slower balls of today are not much faster than the ball we played with in the good old days. What people don't realize is that players have learned to hit the ceiling ball more efficiently. Besides, players are stronger now than ten years ago.

During this period of ball evolution, my power game also evolved. Part of the evolution was by chance, but part was by design. I realized that some tournaments would always use slow balls. I knew that if I wanted to be known as the dominant force in racquetball, I would have to win with any ball.

Slow Ball Adjustments

I make four adjustments when playing with a slow ball: (1) hit more drive shots, (2) use a more conventional swing, (3) use more wrist-snap, and

(4) am more selective with my shots. The reason for making these adjustments is the percentage change with the slower ball (i.e., the return on your investment in power is less with the slower ball).

There are two reasons for more drive shots: First, it wears down my opponent, and second, it sets up my splat ball. With a fast ball, all I have to do is go for a kill shot every opportunity I get. Some of those kills turn out to be pass shots because I mis-hit the ball. On those high kills, the ball is moving so fast that most of the time the other player is not going to end the rally on my first mis-hit. This gives me another chance to kill it.

Therefore, with a faster ball I end up wearing down my opponents more by chance than by intent.

With the slower ball nobody is going to miss an opportunity to put away a mis-hit. But if I keep driving the ball until I get a good shot, my opponents are going to wear down long before I do because I hit the ball so much more efficiently than anyone else. I expend very little energy when I power the ball because the pendulum stroke is designed for maximum power with minimum effort.

Another reason for driving the ball is to set up my deep-court splat ball. By driving the slow ball, I'm forcing the other player out of center court and into the deep back corners. There isn't any one who has the power or accuracy that I do from backcourt. I can duel or slug it out all day with anyone in backcourt, and sooner or later I will get a chance to splat the ball into a corner while my opponent is still roaming around the back corners.

The second adjustment I make is to modify my swing so that it is less of a full pendulum and more of a conventional swing. The pendulum swing is a pure power stroke. I still use it when driving the ball. But when I go for a finer kill shot, I take a little off the ball by using a more conventional swing. This still allows me to take a full swing but it gives me a little more accuracy. I never want to push the ball to get more accuracy. The swing should always be natural and fluid. Every shot should always be natural and fluid. Every shot should keep the adrenalin flowing and give you the thrill of going all out. If you start pushing the ball, you get hesitant and blow the easy shots when the game gets tight.

The third adjustment is that I snap the wrist more. The slower ball gives me more time to really cock the wrist as far back as it will go. It's like stretching a rubber band farther to get more snap. The extra wrist-snap does two things for me: (1) I hit the ball harder, and (2) I keep the ball down better. Because I can't get as much ball speed from a conventional swing as I can from a pendulum swing, the extra wrist-snap makes up for the speed I have lost in going to the more conventional swing. Also, the natural spin from the extra wrist-snap keeps the ball from popping up. In racquetball, putting a lot of effort into spinning the ball like you would in tennis is a waste of time. A little natural spin keeps the ball low on the kill shots, but don't go out of the way to do it. When the ball stays low, your opponent has to bend down to return the ball. Try a few hundred deep knee bends and you'll know the effect of keeping the ball low during the course of a match.

The fourth and final adjustment I make is to be choosy about the shots I take. With a fast ball I can be a little sloppy because I'll usually blow the ball by the other player no matter what I do. But with the slower ball my opponents have more time to react. That's why the drive shot fits into the picture as a fundamental shot in the slow-ball strategy.

The slow ball also means use of more ceiling shots, more patience, and less expectation from power kills. I guess you might say that, with the slow ball, attrition becomes more important, but don't revolve your whole strategy around wearing opponents down like the classic control players do because attrition strategy just doesn't work in the long run.

With a slow ball you also have to change your service strategy to conserve more energy. Pace yourself. It's a question of investment. A drive serve isn't going to give you the same return on your energy investment as a fast ball will. So mix up the serves more. But don't desert the drive serve. A drive serve is good even when it isn't moving at 140 miles per hour as long as it's low.

So there you have it, four adjustments that I make when playing with the slow ball. The Marty Hogan power game isn't just slam, bang racquetball. You have to know the limitations of pure power and adjust accordingly. As I have said over and over again, the proper term is power-based racquetball. All the other elements rest on top of that base.

Slow-Ball Tournament

How do I prepare for a slow-ball tournament? The short answer is, not much. Most of the preparation is mental and very little is physical. For the average player, though, you will have to prepare more because of the attrition factor of the slow ball.

The most important preparation is still mental. You can't expect the shots that are your usual pet winners to be outright winners with the slow ball. Either you will have to throw them out the window or wait for two or three offensive opportunities before winning a point. Patience is the key word here. Don't let the ball frustrate you. Five years ago, the slow ball gave me fits because I expected the same quick results I got from the superball. Forget it. But keep pressuring your opponent. Just because you don't win the point on the first try doesn't mean you should give up the power kill in favor of the pass shot. The kill shot still ends the game faster and better than any shot in the book. You just have to try more times with a slow ball.

I practice with a slow ball only about two weeks before a tournament because it's a lot easier going from a fast to a slow ball than from a slow to a fast ball. The only reason I practice with the slow ball at all is to get my timing down and test whether I have mentally adjusted to the slow-ball strategy or not.

But for the average player, you may have to practice more with a slower ball because if you can't put the ball away, your opponent will grind you into the ground. I've heard some of the local club players say that when they really want to get some exercise, they use a slow ball.

You'll have to use more underspin on the ceiling balls when using a slow ball so that it will carry deeper with about the same effort as the fast ball. If you don't have the strength to blast the ball for an hour or two, hit higher V balls to drive the other player out of center court. But try the adjustments I described. And remember, the slow ball gives you a lot more time to prepare for a kill shot, so go for the kill when you get the chance.

How to Prepare for a Big Tournament

People have short memories. If I lose the Nationals, no one will remember my record even if I win every pro stop during a season. The money is unimportant. I want the recognition as the best player in the world. So I designed a special training program for the big tournament—The Nationals. The details of my program encompass seven fundamental principles that can be used for designing a program for any situation.

Timing

I begin my intensive training about six weeks before the Nationals. If I start too soon, my intensity will burn out before the end of the tournament. If I start too late, I won't reach my target in terms of physical skills and mental preparedness. I want to peak at the Nationals, not before or after.

Overloading

I spend the first three weeks overloading my whole physical and mental system. It's three weeks of pure hell that I endure because it ultimately produces the mental and physical toughness necessary to win the Nationals.

I get up at seven o'clock every morning. I eat a medium-sized breakfast but nothing special. Between 8:00 A.M. and 9:00 A.M., I head to a club where I play for six hours interrupted only for a lunch break. That's right. Six hours per day, five days per week. I keep this schedule up for three straight weeks. It doesn't matter who I play; it's the on-court time that's important.

The first week is almost unbearable. After each workout, I eat dinner and then collapse. The torture goes on for five or six days. But, surprisingly enough, my body adapts to the workload, and I get accustomed to the regimen.

However, one word of caution. This level of intensity is based on early-season workouts of two or three hours of play per day. I've built up a conditioning base that allows me to double my workout intensity just for the Nationals. You'll have to scale down your workout intensity relative to the base you've developed. If you don't, you're open to injury to your skeletal and central nervous systems.

This overload technique is similar to using the overload principle found in weight lifting. To build muscle strength in minimum time, additional weights must be added whenever a muscle adapts to a given weight. By doubling my workout intensity prior to the Nationals, I'm overloading my system in hopes of reaching the next physical plateau. After the first week, my body adapts to the workout intensity just like a weight lifter's muscles adapt to increased weight.

Filling the Reservoir

The intensity of the first three weeks has a second purpose: building up strength in reserve that can then be drawn upon in a real tough match. The workouts have to be longer, harder, and tougher than any match will ever be. That way, if I fall behind in a match, I can still increase the tempo of play by drawing on my reserve strength.

The strength reservoir gives me added confidence: not only from knowing that I can draw from the well but that I endured three weeks of workouts that are tougher than any other player is willing to endure. This means that anytime someone else tries to apply some pressure, I can, in turn, apply even more pressure.

Even though in the first three weeks I've reached the next strength plateau, my energy reserves are pretty low. Three weeks of strenuous workouts have broken down muscle tissue that hasn't had a chance to completely rebuild and has burned up almost all my energy reserves. The last three weeks are designed to do this rebuilding and at the same time build up my energy reserves.

In weeks four and five, I cut back to four hours of playing per day, five days per week, and in the sixth week I cut down to two hours of playing per day. The cutback allows energy which would normally be burnt up to be channeled into reserve. By the end of six weeks, the cutback is translated into increased workout intensity for shorter durations because I have greater energy and endurance.

Although I do not use carbohydrate loading, the energy buildup from my training program is similar to the effects some people get from carbohydrate loading. Carbohydrate loading begins by exercising four or five days at an above-normal activity level while eating below-normal amounts of carbohydrates. This combination is intended to deplete the body of glycogen, the substance that the body uses to generate quick energy. Then by switching to exercising at a normal activity level while eating above-normal amounts of carbohydrates, the body stores the above-normal levels of glycogen that then form the energy reserves.

Shot Flexibility

While the first three weeks are focused on breaking through a physical barrier, the last three weeks are aimed at breaking through the mental barrier. The attack begins by improving my shot flexibility.

Shot flexibility is a measure of the range of shots that can be hit from a given position. I want to be able to hit as many different shots from a given position as I can. The closer I come to attaining that goal, the greater my deception will be.

In order to obtain shot flexibility, you must be relaxed and hit with a fluid, natural swing. You have to hit shots over and over again until the timing is down. That's why I emphasize swinging all out on shots without worrying about the score when practicing. That's also why I play long hours rather than spending endless hours hitting alone. When I hit alone, I'm not under the same pressure to time my shots, and I don't get the same variety of situations that I get when I play someone else. These extra situations under playing conditions toughen muscles that would otherwise go undeveloped when practicing alone.

Maximum flexibility means that I can shoot down the wall, shoot cross-court, drive either direction, hit a pinch, or hit a reverse pinch all from

Figure 17-3. Marty Hogan defeated Mike Yellen in the finals of the 1980 Nationals at the Las Vegas Sporting House (Courtesy Racquetball Illustrated)

the same court position. Substantial wrist strength makes it possible to hit all these shots with almost the same swing.

Specificity

Note that so far I haven't mentioned anything but playing racquetball as part of my intensive training program. I do practice shots alone on the court but not very much this late in the season. It's usually too late too worry about a kink in a shot that can't be solved by playing. I also run about five miles at the end of each day.

But I don't like weight lifting or running agility courses or sprints. Again, it's too late; that should have been done at the beginning of the season. I do occasionally indulge in some push-ups and sit-ups but probably more out of habit than anything else.

In short, I practice racquetball primarily by playing racquetball and exclude anything that is not specifically related to playing racquetball. Although I do include activities such as running in my late-season workouts, I do so mainly for relaxation.

Focus

The final weeks of preparation are aimed at fine-honing my aggressiveness, shot making, and concentration. By cutting back on the workout durations, I channel the same energy level into a short time period. Having stretched my shot range to its maximum extension in the first three or four weeks, I now focus my attention on refining my bread-and-butter shots—the forehand pinch from the deep left corner or my backhand kill of a deep ceiling ball.

By the end of the sixth week, I have developed a true hatred for playing racquetball that has been built up by the long court hours. This hatred manifests itself as a growing, controlled anger directed toward each shot. By this point, I am only interested in winning each point in the quickest possible way. I now literally attack the ball with full power at every possible opportunity. I am no longer interested in developing more shot flexibility or power but rather putting them to their greatest use.

I have often been accused of lackadaisical play in which I seem to toy with my opponents. Those claims are sometimes justified during the season. It's tough to concentrate 365 days out of a year without a challenge. But in the Nationals, no one gets a free ride. If I can win 21–0, I will because I have a totally different state of mind in the Nationals than in all the other tournaments.

During these six weeks before the Nationals, I narrow my focus on only one goal. Even everyday pleasures and vices are forsaken during the quest. The discipline required to endure the six-week training program carries over into tournament week.

Food and Rest

So far I've led you to believe that I spend every waking hour playing racquetball, but adequate rest is as important as all the other elements. Without proper rest you cannot obtain the maximum benefit out of each training day, and you therefore don't play at your maximum potential at the end of the training period.

After each day's workout, I forget about racquetball, and on weekends I engage in activities that are noncompetitive. Your body must be given time to recover. This recovery will depend on your base. It may take a whole season or even years to build up a base where you can play even two hours a day three or four times per week. Successive applications of overload and rest will increase your recovery periods.

I have no recommendations on the subject of food because I'm an occasional junk food addict (Ding Dongs are a favorite). But at some point in the future, age may change my habits. I have no hard vices: I don't drink, smoke, or take drugs.

Conclusion

This has been a glimpse at intensive racquetball training. The general principles can be applied to training for any event.

1. Time the training period for adequate overload and recovery.
2. Use the overload principle to reach the next physical plateau in minimum time.
3. Follow the overload period with workout cutback to build up energy reserves.
4. Workouts should aim at making demands tougher than those of real matches.
5. Work on shot flexibility and timing by playing.
6. Play to improve.
7. Get adequate rest relative to your conditioning and workout intensity.

It would be great if we all had the time and energy to use this program for every tournament. Unfortunately, we don't; even I can only endure such a program once a year. But the basic principles can be used as guidelines to tailor individual programs. Those with dreams of a national title will see that the price of success is high.

The Quick-Draw Forehand

Now that I have established that power racquetball is here to stay, it's time to look at some fundamental principles. And what better way to discuss them than in the most critical situations in which a player doesn't have time to set up for a picture-perfect power shot.

Those situations arise when you are up against the side wall and your opponent jams the ball at you or in the middle of a center-court slug out or when the ball just decides to take a bad bounce. Most players in those situations either top a pitter-patter ball back or hit it somewhere, anywhere, just to get it back into play. But advanced players know better than that. They dig out from their bag of tricks a rapid-fire shot that goes invariably for a winner. Since the quick-draw forehand is easier to hit than the backhand, we'll start with that shot and reserve the backhand and other specialty shots for later discussion.

Basic Principles

There are four main factors involved in hitting a quick-draw forehand: flexible wrist action, good contact point, whip-like arm motion, and controlled weight transfer.

Flexible wrist action is the most important part of the shot. If necessary, you can drive or kill a normal shot with a moderately stiff wrist, but there's no way you can react fast enough to a blazing-fast shot with slow, stiff, weak wrist action. You need to adjust the wrist for any timing problems caused by the rest of the swing or to generate power when you don't transfer enough weight toward the target area.

The contact point can be much deeper than called for in the classical forehand. In fact, a quick forehand can be hit with lots of pace even when the ball is behind the body. Because the contact point is deep in the stance, you will have more time to react to the ball than when you try to contact the ball closer to the instep of the left leg as in the classic forehand.

You will need to learn how to react to the ball with a continuous whipping-arm motion rather than a jerky one. Swinging by the numbers is the worst possible way to try to hit a rapid-fire forehand. Swinging by the numbers tightens up players rather than allowing them to stay loose. The result is paralysis when the pressure mounts in quick-reaction situations.

Finally, even under very severe time limitations, some weight transfer toward the target area can add enough speed to the ball to make the shot a winner rather than just a dink. A tremendous amount of ball speed can be generated by combining just a few of these principles in a rapid-fire forehand.

The rule of thumb is to hit the ball away from the other player, but as I will demonstrate later there are certain situations in which the rule can be bent to give you an extra advantage in the long run. This has to do with the mental part of your game.

The principle of practice and more practice puts emphasis on flexibility, adaptiveness, and creativity. It's great to be able to calculate all sorts of trivial measures such as force and momentum, but those things are only good in locker-room or bar talk. When you have only a split second to respond to a ball coming at 100 miles per hour, you have to react naturally and feel the shot, not think the shot. Practice should be centered around getting this feel and reacting comfortably to balls being shot at you.

The How

Let's look at some factors involved in how to hit the quick-draw fore-hand. Along with the major factors of flexible wrist-action, good contact point, whipping swing, and directed weight transfer, you also have to concentrate on footwork, grip, ball spin, and position recovery.

There's not much you can do about foot position if the ball is already on top of you. But the thing to remember is that you can still hit the ball pretty hard even with an open stance facing the front wall. You just have to learn how to stay calm without trying to get into the ideal position for every shot. Hit the ball within an open stance or in whatever stance you happen to be in at the time.

But do it with an offensive purpose, not a defensive one. You'll notice that even with the feet parallel to the front wall, you can still turn your upper body almost parallel to the side wall. This movement in fact winds you up like a rubber band, ready to be unwound into the ball (i.e., rotating the upper body back parallel to the front wall).

If you do not have a chance to move, then I recommend moving the right foot away from the approaching ball rather than stepping into the ball with the left foot. By beginning the swing during this turning motion, you'll be ready to meet the ball as soon as or sometimes even before the right foot gets into place. This movement take only a split second—just about the amount of time you'll have. Of course, if you have more time than this, you may want to move farther away from the ball to contact it from a lower position.

What about grip? Although the top players will tell you they only use one or two grips, they really have probably five or six different grips, one or two of which are used when they have time to set up for a shot. Grip is only important when you are trying to hit with maximum effi-ciency. When you're jammed, go with what you have. The one-grip player has an advantage because his or her primary grip is always the same. The two-grip player is wise to choose one grip (backhand, forehand, or in between) to use in all cases except when there is time to change the grip. But in either case, don't worry about the grip.

You can adjust the direction of the shot by modifying the wrist-snap and sometimes the swing. But the wrist-snap is the most important part of making a quick-draw shot work. That's why it makes sense sometimes to practice hitting from off-balance positions using irregular grips. It's not so much that you will want to practice those shots 100 times in a row, but you want to feel comfortable making fine adjustments with the wrist.

Ball spin is sometimes helpful but not in the tennis sense. I never pur-posely try to use spin for any advantage because it's more trouble than it's worth. A racquetball just doesn't react like a tennis ball. But if I'm jammed and the ball gets behind me, I'll come over the ball from behind my right hip and put it into a corner or down the line. The purpose of the topspin is not deception but protection and control. If I use a regular flat shot with the ball that far behind my body, I'll either throw my shoulder out or send the ball sailing out of control. So the topspin is used in an effort to let me swing with full force but still be able to control where I want the ball to go. Remember, power players don't push the ball too often. It's bad for the image.

The last point I want to make is that the quick-draw shot has to be followed up. Think in terms of offense. Even if the shot was a great one, the other player may still return it. Think ahead. Anticipate where your opponent's return will go and jump on it.

One other point about flexible wrist action: The wrist-snap is the last point in the sequence involved in hitting any shot. Once your motion starts for any shot, there's very little adjustment you can make—except to modify the wrist-snap. You must be able to feel the plane of the racquet face and, with a few exceptions, snap the wrist in such a manner that the racquet face comes straight through the ball rather than over or under the ball. This means that you can hit a forehand with a backhand grip. The sooner you learn to hit every shot with lots of wrist-snap, the sooner your wrist will be conditioned to make the adjustments mentioned here. Wrist adjustment isn't easy at first, so you'll have to build up to it. But if you start by consciously hitting all the basic shots with wrist-snap, the transition from intermediate to advanced player will be much quicker.

Under "Basic Principles" I said that the contact point at times will be much deeper than you would expect. But in order to get maximum power, you have to pull back the arm and shoulder as far as they will go. Too often, the beginner will not bring the arm all the way back because of the misconception that if the ball takes a bad bounce or the ball isn't in a perfect position, the best way to adjust is by contacting the ball early. Nonsense. The wrist adjustment serves that purpose unless you misjudge the ball by a foot or more. Also, some players don't realize that they have not drawn the racquet back to its maximum possible position. You can tell if that position has been reached if the arm will not pivot any farther when someone pushes on the shoulder.

The swing itself must be a fluid, whipping motion. Imagine yourself in your good old childhood days when you tried to snap someone with a towel. The motion is similar, although not identical, for a quick-draw forehand. The difference is that the arm motion has to adjust to the height of the ball and the lack of time you have before contact.

Proper weight transfer is the third ingredient that is necessary to gain good velocity on the ball.

Even in an awkward body position, you should strive to start with the weight deep in your stance and then transfer it with your legs and hips in the direction of the intended shot. This motion may be as little as thrusting the knees about six inches toward the front wall or as much as a full transfer of your hip weight from rear to front foot. This motion along with the uncoiling of the upper body should be sufficient to hit the ball with good pace. One major mistake is to make contact with the ball too late. The result is usually a ball which sails into the left wall. That's why the ball needs to be contacted deep in the stance so that the uncoiling motion, while in an open or irregular stance, transfers that part of the motion directed at the front wall. The follow-through in this case is just for balance.

The Shots

Once you have some control over the quick-draw forehand, you should still strive to put the ball in the best place. The easiest choice is to hit the ball where the other player isn't. This choice, as simple as it is, will always work to some extent, but there are some situations where other choices may be warranted.

A pinch shot is called for under two conditions. If the other player is caught between you and the side wall or is in deep court, a pinch has the added psychological effect of demoralizing the opposition because he or she is helplessly frozen against the wall. This opens the doors for less precise shots that you may have to or want to hit later in a match. The key is to "legally shove" the other player against the side wall.

Practice Drills

Practicing the quick-draw shot can be dangerous because you start believing that every shot should be hit with the motion described earlier. But with that warning, I'll describe two drills that will make life a little more comfortable under quick-draw situations.

In the first drill, you should stand facing the front wall behind the back service line and tap the ball to the front wall with the feet planted in the open stance. Get the feel of the deep contact point. Then after a few minutes, move closer to the front wall. Do this until you get to the front service line. Then move back and do the same thing but add more wrist and arm motion into the shot to pick up the pace. The final stage is to alternate between setting yourself up and whipping a forehand down the wall (with an open stance). If you have a partner, trade off setting the other person up with faster and faster shots. The ultimate shot is the pinch from this position.

In the second drill, alternate from side to side continuously hitting pinch shots from the back service line. Increase the tempo as your body loosens up. At first, concentrate individually on each separate point I've made but stay loose. The most important things to try are wrist adjustment and the whipping motion. When it seems easy, try moving closer to the wall.

Doubles games are excellent to test what you've learned because you are often at close quarters slugging it out with three other players. The action is fast and the adrenalin is flowing.

The basic principles outlined here apply to both the forehand and the backhand. In fact they apply to all shots. You may not be able to follow every aspect of what I've described, but this should give you a glimpse of what is possible. As you become accustomed to hitting quick draw shots you can refine their execution. Then there will be a day when it will seem like old hat—the day when you've really entered the realm of the advanced player.

The Power Backhand

When I played my first national tournament in 1969, I noticed one thing about most of the players, even some of the top ranked ones: Their backhands were far inferior to their forehands and often were used only in a do-or-die situation. Even today, some of the top pros have weak backhands.

I decided then and there that I would be a player with a balanced offense—a threat from either side. Thus, I practiced the backhand much more than the forehand. The result? A backhand that I think is more accurate and powerful than my forehand. And others have told me it is the most awesome shot in racquetball next to my power drive.

In order to have a balanced attack and prevent your opposition from picking apart your backhand, you should spend a considerable amount of effort to make your backhand as big a threat as your forehand.

The long-run benefits are numerous. Players always attack the backhand first. If you respond with some unexpected backhand kills, they will start hitting to your forehand—a shot you know is even more devastating. Very few players can recognize when an opponent has a better backhand than forehand. They revolve their entire game plan around attacking the backhand. Their mind is locked: Attack the backhand; the forehand is too good.

But the backhand is really not that hard to master. To conquer it requires mostly a psychological victory. We learn to bat forehand, throw forehand, and the masses tell us that the backhand is hard. So when we get around to thinking about the backhand, we have already developed a deep-seated fear of it. But in reality the backhand should be easier to hit than the forehand. The mechanics of the backhand are in your favor because at the point of contact your whole body weight is behind the ball rather than in front of the ball as it is in the forehand. Fear comes from the uncertainty of the untried and lack of backhand muscle development. Hours of proper practice will remove the stigma that a weak backhand is normal and therefore acceptable. It may be normal, but it is definitely not acceptable.

Technique

It is very difficult to effectively describe the mechanics of any stroke, let alone my backhand. A proper education should combine observation and experimentation framed by some basic principles. I will outline my laws of motion below. But you should watch the top players execute their backhands and try to develop a mental image of the essential features of the stroke. Chances are they don't hit the ball quite the same way I do, but at least you will get some approximation of the proper stroke.

There are five main features of my backhand: (1) a universal grip—same as the forehand, (2) a full pendulum swing, (3) a very low posture, (4) a powerful leg thrust into the contact zone, and (5) an explosive wrist-snap.

I use basically one grip for the forehand and the backhand. Tennis players call it a continental grip, midway between conventional forehand and backhand grips. In reality, top players who follow the one-grip school of thought make small adjustments. I am no exception. But the main point is that I make my major adjustments by changing the wrist-snap. The adjustment aims for a flat contact with the ball directed toward the bottom board. This requires good timing, well-developed racquet sense, and a strong wrist. These qualities can only be developed by long hours of practice until the wrist-snap becomes an integral part of every shot and you literally feel the ball.

At first glance, this goal may seem too lofty for the casual player. But that's only because the voices of the past tell you that it's impossible or that it's unorthodox. But if you can learn to hit the forehand and the backhand with just one grip, you will be rewarded with moments of brilliance and a greater range of shots. Never again will you be jammed while changing grips.

A full pendulum swing is necessary to generate maximum power with minimum effort. Many players do not get the full benefit of the pendulum swing because they imitate a bat swing in which the racquet trajectory resembles a roundhouse swing. The proper racquet trajectory is more like a golf swing but with the stroke moving in the plane perpendicular to the floor and in the direction of the intended shot. The stroke is an up and down motion, not a circular one. Of course, the swing must level off at the bottom to prevent excessive skipping.

To start the pendulum swing, your weight must be transferred onto the back foot in a closed stance. Then, as the ball approaches, draw the arm and racquet back along the perpendicular plane of the forward swing and point the forearm straight up to the sky. Many racquetball teachers preach that you should bring the racquet back early and hold the ready position. Unfortunately, if you follow this rule with the full pendulum swing, you will be extremely cramped. You'll lose the rocking effect needed to get a maximum windup. The only important preparation is to constantly shuffle the feet into proper position with your weight ready to spring off the rear foot. The backswing motion should be timed so that you get maximum extension without holding yourself in an awkward set position.

At the apex of the backswing, the wrist should be curled but relaxed, ready to explode toward the ball. At this point, all the muscles from the waist up that will contribute to the power component of the stroke should be at maximum extension like a taut rubber band ready to snap. This means lifting the racquet (which is now behind the left ear) further up towards the sky. You should feel like someone yanked you from the ceiling. The shoulders rotate away from the oncoming ball with the right shoulder dropping. The hips shift farther toward the back foot. This position should be reached in one smooth motion and held only for a split second.

Preparation for the wrist curl is much like a karate punch. The wrist is relaxed, almost floppy, when it is brought back to its maximum extension at the apex of the backswing. This reduces wrist fatigue and lets you easily adjust to unpredictable shots. But as the racquet begins its journey toward the contact point, the wrist muscles reach their maximum extension in a fully cocked position.

During this setup phase of the stroke, you should already have low posture in which the legs are bent, almost a squat. Your upper body should be bent at the waist. It is extremely important to be low to the ground when hitting a kill shot. If you have never tried this, you may find that you will need to do some exercises to strengthen the leg muscles, a requirement for this semicrouched position.

As I begin the downward swing of the racquet, I squeeze the grip, pull down with the racquet, push off with my rear leg, and accelerate toward the contact zone. My shoulders and hips begin to uncoil. The contact zone is in front of my starting position but just anterior to my right knee. As I step into the ball, I form a closed stance. In order to keep the ball from sailing on contact, the right shoulder must level out just like the racquet trajectory. In a setup, most of my power is generated from my legs, not my arms or upper body.

In the final phase of the stroke, the swing levels out just before impact and the wrist snaps with a level follow-through. The ball should explode off the racquet strings. If the stroke is not level at the contact point, the ball will either skip or sail.

The powerful thrust and step will tax the muscles in your right thigh. To avoid this, transfer the weight in the direction of the shot and follow through naturally. Snap the wrist so that the ball is hit almost flat. This gives maximum power and minimizes the chances for error when fatigue sets in. With underspin or topspin, the ball will float or skip when you get tired. The wrist-snap is to be made right before impact. Snap too early and you will lose valuable energy. Snap too late and you will not generate maximum power.

Timing, of course, is the key to hitting with maximum power while expending a minimum amount of effort. It can't be taught on a point-by-point basis. Rather it must be learned by the feel technique in which you spend time on the court feeling the racquet make contact with the ball, feeling the flow of the backhand swing. In all cases, strive for a relaxed swing in which the arm moves freely without different techniques to increase your racquet awareness.

Strategy

Although the backhand down-the-line shot is more difficult than its forehand counterpart, the best strategy is still to hit about 75 percent of the backhands straight down the line. Mix in about 25 percent backhand pinches or crosscourt kills. Three shots down the line and one complementary shot are a good frame of reference. The reason behind this strategy is that, as the backhand explodes down the left wall, your opponent will have to contend with the side wall. In addition, it takes much less time for the ball to travel to the front wall when hitting down the line than crosscourt.

At worst, if the ball does not catch the side wall, any kill attempt that stays up will carry your opponent to the backcourt on his backhand side. The three shots down the wall should prime your opponent for the second of the one–two punch. A reliable, straight-in kill shot will be feared and will make your opponent tend to lean to the backhand side. This sets him or her up for other shots, the best of which is the pinch.

I also follow the same strategy on the backhand return of service. Other pros respond to a drive serve left with a ceiling or pass shot. I choose to shoot into the left corner. Since the backhand is my strength, I go on the offensive whenever I can. I have timed the drive serves of some pros to the point where my backhand kill off their serve is automatic. That's why a lot of players are now lobbing my backhand because they know it's suicide to hit any other serve.

Unfortunately, the technique and strategy that I have outlined so far are not all there is to the Hogan backhand. The real difference that sets my backhand apart from all the other backhands is that I can take any shot with my feet in any position and still power the ball into the left corner. This comes from avoiding the early set-and-hold technique advocated by most racquetball teachers. I use a compact but fully extended backswing, and I practice fluid weight transfer and body flow into the contact zone. In short, my backhand is extremely versatile because I have avoided some of the very checkpoints demanded by other racquetball teachers. Instead, I stress timing and stroke creativity. In a match, the ball is hardly ever in a position where you can take the ideal stroke. Why then force yourself into waiting for these few opportunities? Why not create your own opportunities by learning to adjust to the situation at hand?

Get out of the straightjacket forced on you by the old school. Start hitting backhands with a free swing to develop the backhand muscles. Then learn to adjust to changing situations by hitting backhands with lots of wrist-snap. Finally, work on fully extending the backswing. At first the results may be frustrating. But at some point you will discover that as long as you stay relaxed, flow into the contact area, and snap the wrist, the backhand will no longer be just a popgun in your arsenal but a cannon that will explode you to the next higher level of play.

Fast Formulas For A Better Backhand

Imitate Your Forehand

Your backhand stroke should ideally be almost exactly like your forehand stroke. I consider the backhand the easiest stroke to make in racquetball. I have more confidence hitting my backhand than I do in hitting my forehand. My backhand is such a nice, fluid motion. I am also able to maintain the consistency in my backhand regardless of my positioning on the court.

You should develop the same fluid motion with your backhand as you have with your forehand. Make sure you get a high backhand swing and good follow-through on each backhand stroke. It doesn't matter if you are in the frontcourt or if you are in the backcourt, every stroke should look the same. I think the worst thing anyone could do in learning a backhand is learning a particular stroke that is going to handicap you in certain shot selections.

Build Your Confidence

My game style has enabled me to hit a backhand anywhere on the court. I've been able to hit my backhand better than head high, 39 feet away in the backcourt for an outright kill. I think anyone who learns the fluid power of my backhand stroke will also have greater range in his or her stroke and shot selection.

If you're weak in hitting your backhand in the deep parts of the court, your opponent will soon catch on. As a result, these are the only shots your opponent will be hitting during the course of the match. So the most important thing to remember is find a backhand stroke you can incorporate into your game. This way you will not be at a disadvantage during the game. Racquetball is played on a 20 by 40 by 20 foot court, and it's fairly easy for your opponent to isolate certain areas of the court, especially if he or she knows you have a weak return.

Use a Solid Stroke

The one tip I give everybody is hit your backhand solidly. When you go to hit the backhand, hit it like you would your forehand. To hit a forehand you should step up and execute a good, hard swipe. Make good, firm contact.

The same should go with your backhand. Don't push your backhand stroke. Don't ease up when you are hitting crosscourt or going for kills because you feel like you don't have enough accuracy. Hit the ball solidly with your backhand. Create a backhand stroke you are going to be as confident with as you are with your forehand.

The Secret Splat Shot

One shot I think is very effective is a backhand splat shot (side wall, front wall, and then sort of splats out on court). This shot is so tough to judge and cover you'll find that even if you don't hit it just right, the ball will go in for a winner. There's no player in the game who can cover a splat shot with 100 percent efficiency. This is because no one expects you to hit down hard on your backhand. It's also hard to judge whether the ball is going to splat out wide or splat out short. So covering the splat shot becomes extremely difficult for your opponent.

The Secret Struggle

Appendix A
Racquetball Rules

Rules may be obtained from the American Amateur Racquetball Association, 815 North Weber, Suite 203, Colorado Springs, CO 80903. Rules are reprinted with permission.

I. *The Game.*
   A. *Types of Games.* Racquetball may be played by two, three, or four players. When played by two it is called singles, when played by three, cutthroat, and when played by four, doubles.
   B. *Description.* Racquetball is a competitive game in which only one racquet is used by each player to serve and return the ball.
   C. *Objective.* The objective is to win each rally by serving or returning the ball so that the opponent is unable to keep the ball in play. A rally is over when a side makes an error, is unable to return the ball before it touches the floor twice, or if a hinder is called.
   D. *Points and Outs.* Points are scored only by the server or serving team when that side serves an ace or wins a rally. When the serving side loses a rally, it loses the serve. Losing the serve is called an out in singles, and a handout or side-out in doubles.

E. *Game.* A game is won by the side first scoring 15 points (or 11 points in the tiebreaker). A one-point advantage is sufficient.

F. *Match.* A match is won by the first side winning two games. The first two games of a match are played to 15 points. In the event that each participant or team wins one game, the match shall be decided by an 11-point tiebreaker.

G. *Doubles Team.* A doubles team shall consist of two players that meet either the age requirements or player classification requirements to participate in a particular division of play. A team must be classified by the ability level (or player classification) of the higher-ranked player on the team.

   A change in playing partners may not be made after the final draw has been made and posted. Under no circumstances can a partner change be made during the course of a tournament without the consent of the Tournament Director.

H. *Consolation Matches.*
   1. Consolation matches may be waived at the discretion of the Tournament Director, but this waiver must be in writing on the tournament application.
   2. In all AARA sanctioned tournaments, each entrant shall be entitled to participate in a minimum of two matches. This means that losers of the first match shall have the opportunity to compete in a consolation bracket of their own division. In draws of fewer than seven players, a round-robin format may be offered.

II. *Courts and Equipment.*
   A. *Regulation Court.*
      1. *Dimensions.* The dimensions shall be 20 feet wide, 20 feet high, and 40 feet long, with a back wall at least 12 feet high. All surfaces within the court shall be deemed in play with the exception of any gallery openings or surfaces designated as court hinders.
      2. *Lines and Zones.* Racquetball courts shall be divided and marked with lines one and one-half inches wide as follows:
      a) Short Line. The back edge of the short line is midway between and parallel to the front and back walls, thus dividing the court into an equal frontcourt and backcourt.
      b) Service line. The front edge of the service line is parallel to and located five feet in front of the back edge of the short line.

c) Service Zone. The service zone is the area between the outer edges of the short and service lines.

d) Service Boxes. The service boxes are located at each end of the service zone and are designated by lines parallel with each wall. The inside edge of the lines are 18 inches from the side walls.

e) Receiving Line. A broken line parallel to the short line. The back edge of the receiving line will be five feet from the back edge of the short line. The receiving line will begin with a line 21 inches long that extends from each side wall: The two lines will be connected by an alternate series of six-inch spaces and six-inch lines (17 six-inch spaces and 16 six-inch lines).

f) Safety Zone. The five-foot area bounded by the short line and the receiving line. The zone is observed only during the serve. If the receiver enters the zone prematurely, it results in a point. If the server enters the zone prematurely, it results in the loss of serve.

B. *Ball Specifications.*
1. The standard racquetball shall be two and one-quarter-inches in diameter, weigh approximately 1.4 ounces, and, at a temperature of 70 to 74°F with a 100-inch drop, rebound is to be 68 to 72 inches; hardness, 55- to 60-inch durometer measurement.
2. Any ball that carries the endorsement stamp of approval from the AARA is an official ball. Only AARA approved balls may be used in AARA sanctioned tournaments.

C. *Ball Selection.*
1. A ball shall be selected by the referee for use in each match. During the match the referee may, at his or her discretion or at the request of a player or team, replace the game ball. Balls that are not round or that bounce erratically shall not be used.
2. In tournament play, the referee and the players shall agree to an alternate ball so that, in the event of breakage, the second ball can be put into play immediately.

D. *Racquet Specifications.*
1. *Dimensions.* The racquet, including bumper guard and all solid parts, may not exceed 21 inches in length.
2. The regulation racquet frame may be of any material as long as it conforms to the above specifications.

3. The regulation racquet must include a thong that must be securely attached to the player's wrist.

4. The string of the racquet should be gut, monofilament, nylon, graphite, plastic, metal, or a combination thereof as long as the strings do not mark or deface the ball.

E. *Uniform.*

1. The uniform and shoes may be of any color but must have soles that do not mark or damage the court floor. The shirt may contain any insignia or writing considered in good taste by the Tournament Director. Players are required to wear shirts. Extremely loose fitting or otherwise distracting garments are not permissible.

2. Eye protection is required for any participant under the age of 19 in all AARA-sanctioned tournaments.

III. *Officiating and Play Regulations.*

Rule 1.   *Tournament Officiating*

a) *Tournaments.* All tournaments shall be managed by a committee or Tournament Director who shall designate the officials.

b) *Officials.* The official shall be a referee designated by the Tournament Director or the floor manager or one agreed to by both participants (teams in doubles). Officials may also include, at the discretion of the Tournament Director, a scorekeeper and two linespeople.

c) *Removal of Referee.* A referee may be removed upon the agreement of both participants (teams in doubles) or at the discretion of the Tournament Director or rules officials. In the event that a referee's removal is requested by one player (team) and not agreed to by the other, the Tournament Director or officials may accept or reject the request.

d) *Rule Briefing.* Before all tournaments, all officials and players shall be briefed on rules and on court hinders or regulations or modifications the Tournament Director wishes to impose. This briefing should be made in writing. The current AARA rules will apply and be made available. Any modifications the Tournament Director wishes to impose must be stated in writing on the entry form and be available to all players at registration.

e) *Referees.* (1) *Prematch Duties.* Before each match begins, it shall be the duty of the referee to: (a) check on adequacy or preparation of the court with respect to cleanliness, light-

ing, and temperature; (b) check on availability and suita-
bility of materials necessary for the match such as balls,
towels, score cards, pencils, and time piece; (c) instruct
players on court; (d) point out court hinders and local regulations; (e) inspect equipment and toss coin; (f) check
linespeople and scorekeeper and ask for reserve game ball
upon assuming officiating position; (g) review any rule
modifications in effect for this particular tournament. (2)
Decisions. During the match, the referee shall make all decisions with regard to the rules. When linespeople are used,
the referee shall announce all final judgments. If both
players in singles and three out of four in a doubles match
disagree with a judgment call made by the referee, the
referee is overruled. The referee shall have jurisdiction over
the spectators as well as players while the match is in
progress. (3) *Protests.* Any decision not involving the judgment of the referee may, on protest, be decided by the
Tournament Director or a designated official. (4) *Forfeitures.*
A match may be forfeited by the referee when: (a) any
player refuses to abide by the referee's decision or engages
in unsportsmanlike conduct; (b) a player's or team's
matches may be forfeited by the Tournament Director or
official for failure to comply with the tournament or host
facility's rules while on the premises, for failure to referee,
for improper conduct on the premises between matches,
or for abuse of hospitality, locker room, or other rules and
procedures; (c) any player or team fails to report to play
ten minutes after the match has been called to play. (The
Tournament Director may permit a longer delay if circumstances warrant.)

f) *Linespeople.* (1) Two linespeople are recommended for all
matches from the semifinals on up, subject to availability
and the discretion of the tournament officials. The linespeople shall be selected by the officials and situated as
designated by the officials. If any player objects to the selection of a linesperson before the match begins, all reasonable effort shall be made to find a replacement acceptable
to the officials and players. If a player or team objects to
a linesperson after the match begins, replacement shall be
at the discretion of the referee and officials. (2) Linespeople
are designated in order to help decide appealed rulings.

Two linespeople will be designated by the referee and shall, at the referee's signal, either agree or disagree with the referee's ruling. The signal by a linesperson to show agreement with the referee is thumbs up. The signal to show disagreement is thumbs down. The signal for no opinion is open palm down. If both linespeople signal no opinion, the referee's call stands. If both linespeople disagree with the referee, the referee must reverse the ruling. If one linesperson agrees and one disagrees or has no opinion, the referee's call shall stand. If one linesperson disagrees and one has no opinion, the rally or serve shall be replayed. Any replays will result in two serves with the exception of appeals on the second serve itself.

g) *Appeals.* In any match using linespeople a player or team may appeal only the following calls made or not made by the referee: (1) *Kill Shots*, skip balls, fault serves, out serves, double-bounce pickups. The appeal must be directed to the referee, who will then request opinions simultaneously from the two linespeople. Any appeal made directly to a linesperson by a player or team or made after an excessive demonstration or complaint by the player(s) will be considered null and void and will forfeit any appeal rights for that player or team for that particular rally. (2) *Kill Shot Appeals.* If the referee makes a call of good on a kill shot attempt that ends in a rally, the loser of the rally may appeal the call. If the appeal is successful and the referee's original call is reversed, the side which originally lost the rally is declared the winner of the rally. If the referee makes a call of bad or skip on a kill shot attempt, the rally has ended and the side against which the call was made has the right to appeal the call. If the appeal is successful and the referee's original call is reversed, the referee must then decide if the shot could have been returned had play continued. If the shot could have been (or was) returned, the rally shall be replayed. If the shot was a kill or pass that the opponent could not have retrieved (in the referee's opinion), the side that originally lost the rally is declared the winner of the rally. The referee's judgment in this matter is final. Any rally replayed shall afford the server two serves. (3) *Fault Serve Appeals.* If the referee makes a call of fault on a serve, the server may appeal the call. If the appeal is successful, the server is entitled to replay the serve. If the referee makes no call on a serve (indicating that the serve was good), the receiver may appeal. If the appeal is successful, a fault is called. If it was a first service, one more serve is allowed. If the serve was a second serve, then the fault serve would cause an out. (4) *Out-Serve Appeals.* If the referee makes a call of out serve, thereby stopping the play, the serving side may appeal the call. If the appeal is successful, the referee shall revise the call to the proper call and the service shall be replayed or a point awarded if the resulting serve was an ace. If the referee makes no call or calls a fault serve, and the receiver thinks it was an out serve, the receiver may appeal. If the appeal is successful the service results in an out. (5) *Double-Bounce Pickup Appeals.* If the referee makes a call of two bounces, thereby stopping play, the side against which the call was made has the right of appeal. If the appeal is upheld, the rally is replayed or the referee may award the rally to the hitter if the resulting shot could not have been retrieved by the opponent (and providing the referee's call did not cause the opponent to hesitate or stop play). If the referee makes no call on a particular play, indicating thereby that the player hit the ball before the second bounce, the opponent has the right to appeal at the end of the rally. However, because the ball is in play, the side wishing to appeal must clearly motion to the referee and linespeople by raising the nonracquet hand, thereby alerting the officials as to the exact shot which is being appealed. At the same time, the player appealing must continue to play. If the appealing player should lose the rally and the appeal is upheld, the player who appealed then becomes the winner of the rally. All rallies replayed as the result of a double-bounce pickup appeal shall result in the server getting two serves.

h) *Rules Interpretations.* If a player feels that the referee has interpreted the rules incorrectly, he or she may require the referee or Tournament Director to show him or her the applicable rule in the rule book.

Rule 2.   *Serve*

a) *Order.* The player or side winning the toss becomes the first server and starts the first game. The loser of the toss will serve first in the second game. The player or team scoring the most total points in games one and two shall serve first in the tiebreaker. In the event that both players or teams score an equal number of points in the first two games, another coin toss shall determine service in the tiebreaker.

b) *Start*. The serve is started from any place within the service zone. No part of either foot may extend beyond either line of the service zone. Stepping on but not over the line is permitted. The servers must remain in the service zone from the moment the service motion begins until the served ball passes the short line. Violations are called foot faults. The server may not start any service motion until the referee has called the score or second serve.

c) *Manner*. While standing within the service zone the server must bounce the ball on the floor and strike it with his or her racquet; the ball must hit the front wall first and on the rebound hit the floor behind the back edge of the short line either with or without touching one of the side walls. A balk serve or fake swing at the ball shall be deemed an infraction and be judged an out, handout or side out.

d) *Readiness*. Serves shall not be made until the receiving side is ready and the referee has called the score. The referee shall call the score as both server and receiver prepare to return to their respective positions, shortly after the previous point has ended.

e) *Delays*. Delays on the part of the server or receiver exceeding ten seconds shall result in an out or point against the offender. (1) This ten second rule is applicable to both server and receiver, each of whom is allowed up to ten seconds after the score is called to serve or to be ready to receive. It is the server's responsibility to be certain that the receiver is ready. If the receiver is not ready, he or she must signal so by either raising the racquet above the head or completely turning the back to the server. These are the only two acceptable signals. (2) If the server serves the ball while the receiver is signaling not ready, the serve shall go over with no penalty and the server shall be warned by the referee to check the receiver. If the server continues to serve without checking the receiver, the referee may award a technical for delay of game. (3) After the score is called, if the server looks at the receiver and the receiver is not signaling not ready, the server may then serve. If the receiver attempts to signal not ready after that point, such signal shall not be acknowledged and the serve becomes legal.

Rule 3.   *Serve In Doubles*
a) *Server.* At the beginning of each game in doubles, each side shall inform the referee of the order of service that shall be followed throughout the game. When the first server is out the first time up, the side is out. Thereafter, both players on each side shall serve until each receives a handout.
b) *Partner's Position.* On each serve the server's partner shall stand erect with back to the side wall and with both feet on the floor within the service box from the moment the server begins his service motion until the ball passes the short line. Violations are called foot faults.

Rule 4.   *Defective Serves.* Defective serves are of three types resulting in penalties as follows:
a) *Dead Ball Serve.* A dead ball serve results in no penalty and the server is given another serve (without cancelling a prior illegal serve).
b) *Fault Serve.* Hitting two fault serves results in a handout.
c) *Out Serve.* An out serve results in a handout.

Rule 5.   *Dead Ball Serves.* Dead ball serves do not cancel any previous illegal service. They occur in the following circumstances:
a) *Legal Serve Hits Partner.* Ball hits the server's partner on the fly on the rebound from the front wall while the server's partner is in the service box. Any serve that touches the floor before hitting the partner in the box is short.
b) *Screen Balls.* Ball passes so close to the server or server's partner as to obstruct the view of the returning sides. Any serve passing behind the server's partner and the side wall is an automatic screen.
c) *Court Hinders.* Ball hits any part of the court that under local rules is a dead ball.
d) *Broken Ball.* If the ball is determined to have broken on the serve, a new ball shall be substituted and the serve shall be replayed (not canceling any prior fault serve).

Rule 6.   *Fault Serves.* The following serves are faults and any two in succession result in an out.

a) *Foot Faults.* A foot fault results when: (1) The server does not begin the service motion with both feet in the service zone. (2) The server leaves the service zone before the served ball passes the short line. (3) In doubles, the server's partner is not in the service box with both feet on the floor and back to the side wall from the time the server begins the service motion until the ball passes the short line.

b) *Short Service.* A short serve is any served ball that hits the front wall and on the rebound hits the floor on or in front of the short line (with or without touching a side wall).

c) *Three-Wall Serve.* Any served ball that first hits the front wall and on the rebound hits the two side walls on the fly.

d) *Ceiling Serve.* Any served ball that first hits the front wall and then touches the ceiling (with or without touching a side wall).

e) *Long Serve.* Any served ball that first hits the front wall and rebounds to the back wall before touching the floor (with or without touching a side wall).

f) *Out-of-Court Serve.* Any served ball that first hits the front wall and then goes out of the court.

Rule 7.   *Out Serves.* Any of the following serves results in an out:

a) *Failure of Server.* Failure of server to put the ball into play within ten seconds of the calling of the score by the referee.

b) *Missed Ball.* Any attempt to strike the ball that results in a total miss or in touching any part of the server's body other than the racquet.

c) *Nonfront Serve.* Any served ball that does not strike the front wall first.

d) *Touched Serve.* Any served ball that on the rebound from the front wall touches the server or server's racquet on the fly or any ball intentionally stopped or caught by the server or server's partner.

e) *Crotch Serve.* If the served ball hits the crotch of the front wall and floor, front wall and side wall, or front wall and ceiling, it is considered no good and is an out serve. A serve into the crotch of the ball wall and the floor is good and in play. A served ball hitting the crotch of the side wall and floor (as in a Z serve) beyond the short line is good and in play.

f) *Illegal Hit.* Any illegal hit (contacting the ball twice, carrying, or hitting the ball with the handle of the racquet or any part of the body or uniform) results in an out serve.

g) *Fake or Balk Serve.* Such a serve is defined as a noncontinous movement of the racquet towards the ball as the server drops the ball for the purpose of serving and results in an out serve.

h) *Out-of-Order Serve.* In doubles, when either partner serves out of order, any points scored during an out-of-order serve will be automatically void with the score reverting to the score prior to the out-of-order serve. The out serve shall be applied to the first server and the second server shall then be allowed to serve.

Rule 8.   *Return of Serve*

a) *Receiving Position.* The receiver may not enter the safety zone until the ball bounces. On the fly return attempt, the receiver may not strike the ball until the ball breaks the plane of the receiving (five-foot) line. The follow-through may carry the receiver or his or her racquet past the receiving line. Neither the receiver nor his or her racquet may break the plane of the short line during the service return. Any violation by the receiver results in a point for the server.

b) *Defective Serve.* The receiving side shall not catch or touch a defectively served ball until a call by the referee has been made or it has touched the floor for the second time.

c) *Legal Return.* After the ball is legally served, one of the players on the receiving side must strike the ball with the racquet either on the fly or after the first bounce and before the ball touches the floor the second time and return the ball to the front wall either directly or after touching one or both sidewalls, the back wall, the ceiling, or any combination of those surfaces. A returned ball may not touch the floor before touching the front wall.

d) *Failure to Return.* The failure to return a serve results in a point for the serving side.

Rule 9.   *Changes of Serve*

a) *Outs.* A server is entitled to continue serving until:

(1) *Out Serve.* The player commits a violation of Rule 7. (2) *Fault Serves.* The player commits two fault serves in succession per Rule 6. (3) *Hits Partner.* The player hits partner with an attempted return. (4) *Return Failure.* The server or partner fails to hit the ball on one bounce or fails to return the ball to the front wall on the fly (with or without hitting any combination of walls and ceiling). (5) *Avoidable Hinder.* The server or partner commits an avoidable hinder per Rule 12.

b) *Side Out.* In singles, a single handout or out equals a side out and retires the server. In doubles a single handout equals a side out on the first service of each game; thereafter, two handouts equal a side out and thereby retire the serving team.

c) *Effect.* When the server or the serving team receives a side out, the server(s) become the receiver(s) and the receiver(s) become the server(s).

Rule 10. *Rallies.* Each legal return after the serve is called a rally. Play during rallies shall be according to the following rules:

a) *Legal Hits.* Only the head of the racquet may be used at any time to return the ball. The racquet may be held in one or both hands. Switching hands to hit the ball, touching the ball with any part of the body or uniform, or removing the wrist thong will result in loss of the rally.

b) *One Touch.* In attempting returns, the ball may be touched or struck only once by a player or team or the result is a loss of rally. The ball may not be carried. (A carried ball is one that rests on the racquet in such a way that the effect is more of a sling action or throw than a hit.)

c) *Failure to Return.* Any of the following constitutes a failure to make a legal return during a rally: (1) The ball bounces on the floor more than once before being hit. (2) The ball does not reach the front wall on the fly. (3) The ball caroms off a player's racquet into a gallery or wall opening without first hitting the front wall. (4) A ball that obviously did not have the velocity or direction to hit the front wall strikes another player on the court. (5) A ball struck by one player on a team hits that player's partner, or a player is struck by a ball which was previously hit by that player or partner. (6) An avoidable hinder (Rule 12) is committed.

d) *Effect.* Violations of Rule 10, sections a, b, or c, result in a loss of rally. If the serving player or team loses the rally it is an out (handout or side out). If the receiver(s) loses the rally, it results in a point for the service side.

e) *Return Attempts.* (1) In singles if a player swings at but misses the ball, the player may continue to attempt to return the ball until it touches the floor the second time. (2) In doubles if one player swings at but misses the ball, both partners may make further attempts to return the ball until it touches the floor the second time. Both partners on a side are entitled to return the ball.

f) *Out-of-Court Ball.* (1) *After Return.* Any ball returned to the front wall that on the rebound or on the first bounce goes into the gallery or through any opening in a side wall shall be declared dead and the server shall receive two serves. (2) *No Return.* Any ball not returned to the front wall that caroms off a player's racquet into the gallery or into any opening in a side wall either with or without touching the ceiling, side, or back wall, shall be an out or point against the player(s) failing to make the return.

g) *Broken Ball.* If there is any suspicion that a ball has broken on the serve or during a rally, play shall continue until the end of the rally. The referee or any player may request that the ball be examined. If the referee decides the ball is broken, a new ball shall be put into play and the server given two serves. The only proper way to check for a broken ball is to squeeze it by hand. Checking the ball by striking it with a racquet will not be considered a valid check and shall work to the disadvantage of the player or team which struck the ball after the rally.

h) *Stopping Play.* If a player loses a shoe or other equipment or foreign objects enter the court or any other outside interference occurs, the referee shall stop the play if such occurrences interfere with ensuing play or players' safety.

i) *Replays.* Any rallies that are replayed for any reason without the awarding of a point or side out shall result in cancellation of any previously called faults and the server being awarded two serves.

Rule 11. *Dead-Ball Hinders.* Dead-ball hinders result in the rally being replayed without penalty and the server receiving two serves.

a) *Situations.* (1) *Court Hinders.* A ball that hits any part of the court that has been designated as such is a court hinder, or any ball that takes an irregular bounce off a rough or irregular surface in such a manner as the referee determines that said irregular bounce affected the rally. (2) *Hitting Opponent.* Any returned ball that touches an opponent on the fly before it returns to the front wall is a dead ball. The player that has been hit or nicked by the ball may make this call, but it must be made immediately and acknowledged by the referee. Any ball that hits an opponent but obviously did not have the velocity or direction to reach the front wall shall not result in a hinder (and shall cause the player or team that hit the ball to lose the rally). (3) *Body Contact.* If body contact occurs that the referee believes was sufficient to stop the rally, either for the purpose of preventing injury by further contact or because the contact prevented a player from being able to make a reasonable return, the referee shall award a hinder. Body contact, particularly on the follow-through, is not necessarily a hinder. (4) *Screen Ball.* Any ball rebounding from the front wall close to the body of a player on the side that just returned the ball and interfering with or preventing the returning side from seeing the ball is a hinder. (5) *Back Swing Hinder.* Any body contact either on the back swing or enroute to or just prior to returning the ball that impairs the hitter's ability to take a reasonable swing is a hinder. This call may be made by the player attempting to return if it is made immediately, and it is subject to acceptance and approval by the referee. (6) *Safety Holdup.* Any player about to execute a return who believes he or she is likely to strike the opponent with the ball or racquet may immediately stop play and request a dead-ball hinder. This call must be made immediately and is subject to acceptance and approval by the referee. (The referee will grant a dead-ball hinder if he or she believes the holdup was reasonable and the player would have been able to return the shot, and the referee may also decide to call an avoidable hinder if warranted.)

(7) *Other Interference.* Any other unintentional interference that prevents an opponent from having a fair chance to see or return the ball is declared a dead-ball hinder.

b) *Effect.* A call by the referee of a hinder stops the play and voids any situation following (such as the ball hitting a player). The only hinders a player may call are specified in Rules 11a(2), 11a(5), and 11a(6) and are subject to the acceptance of the referee. The effect of a dead-ball hinder is that the player who served shall serve again and shall be awarded two serves.

c) *Avoidance.* While making an attempt to return the ball, a player is entitled to a fair chance to see and return the ball. It is the responsibility of the side that has just served or returned the ball to move so that the receiving side may go straight to the ball and have an unobstructed view of the ball after it leaves the front wall. In the judgment of the referee, however, the receiver must make a reasonable effort to move toward the ball and have a reasonable chance to return the ball in order for a hinder to be called.

Rule 12. *Avoidable Hinders.* An avoidable hinder results in the loss of a rally. An avoidable hinder does not necessarily have to be an intentional act and is a result of any of the following:

a) *Failure to Move.* Player does not move sufficiently to allow an opponent a shot.

b) *Blocking.* Player moves into a position effecting a block on the opponent about to return the ball; in doubles one partner moves in front of an opponent as the partner of that opponent is returning the ball.

c) *Moving Into The Ball.* Player moves in the way of and is struck by the ball just played by the opponent.

d) *Pushing.* Player deliberately pushes or shoves opponent during a rally.

e) *Moves.* Player movement that restricts opponent's swing so that the player returning the ball does not have an unimpeded swing.

f) *Intentional Distractions.* Deliberate shouting, stamping of feet, waving of a racquet, or any manner of disrupting the player who is hitting the ball.

g) *Wetting The Ball.* The players, particularly the server, have the responsibility to see that the ball is kept dry at all times. Any wetting of the ball whether deliberate or accidental that is not corrected prior to the beginning of the rally shall result in an avoidable hinder.

Rule 13. *Time-Outs.*

a) *Rest Periods.* During games to 21, each player or team is allowed up to three thirty-second time-outs (two per side in games to 11). Time-outs may not be called by either party after the server begins the service motion.

b) *Injury.* If a player is injured during the course of a match as a result of contact with the ball, racquet, opponent, wall, or floor he or she shall be granted an injury time-out. An injured player shall not be allowed more than a total of 15 minutes of rest during the match. If the injured player is not able to resume play after rest totaling 15 minutes, the match shall be awarded to the opponent(s). Muscle cramps, pulls, fatigue, and other ailments that are not caused by direct contact on the court will not be considered an injury.

c) *Equipment Time-Outs.* Players are expected to keep all clothing and equipment in playable condition and are expected to use regular time-outs and time between games for adjustment and replacement of equipment. If a player or team is out of time-outs and the referee determines that an equipment change or adjustment is necessary for fair and safe continuation of the match, the referee may award an equipment time-out not to exceed two minutes.

d) *Between Games.* A five-minute rest period is allowed between all games of a match.

e) *Postponed Games.* Any games postponed by referees shall be resumed with the same score as when postponed.

Rule 14. *Technicals.*

a) *Technical Fouls.* The referee is empowered to deduct one point from a player's or team's score when in the referee's judgment the player is being overtly and deliberately abusive. The actual invoking of this penalty is called a Referee's Technical. If, after the technical is called against the abusing player, play is not immediately continued, the referee is empowered to forfeit the match in favor of the abusing player's opponent(s). Some examples of actions which may result in technicals are: (1) Profanity. Profanity is an automatic technical and should be invoked by the referee whenever it occurs. (2) Excessive arguing. (3) Threat of any nature to opponent(s) or referee. (4) Excessive or hard striking of the ball between rallies. (5) Slamming of the racquet against walls or floor, slamming the door, or any action that might result in injury to the court or other player(s). (6) Delay of game, either in the form of taking too much time during time-outs and between games, in drying the court, in excessive questioning of the referee on the rules, or in excessive or unnecessary appeals. (7) Anything considered to be unsportsmanlike behavior.

b) *Technical Warning.* If a player's behavior is not so severe as to warrant a Referee's Technical, a technical warning may be issued without point deduction.

c) *Effect.* If a referee issues a Technical Warning, it shall not result in a loss of rally or point and shall be accompanied by a brief explanation of the reason for the warning. If a referee issues a Referee's Technical, one point shall be removed from the offender's score. The awarding of the technical shall have no effect on service changes or side outs. If the technical occurs either between games or when the offender has no points, the result will be that the offender's score will revert to minus one.

Rule 15. *Professional.* A professional shall be defined as any player (male, female, or junior) who has accepted prize money regardless of the amount in any professionally sanctioned tournament (WPRA, CATALINA) or any other association so deemed by the AARA Board of Directors. A player may participate in a professionally sanctioned tournament that awards cash prizes but will not be considered a professional if no prize money is accepted. The acceptance by a player of merchandise or travel expenses shall not be considered as prize money and does not jeopardize a player's amateur status.

Rule 16. *Return to Amateur Status.* Any player who has been classified as a professional (see Rule 15) can recover amateur status by requesting, in writing, to be reclassified as an amateur. This application shall be tendered to the Executive Director of the American Amateur Racquetball Association and shall become effective immediately as long as the player making application for reinstatement of amateur status has received no money for that year.

Rule 17. *Age Group Divisions.* Age is determined as of the first day of the tournament.

Men's Age Divisions:

Open—all players other than pro
Junior Veterans Open—amateurs 25+
Veterans Open—amateurs 30+
Seniors—amateurs 35+
Veteran Seniors—amateurs 40+
Masters—amateurs 45+
Veteran Masters—amateurs 50+
Golden Masters—amateurs 55+
Senior Golden Masters—amateurs 60+
Veteran Golden Masters—amateurs 65+
Advanced Golden Masters—amateurs 70+

Women's Age Divisions:

Open—all players other than pro
Junior Veterans Open—amateurs 25+
Veterans Open—amateurs 30+
Seniors—amateurs 35+
Veteran Seniors—amateurs 40+
Masters—amateurs 45+
Veteran Masters—amateurs 50+
Golden Masters—amateurs 55+
Senior Golden Masters—amateurs 60+
Veteran Golden Masters—amateurs 65+
Advanced Golden Masters—amateurs 70+

Other Divisions:

Mixed Doubles
Disabled

Junior Divisions:

Age determined as of January 1st of each calendar year.

Junior Boys:

18 years and under
16 years and under
14 years and under
12 years and under
10 years and under
8 years and under (no bounce)
Doubles Team—ages apply as above.

Junior Girls:

18 years and under

16 years and under

14 years and under

12 years and under

10 years and under

8 years and under (no bounce)

Scoring—All matches in Junior divisions will be the best of three games to 15 points (win by one point). If a tiebreaker third game is necessary the game is played to 15 points (win by two points) or up to 21 points (win by one point).

Junior Players should abide by all AARA rules with the following exceptions:

a) *Eyeguards.* Eyeguards *must* be worn in all AARA sanctioned events.

b) *Time-Outs.* Three in each game.

IV. *Tournaments*

Rule 18. *Draws.* (a) If possible, all draws shall be made at least two days before the tournament commences. The seeding method of drawing shall be approved by the American Amateur Racquetball Association. (b) The draw and seeding committee shall comprise the AARA's Executive Director, National Commissioner, and the host Tournament Director. No other persons shall participate in the draw or seeding unless at the invitation of the draw and seeding committee. (c) In local, state, and regional tournaments the draw shall be the responsibility of the tournament chairperson. In regional play the tournament chairperson should work in coordination with the AARA Regional Commissioner at the tournament.

Rule 19. *Scheduling Preliminary Matches.* If one or more contestants are entered in both singles and doubles it is recommended that the doubles match be played on the day preceding the singles. This should ensure sufficient rest between the final matches. If both final matches must be played on the same day or night, the following procedure is recommended:

1. The singles match be played first.

2. A rest period of not less than one hour be allowed between the finals in singles and doubles.

Rule 20. *Notice of Matches.* After the first round of matches, it is the responsibility of each player to check the posted schedules to determine the time and place of each subsequent match. If any change is made in the schedule after posting, it shall be the duty of the committee or chairperson to notify the players of the change.

Rule 21. *Third Place.* Players are not required to play off for third place or fourth place. However, for point standings, if one semifinalist wants to play off for third and the other semifinalist does not, the one willing to play shall be awarded the third place. If both semifinalists do not wish to play off for third or fourth position, then the points shall be awarded evenly.

Rule 22. *AARA Regional Tournaments.* The United States and Europe are divided into a combined total of sixteen regions. a) A player may compete in only one regional tournament per year. b) The defined area of eligibility for a person's region is that of his or her permanent residence. The only exception is when the locale of the adjoining regional tournament is closer to a player's residence than the site of their own home regional. In such a case the player is afforded the option of playing in either tournament but not in both tournaments. c) A player can participate in only two events in a regional tournament. d) Awards and remuneration to the AARA National Championships will be posted on the entry blank.

Rule 23. *Tournament Management.* In all AARA-sanctioned tournaments the Tournament Director and/or the National AARA official in attendance may decide on a change of courts after the completion of any tournament game if such a change will accommodate better spectator conditions.

Rule 24. *Tournament Conduct.* In all AARA-sanctioned tournaments the referee is empowered to default a match if a player or team is deemed guilty of conduct detrimental to the tournament and the game.

Rule 25. *AARA Eligibility.* Any paid-up AARA member in good standing who has not been classified as a professional (see Rules 15 and 16) may compete in any AARA sanctioned tournament.

Rule 26. *AARA National Championship.* The National Singles and National Doubles will be played on different weekends. There will be consolation rounds in all divisions.
AARA Regions
Region 1: Maine, New Hampshire, Vermont, Massachusetts, Rhode Island, Connecticut

Region 2: New York, New Jersey

Region 3: Pennsylvania, Maryland, Virginia, Delaware, District of Columbia

Region 4: Florida, Georgia, North Carolina, South Carolina

Region 5: Alabama, Mississippi, Tennessee

Region 6: Arkansas, Kansas, Missouri, Oklahoma

Region 7: Texas, Louisiana

Region 8: Wisconsin, Iowa, Illinois

Region 9: West Virginia, Ohio, Michigan

Region 10: Indiana, Kentucky

Region 11: North Dakota, South Dakota, Minnesota, Nebraska

Region 12: Arizona, New Mexico, Utah, Colorado

Region 13: Wyoming, Montana

Region 14: Nevada, California, Hawaii

Region 15: Washington, Idaho, Oregon, Alaska

Region 16: Americans in Europe

a) The National Ratings Committee may handle the rating of each region and determine how many players shall qualify from each regional tournament.

b) All National finalists in each division may be exempt from qualifying for the same division the following year.

c) There may be a tournament one day ahead of the National Tournament at the same site to qualify eight players in each division who were unable to qualify or who failed to qualify in the Regionals.

d) This rule is in force only when a division is obviously oversubscribed.

(1) Qualifying Singles. A player may have to qualify at one of the sixteen regional tournaments.

(2) Qualifying Doubles. There will be no regional qualifying for doubles.

Rule 27. *Intercollegiate Tournament.* It will be conducted at a separate date and location.

V. *One-Wall and Three-Wall Rules*

Rule 28. *One-Wall and Three-Wall Rules.* Racquetball rules for one-wall, three-wall, and four-wall are the same with the following exceptions:

a) *One Wall.* Court Size: wall shall be 20 feet wide and 16 feet high, floor 20 feet wide and 34 feet from the wall to the back edge of the long line. There should be a minimum of three feet beyond the long line and six feet outside each side line and behind the long line to create a movement area for the players.

b) *Short Line:* Back edge 16 feet from the wall.

c) *Service Markers:* Lines at least six inches long parallel to and midway between the long and short lines, extending in from the side lines. The imaginary extension together of these lines indicates the service line. Lines are one and one-half inches in width.

d) *Service Zone:* Floor area inside and including the short, side, and service lines.

e) *Receiving Zone:* Floor area in back of short line bounded by and including the long and side lines.

f) *Three-Wall Serve:* A serve that goes beyond the side walls on the fly is considered long. A serve that goes beyond the long line on a fly, but within the side walls, is the same as short.

g) *Court Size—short side wall:* 20 feet wide and 20 feet high and 20 feet long. Side wall shall extend back on either side from the front wall 20 feet along the side wall markers. Side wall may extend from 20 feet at the front wall and taper down to 12 feet at the end of the side wall. All other markings are the same as in four-wall.

h) *Court Size—long side wall:* 20 feet wide and 20 feet high and 40 feet long. Side wall shall extend back on either side 40 feet. The side wall may but is not required to taper from 20 feet high at the front wall down to 12 feet at the 40-foot marker. All lines are the same as in four-wall racquetball.

VI. *Rules for Eight Years and Under—No-Bounce*

Use AARA Racquetball rules with the following modifications.

After a legal serve, the ball may bounce as many times as the receiver wants until he or she swings once to return the ball to the front wall.

The ball may be hit after the serve or during a rally at any time but must be hit before it crosses the short line on its way back to the front wall.

The receiver can hit the ball before it hits the back wall or may play it off the back wall but cannot cross the short line after the ball contacts the back wall.

The only exception to crossing the short line is if the ball is returned to the back wall from the front wall on the fly (without touching the floor), the receiver may cross the short line and play the ball on the first bounce.

New additions are lines on the front wall (use tape) at three feet and one foot high. If the ball is hit below the three-foot and above the one-foot lines during a rally, it has to be returned before it bounces the third time. If the ball hits below the one-foot line during the rally, it must be played or returned to the front wall before it bounces twice as in regulation racquetball. This gives incentive to keeping the ball low.

Games are played best two out of three games to 11 points.

VII. *How To Referee When There Is No Referee*

Rule 1. Safety. Safety is the primary and overriding responsibility of every player who enters the court. At no time should the physical safety of the participants be compromised. Players are entitled *and expected* to hold up their swing *without penalty* any time they believe there might be a risk of physical contact. Any time a player says he or she held up to avoid contact, even if it seems overcautious, he or she is entitled to a hinder (rally replayed without penalty).

Rule 2. Score. Because there is no referee or scorekeeper, it is important to see that there is no misunderstanding in this area; so *the server is required* to announce both the server's and receiver's score before *every* first serve.

Rule 3. During Rallies. During rallies, it is generally the *hitter's* responsibility to make the call—the possibility of a skip ball, double-bounce, or illegal hit. Play should continue until the *hitter* makes the call against himself or herself. If the hitter does not make the call and goes on to win the rally, and the opponent thinks that one of the *hitter's* shots was not good, he or she may appeal to the hitter by pointing out which shot was out and request the hitter to reconsider. If the hitter is sure of his or her call *and* the opponent is still sure the hitter is wrong, the rally is replayed. As a matter of etiquette, the players are *expected* to make calls against themselves any time they are not sure. If a shot is a very close call, unless the hitter is sure the shot was good, he or she should call it an out.

Rule 4. Service.

a) *Fault Serves (Long, Short, Ceiling, and Three-Wall).* The *receiver* has the primary responsibility to make these calls, and should give the benefit of the doubt to the opponent whenever it is close. The receiver must make the call immediately and not wait until after hitting the ball and seeing how good a shot it was. *It is not an option play.* The receiver does not have the right to play a short serve just because he or she thinks it's a setup.

b) *Screen Serves.* When there is no referee, a screen serve *does not become an option play.* When the receiver believes his or her vision of the ball was sufficiently impaired to give the server too great an advantage on the serve, the receiver may hold up his or her swing and call a screen serve, or if he or she still feels that a good shot at the ball can be taken, he or she can say nothing and continue playing. *The receiver may not call a screen after attempting to hit the ball.* Furthermore, the server may not call a screen under any circumstances. He or she must expect to play the rally until the receiver makes a call. (In doubles, unless the ball goes behind the back of the server's partner, no screens should be called.)

c) *Technical Calls.* Footfaults, ten-second violations, receiving-line violations, service-zone infringement, and other technical calls really require a referee. *However,* if either player believes the opponent is abusing any of these rules, between rallies they should discuss it to be sure there is agreement on what the rule is and to put each other on notice that the rules should be followed.

Rule 5. Hinders. Generally, the hinder should work like the screen serve—as an option play for the hindered party. *Only* the person going for the shot can stop play by calling a hinder, and he or she must do so immediately—not wait to see how good a shot can be hit. If the hindered party believes he or she can make an effective return in spite of some physical contact or screen that has occurred, he or she may continue to play. *However,* as safety is the overriding factor, *either party* may call a hinder if it is to prevent contact.

Rule 6. Avoidable Hinders. Since avoidable hinders are usually not intentional, they occur even in the friendliest matches. When a player turns the wrong way and gets in the way of the opponent's setup, there should be a better way than saying "I'm sorry" to make up for the mistake. Instead of an "I'm sorry," the player who makes the error should simply award the rally to the opponent. If a player thinks the opponent was guilty of an avoidable hinder, and the opponent did not call it, the offended player should appeal to the opponent by pointing out that the hinder seemed avoidable. The opponent may then call it or disagree, but the call can only be made on yourself. Often, just pointing out what you think is an avoidable hinder will put the opponent on notice for future rallies and prevent recurrences.

Rule 7. Disputes. If either player for any reason desires to have a referee, it is considered common courtesy for the other player to go along with the request, and a referee acceptable to both sides should be found. If no referee is available and a question about a rule or rule interpretation comes up, seek out the club pro or a more experienced player for guidance. If you're still unclear after the match, contact your local state racquetball association for the answer.

Appendix B
Additional Resources

Books

Allsen, P.E., & Witbeck, A.R. (1972). *Racquetball/Paddleball*. Dubuque, IA: Wm. C. Brown.

Allsen, P.E., & Witbeck, A.R. (1977). *Racquetball/Paddleball* (2nd ed.). Dubuque, IA: Wm. C. Brown.

Allsen, P.E., & Witbeck, A.R. (1981). *Racquetball*. Dubuque, IA: Wm. C. Brown.

Boccaccio, T. (1979). *Racquetball basics*. Englewood Cliffs, NJ: Prentice-Hall.

Brumfield, C., & Bairstow, J. (1978). *Off the wall*. Pinebrook, NJ: Dial Press.

Collins, D.R., Hodges, P.B., & Marshall, M. (1983). *The art and science of racquetball*. Bloomington, IN: Tichenor.

Darden, E. (1981). *Power racquetball: Featuring PST*. West Point, NY: Leisure Press.

Dowell, L.J., & Grice, W.A. (1979). *Racquetball*. Boston: American Press.

Fabian, L. (1986). *Racquetball: Strategies for winning*. Dubuque, IA: Eddie Bowers.

Fichter, G.S. (1979). *Racquetball*. New York: Watts.

Fleming, A.W., & Bloom, J.A. (1973). *Paddleball and racquetball*. Pacific Palisades, CA: Goodyear.

Garfinkel, C. (1978). *Racquetball the easy way*. New York: Atheneum.

Hogan, M., & Brumfield, C. (1978). *Power racquetball*. Chicago: Contemporary Books.

Keeley, S. (1976). *The complete book of racquetball*. Northfield, IL: DBI Books.

Kramer, J. (1979). *Beginner's racquetball book*. Mountain View, CA: Anderson World.

Leve, C. (1973). *Inside racquetball*. Chicago: Regnery.

Lubarsky, S., Kaufman, S., & Scagnetti, J. (1980). *How to improve your racquetball*. North Hollywood, CA: Wilshire.

Lubarsky, S. (1978). *Racquetball made easy*. North Hollywood, CA: Wilshire.

Maclean, N. (1977). *Platform tennis, racquetball and paddleball*. Orlando, FL: Drake.

Moore, A.C. (1979). *Racquetball for all*. Dubuque, IA: Kendall-Hunt.

National Association for Girls and Women in Sport. (1978). *Team handball, racquetball, orienteering*. Washington, DC: AAHPER.

Norton, C., & Bryan, J. (1984). *Racquetball: A guide for the aspiring player*. Englewood, CO: Morton.

Pahgrazi, R.P. (1986). *Racquetball*. Glenview, IL: Scott Foresman.

Poynter, M. (1980). *The racquetball book*. New York: Messner.

Reznik, J.W. (1979). *Racquetball*. New York: Sterling.

Reznik, J.W. (1976). *Championship racquetball: By the experts*. West Point, NY: Leisure Press.

Reznik, J.W. (1983). *Racquetball for men and women*. Champaign, IL: Stipes.

Rich. J. (1975). *Fundamentals of racquetball*. Dubuque, IA: Kendall-Hunt.

Sauser, J., & Shay, A. (1981). *Beginning racquetball drills*. Chicago: Contemporary Books.

Sauser, J., & Shay, A. (1977). *Inside racquetball for women*. Chicago: Contemporary Books.

Sauser, J., & Shay, A. (1977). *Intermediate racquetball drills*. Chicago: Contemporary Books.

Sauser, J., & Shay, A. (1979). *Racquetball strategy*. Chicago: Contemporary Books.

Sauser, J., & Shay, A. (1978). *Teaching your child racquetball.* Chicago: Contemporary Books.

Scott, E.L. (1979). *Racquetball: The cult.* Garden City, NY: Doubleday.

Scott, R.S. (1980). *The Physician and Sportsmedicine guide to racquetball and squash.* New York: McGraw.

Shay, A., & Francher, T. (1979). *40 common errors in racquetball and how to correct them.* Chicago: Contemporary Books.

Shay, A., & Leve, C. (1976). *Winning racquetball.* Chicago: Regnery.

Sheftel, C., & Shay, A. (1978). *Contemporary racquetball.* Chicago: Contemporary Books.

Spear, V.I. (1976). *How to win at racquetball.* Chicago: Rand McNally.

Spear, V.I. (1979). *Sports Illustrated racquetball.* New York: Lippincott.

Stafford, R. (1982). *Racquetball: The sport for everyone* (rev. ed.). Memphis: S.C. Toof.

Strandemo, S., & Bruns, B. (1981). *Advanced racquetball.* New York: Pocket Books.

Strandemo, S., & Bruns, B. (1977). *The racquetball book.* New York: Pocket Books.

Verner, B., & Skowrup, D. (1977). *Racquetball.* Palo Alto, CA: Mayfield.

Weckstein, J. (1975). *Racquetball for women.* Royal Oak, MI: Lincoln Press.

Wickstrom, R., & Larson, C. (1972). *Racquetball and paddleball fundamentals.* Columbus, OH: Merrill.

Wright, S., & Keeley, S. (1980). *The women's book of racquetball.* Chicago: Contemporary Books.

Periodicals

National Racquetball. Publication Management, Inc., 4350 Dipaolo Center, Dearlove Road, Glenview, IL 60025.

Racquetball. Monthly publication of American Amateur Racquetball Association (AARA). 5545 Murray Road, Memphis, TN 38117.

Racquetball Illustrated. Bi-monthly publication. 7011 Sunset Boulevard, Hollywood, CA 90028. Issued July 1978, Vol. 1, No. 1, until February-March, 1984, Vol. 7 No. 2. Now incorporated into *National Racquetball.*

Racquetball Industry. Bi-monthly publication. 1545 N.E. 123rd Street, Suite 2-C, North Miami, FL 33161. Now incorporated into *Fitness Industry* (same address).

Selected Periodical Articles on Racquetball Injuries

Ardito, J. (1978). Should we make eye guards a must? *National Racquetball*, **6**, 12.

Bishop, P., Kozey, J., & Caldwell, G. (1982, March). Performance of eye protectors for squash and racquetball. *The Physician and Sportsmedicine*, **10**, 63–69.

Buetstein, R.J. (1981). Heal thyself. *Racquetball*, **10**, 22–25.

Carlson, T. (1979). Playing hurt. *Racquetball*, **8**, 15–20.

Carlson, T. (1979). Wounded knee. *Racquetball*, **8**, 27–30.

Della-Guistine, D. (1980). Racquetball safety problems. *Athletic Purchasing and Facilities*, **4**, 40.

Easterbrook, M. (1981). Eye injuries in racket sports: A continuing problem. *Physician and Sportsmedicine*, **9**, 91–94, 97, 100–101.

Easterbrook, M. (1981). Eye protection for squash and racquetball players. *Physician and Sportsmedicine*, **9**, 79–82.

Easterbrook, M. (1982). Working to save your eyes. *National Racquetball*, **11**, 6–9.

Feigelman, M.J., et al. (1983, December 23/30). Assessment of ocular protection for racquetball. *Journal of the American Medical Association*, **250**, 3305–3308.

Goulart, F.S. (1980). The aspirin alternative: Racquetball without pain. *National Racquetball*, **9**, 76–79.

Huey, L. (1983, June). For your eyes only. *Racquetball Illustrated*, **6**, 11–17.

Kort, M. (1980). Eye injuries. *Racquetball Illustrated*, **3**, 58, 60.

La Bonne, M. (1980). Eye injuries. *Racquetball*, **9**, 23–24.

McDonough, T. (1980). A little dab will do you. *Racquetball*, **9**, 21–22, 26.

Meagher, J., & Broughton, P. (1979). Sports massage. *Racquetball Illustrated*, **2**, 59–61.

Meyers, L. (1980). Keep your eye on the ball, not the other way around. *National Racquetball*, **9**, 38–39.

Miller, A. (1981). First aid: What you don't know can hurt you. *Racquetball*, **10**, 22–24.

Newman, D.J. (1981). Two ways to cure racquetball elbow: Acupuncture (Part 2). *National Racquetball*, **10**, 20–21.

Rose, C.P., & Morse, J.O. (1979). Racquetball injuries. *Physician and Sportsmedicine*, **7**, 72–75, 78.

Scott, R. (1978). From beans to bursa. *Racquetball Illustrated*, **1**, 56–58.

Scott, R. (1978). Let's look at eye injuries. *Racquetball Illustrated*, **1**, 53–54.

Turley, S. (1979). How dry I am: It's called dehydration, and it isn't funny. *Racquetball*, **8**, 21–23, 26.

Vinger, P.F. (1983, June). Eye protection for racquet sports. *Journal of Physical Education, Recreation and Dance*, **54**, 46–48.

Vinger, P.F., & Tolpin, D.W. (1978, June 16). Racket sports an ocular hazard. *Journal of The American Medical Association*, **239**, 2575–2577.

Wolf, C.J. (1979). Recognizing foot injuries. *Racquetball Illustrated*, **1**, 68, 70–71.

Ziehm, L. (1981). What's being done to decrease eye injuries in racquetball? *Racquetball*, **10**, 17, 19.

Selected Periodical Articles on Racquetball Skills Tests

Bartee, H., & Fothergill, R.W. (1980). Tests of racquetball skills. *Texas Association for Health, Physical Education and Recreation Journal*, **48**, 8, 32.

Collins, R., & Hodges, P. (1982). Racquetball skills test investigation. *Minnesota Journal for Health, Physical Education, Recreation and Dance*, **10**, 10–12.

Durstine, J.L., & Drowatsky, J.N. (1979, Fall). Racquetball success: Skill and more. *Learning and Physical Education Newsletter*, p. 12.

Hensley, L.D., East, W.B., & Stillwell, J.L. (1979). A racquetball skills test. *Research Quarterly*, **50**, 114–118.

Dissertations

Buschner, C.A. (1976). The validation of a racquetball skills test for college men. (Doctoral dissertation, Oklahoma State University). *Dissertation Abstracts International*, **38**, 5330.

Grant, R.H. (1980). The effects of subliminally projected visual stimuli on skill development, selected attention, and participation in racquetball by college students. (Doctoral dissertation, East Texas State University). *Dissertation Abstracts International, 41*, 585.

Grice, W.A. (1980). An analysis of exercise intensity, glucose and lactic acid concentration, and heart rate response in selected college male racquetball players during competition. (Doctoral dissertation, Northwestern State University of Louisiana). *Dissertation Abstracts International, 41*, 4643.

Klass, R.A. (1977). The validation of a battery of reaction time tests to predict racquetball ability for college men. (Doctoral dissertation, Oklahoma State University). *Dissertation Abstracts International, 37*, 6258.

Shemwell, J.A., Jr. (1980). Validation of the James-Lowell racquetball test: A skills and ability test for use in instructional racquetball. (Doctoral dissertation, Middle Tennessee State University). *Dissertation Abstracts International, 41*, 4645.

Theses

Dennis, D.C. (1979). *Racquetball skill level and maximal oxygen uptake.* Unpublished master's thesis, California State University, Fullerton.

Epperson, S. (1977). *Validation of the Reznik racquetball test.* Unpublished master's thesis, Washington State University, Pullman.

Rudisell, M.E. (1982). *The effects of blue, red, and white lighting on selected physiological factors and motor performance of skilled and highly skilled racquetball players.* Unpublished master's thesis, Appalachian State University, Boone, NC.

Weston, M. (1980). *The effects of normal, decreased, masked and abnormal auditory cues on the performance of skilled and highly skilled racquetball players.* Unpublished master's thesis, Appalachian State University, Boone, NC.

Racquetball Organizations

AMERICAN AMATEUR RACQUETBALL ASSOCIATION (AARA)
815 N. Weber, Suite 203, Colorado Springs, CO 80903

Promotes racquetball as a sport; organizes racquetball to be a self-governing sport of, by, and for the players; encourages building facilities for the sport; conducts racquetball events including annual national tournaments; recognized by the United States Olympic Committee as the official ruling body of racquetball; formerly International Racquetball Association.

AMERICAN PROFESSIONAL RACQUETBALL ORGANIZATION (APRO), 730 Pine, Deerfield, IL 60015

Racquetball's equivalent to the United States Professional Tennis Association (USPTA).

WOMEN'S PROFESSIONAL RACQUETBALL ASSOCIATION (WPRA) 3727 Centennial Circle, Las Vegas, NV 89121

The racquetball organization for professional women players.

Racquetball Equipment Sources

AMF HEAD, 4801 N. 63rd Street, Boulder, CO 80301

AMF VOIT, Santa Ana, CA 92704

BALL HOPPER PRODUCTS, INC., 3026 Commercial Avenue, Northbrook, IL 60062

CARRERA, P.O. Box 2, Norwood, NJ 07648

CHAMPION GLOVE COMPANY, 2200 E. Ovid, Des Moines, IA 50313

D.P. DIVERSIFIED PRODUCTS, 309 Williamson Avenue, Opelika, AL 36802

EKTELON, 8929 Aero Drive, San Diego, CA 92123

FOOT-JOY, INC., 144 Field Street, Brockton, MA 02403

GENERAL SPORTCRAFT COMPANY, 140 Woodbine Street, Bergenfield, NJ 07621

MARTY HOGAN RACQUETBALL—A division of PRO-KENNEX, 7444 Trade Street, San Diego, CA 92121

OLYMPIAN RACQUETBALL, 5567 Kearny Villa Road, San Diego, CA 92123

OMEGA SPORTS, 9200 Cody, Overland Park, KS 66212

PENN ATHLETIC PRODUCTS COMPANY, 200 Mall Blvd., Monroeville, PA 15146

RAM RACQUETBALLS BY RIGHT-GUARD CORPORATION, Montgomeryville, PA 18936

RICHCRAFT RACQUETBALL, 2817 Empire Avenue, Burbank, CA 91504

SARANAC GLOVE COMPANY, P.O. Box 786, 1263 Main Street, Green Bay, WI 54305

SEAMCO, INC., Hatfield, PA 19440

WILSON SPORTING GOODS, 2233 West Street, River Grove, IL 60171

Glossary

AARA. American Amateur Racquetball Association. Formerly known as IRA or International Racquetball Association.

Ace. A legal serve that eludes the receiver and results in a point for the server.

Alley. The area on both sides of the court near the side walls that is formed by extending an imaginary line from the doubles service box to the front and rear walls.

Angle serve. A power serve that first strikes the front wall and then hits low on the side wall without touching the floor before bouncing in the backcourt.

Anticipation. The act of predicting and moving into position to return an opponent's shot.

APRO. American Professional Racquetball Organization. This organization sets standards and certifies teaching professionals.

Around-the-wall shot. A defensive shot that strikes three walls—the side wall, the front wall, and then the other side wall—before hitting the floor.

Avoidable hinder. An intentional interference with an opponent's shot.

Backhand corner. Area of the court where a side wall and the back wall meet on the same side as the player's backhand.

Backhand grip. The method of holding the racquet to execute a backhand shot.

Backspin. The reverse or backward rotation of the ball. Also called bottom spin.

Backswing. The part of the stroke in which the racquet is brought back behind the body in preparation for hitting the ball.

Back wall. The rear wall of the racquetball court.

Back-wall–back-wall shot. Ball that is played off back wall and driven back into back wall and travels on the fly to the front wall.

Back-wall shot. Ball that is played off back wall and driven on the fly to the front wall.

Base. The butt-end of the racquet handle.

Block. The act of preventing your opponent from hitting the ball by using some part of your body.

Body contact. Physical contact that interferes with your opponent's opportunity to hit the ball.

Butt. The enlarged bottom end of the racquet handle.

Ceiling serve. A fault serve that contacts the ceiling after hitting the front wall.

Ceiling shot. Hitting the ball against the ceiling of the court before striking the front wall. The ball then bounces off the floor in a high arc to a spot deep in the back court. See **reverse ceiling shot.**

Center court. The most strategic area of the court located in the middle about four to five feet in back of the short service line.

Change-of-pace serve. A slow, off-speed semilob serve used to change the tempo of play.

Choke. (1) To move the hand up or down on the racquet handle. (2) To play poorly under pressure.

Continental grip. A one-grip system for holding the racquet. The hand position is somewhere between the forehand and the backhand grips.

Control. The ability to hit the ball to a predetermined spot.

Control player. A player who relies primarily on shot placement rather than on the force (power) of shots.

Corner kill shot. See **pinch shot.**

Court. The playing area, the dimensions of which are 40 feet long by 20 feet wide by 20 feet high.

Court hinder. Any obstacle on the court that deflects the ball and interferes with play, such as a door latch, transoms, thermostat, and so forth.

Crosscourt shot. A shot hit diagonally from one side of the court to the other.

Crotch ball. A ball that strikes the juncture where two playing surfaces meet.

Crotch serve. A serve that hits the juncture of the front wall and the floor, side wall, or ceiling. It results in a loss of serve.

Crowding. Standing or playing unreasonably close to your opponent.

Cutthroat. Game involving three players; each one serves in turn and plays against the other two.

Dead ball. A ball no longer in play.

Dead ball hinder. An unintentional hinder resulting in a replay of the point.

Dead ball serve. An illegal serve that is replayed. It does not result in a penalty to the server or the receiver, nor does it cancel any previous illegal serve.

Default. The failure of a player or team to compete in a contest because of injury, illness, and so on. It results in an automatic win for the opponent.

Defective serve. Any illegal serve—dead ball, fault, or out serve.

Defensive player(s). The receiver or receiving team.

Defensive position. The back area of the racquetball court. The position assumed to return an opponent's shots.

Defensive shot. Any shot used to continue a rally or gain some resting time.

Diagonal formation. A method of doubles play in which the court coverage and responsibilities are assigned by dividing the court diagonally from the left front corner to the right rear corner of the court.

Die. When a ball loses momentum and fails to bounce high enough to be returned.

Dig. To make a good return of a difficult shot that might ordinarily have been a winner.

Dive. A maneuver extending the body into the air in order to dig for a ball.

Doubles. Competition played by two teams with each having two players on a side.

Down-the-wall. A shot hit parallel to and near the side wall. Also called a wallpaper shot or down-the-line shot.

Drill. The act of repeating an exercise again and again in order to develop a skill.

Drive serve. See **power serve.**

Drive shot. A hard-hit ball. Also see **pass shot.**

Drop shot. A finesse shot hit with little speed and designed to barely make contact with the front wall.

Error. The act of unsuccessfully returning a ball during play.

Eyeguard. A protective device worn over the eyes to prevent injury.

Face. The hitting surface of the racquet; the plane formed by the racquet strings.

Fault. An infraction of the service rule.

Five-foot line. The short, red line on the floor or side wall five feet behind the short line of the service box. Also called the restraining line.

Fly kill. A kill shot that is executed while the ball is still in the air after rebounding from the front wall and before it bounces on the floor.

Follow-through. The continuation of the swing after the ball has been contacted. It lends control and direction to the shot.

Foot fault. An illegal position of the server's feet during the serve.

Footwork. The act of moving the feet in coordination with the body to a position to hit the ball in an efficient manner.

Forehand. The stroke made with the palm of the hand turned in the direction of the movement of the racquet.

Front-and-back formation. See **I formation.**

Front-wall–side-wall kill shot. A kill shot that hits the front wall first and then the side wall. Also called a **reverse pinch shot.**

Game. Competition played between players or teams until one of them scores 11 or 15 points.

Game point. The point that decides the winner of the game.

Garbage serve. A half-speed serve that hits midway up on the front wall and returns to the receiver around shoulder height in either of the rear court corners.

Grip. The way in which the racquet is held; the part of the handle grasped by the hand.

Half-and-half formation. See **side-by-side formation.**

Half-lob serve. Same as garbage serve.

Half-volley. The act of hitting the ball immediately after it bounces on the floor.

Handout. Loss of serve by the first partner of the doubles team.

Handshake grip. The most common method of gripping the racquet, like shaking hands with a person.

Head. The oval-, rectangular-, or teardrop-shaped part of the racquet that contains the strings.

High-lob serve. Ball touches the side wall on its descent into the back court but does not come off the back wall.

Hinder. Interfering with a player during a rally or serve.

I formation. A system of positioning in doubles play in which one player lines up in front of the other; the forward player covers the front-court area and the other covers the backcourt area.

Inning. A round of play that permits the gain and loss of a serve by each side.

IRA. International Racquetball Association (see **AARA**).

Kill shot. The act of hitting the ball so low on the front wall that it is practically impossible for your opponent to make a return.

Linespeople. The referee's two aides who are called upon to judge an appeal call made by one of the players.

Live ball. A ball in play or one that bounces exceptionally high.

Lob. See **lob shot.**

Lob serve. A serve hit high and softly to the front wall that rebounds in a high arc towards the back wall.

Lob shot. Similar to the lob serve except that it is hit during a rally.

Long serve. A fault serve that rebounds from the front wall to the back wall without hitting the floor.

Match. A contest that consists of winning two out of three games.

Match point. The point that decides the outcome of a match.

Midcourt. The area of the court between the service line and the receiving line.

Non-front-wall serve. An illegally served ball that strikes any surface of the court before hitting the front wall.

No man's land. Area in court where you do not want to be in relation to the ball and the opponent.

Novice. A beginner or an unskilled player.

Offensive position. Center-court position, the most desirable spot for offensive play. Same as advantage or percentage position.

Offensive shot. Any shot designed to score a point or end a rally.

One-on-two. Game with three players in which the server plays the other two for the entirety of the game.

One-wall racquetball. An outdoor variety of the sport in which only a front wall is utilized.

Open face. The angle of the racquet–ball contact whereby the hitting surface is slanted toward the ceiling; this causes unwanted slicing or backspin on the ball.

Out. Failure to return a ball during play.

Out-of-court ball. Any ball that leaves the court. Balls that strike the front wall before leaving the court are replayed, otherwise a point or loss of serve results against the player hitting it.

Out-of-court serve. A fault serve in which a legally served ball travels out of the court area.

Out-of-order serve. When either partner in doubles serves in the wrong rotation.

Out serve. Any serve that results in a loss of serve.

Overhead shot. A shot made during a rally by hitting the ball when it is in the air above your head.

Oversized racquet. A racquet with a large head.

Paddleball. Racquetball's immediate predecessor, which is played on the same court and with the same rules as racquetball but with a wooden paddle and a different ball.

Pass shot. A shot hit near the side wall and out of reach of your opponent.

Pinch shot. A kill shot that strikes the side wall first and then the front wall.

Placement. A target area of a player's service or return, usually out of the opponent's reach.

Plum. See **setup**.

Point. The unit of scoring. Only the serving side can score points.

Point-of-contact. Where the racquet meets the ball during the stroke.

Power player. A player who relies primarily on hitting the ball hard rather than emphasizing accuracy and/or finesse.

Power serve. A serve that is hit low and fast to a rear corner of the court. Also called a drive serve.

Rally. The continuing exchange of shots that occurs between the serve and the failure to legally return a shot.

Ready position. The body position or stance a player assumes while waiting to make a return of the serve or a shot during play.

Receiver. The player receiving the service.

Receiving line. The line five feet in back of and parallel to the short line. It is marked by three-inch vertical lines on the side wall.

Receiving zone. The area of the racquetball court that extends from the rear wall to the receiving line.

Referee. The individual who officiates the match.

Rest period. The intervals of rest during and between games taken in accordance with the rules.

Restraining line. See **five-foot line.**

Reverse ceiling shot. A ceiling shot where the ball hits the front wall before it hits the ceiling.

Reverse pinch. See **front-wall–side-wall kill shot.**

RMA Pro Tour. Racquetball manufacturers' pro tour for the top male professional players.

Roll-out. A kill shot that is hit so low that it rolls on the floor after rebounding from the front wall.

Rotation formation. A system of doubles play in which the methods of doubles strategy and position are determined by the flow of the rally.

Safety zone. The area between the restraining line and the short service line.

Screen ball. A ball that passes so close to a player during a rally or serve that the view of the returning side is obstructed.

Serve. The method of initiating play.

Service. See **serve.**

Service box. The area on either side of the service zone in which the non-serving partner of the doubles team must stand until a legal serve is made.

Service line. The line parallel to and five feet in front of the short line. The front line of the service zone.

Service zone. The area between and including the service and short lines.

Setup. A weak return of a shot that results in an easy opportunity for a player to hit the ball for a winner.

Shadow ball. See **screen ball.**

Shoot. To attempt to hit kill shots.

Shooter. A player who relies mainly on kill shots.

Short. See **short serve.**

Short line. The line midway between and parallel to the front and back walls. The back line of the service zone.

Short serve. A serve that rebounds from the front wall and strikes the floor in front of the short line.

Side-by-side formation. A system of doubles play in which court coverage and responsibilities are assigned by dividing the racquetball court in half from the front wall to the back wall.

Side out. The loss of serve by a player or team.

Side-wall–front-wall kill shot. See **pinch shot.**

Singles. One player playing against another player.

Skip ball. A ball that strikes the floor before hitting the front wall.

Splat. A shot that hits the side wall close to the hitter and then hits the front wall for a winner.

Straddle ball. A ball that goes between the legs of a player.

Straight kill shot. A low shot that goes directly to and rebounds from the front wall in approximately the same direction from which it came.

Tension. The amount of pressure with which a racquet is strung.

Thong. The rope or strap attached to the bottom of the handle of the racquet and worn around a player's wrist.

Three-wall racquetball. An outdoor variety of the sport in which a front wall and two partial or full side walls are utilized; the back wall is replaced by a line on the playing surface.

Three-wall serve. A fault serve in which the ball strikes three walls in succession before bouncing on the floor. Also called a two-side serve.

Three-wall shot. See **Z ball.**

Throat. The part of the racquet where the handle meets the head.

Tiebreaker. The third game of a match, which is usually played to 11 points.

Time-out. A rest period when play stops. Each player is allowed three per game and two in a tiebreaker. The length is usually 30 to 60 seconds.

Topspin. The forward rotation of the ball that causes it to travel downward and pick up speed after bouncing off the floor.

Touch. Superb racquet control.

Tournament play. Organized competition in which a champion is determined.

Trick shots. An unorthodox shot used as a last-ditch attempt to return a ball. Usually used when you are out of position.

Two-handed backhand. A backhand shot hit using two hands in two forehand grips on the handle, one hand above the other.

Two-side serve. See **three-wall serve.**

Unavoidable hinder. An unintentional obstruction of a player by an opponent during play. Also see **hinder.**

Up-and-back. See **I formation.**

USRA. United States Racquetball Association. A former governing body of racquetball competition.

Volley. A ball hit before it bounces on the floor.

Wall ball. See **wallpaper shot.**

Wallpaper shot. A ball that hugs the side wall as it travels to the rear area of the court making it difficult to return.

Winner. Any shot that ends a rally or scores a point.

Wrist-snap. The combination of wrist rotation and wrist flexion at racquet–ball impact.

Z ball. A defensive shot that strikes three walls before touching the floor. The ball strikes the front wall, a side wall, and then the opposite side wall.

Z serve. A legally served ball in which the front wall is hit, then a side wall, followed by the ball bouncing on the floor behind the short line before striking the opposite side wall. After hitting the second side wall, it should rebound parallel to the rear wall.

Index

About the Authors

Ed Turner, PhD, is a professor of health, physical eduction, and leisure studies at Appalachian State University in Boone, North Carolina. At Appalachian State Ed teaches racquetball and methods courses and co-directs the Interdisciplinary Creativity Center. He has authored many articles on a variety of topics and co-authored the book *Innovative Theory and Practice of Badminton* in 1984. Ed has taught racquet sports for 23 years and has taught and played racquetball for the last 10 years. His other leisure-time pursuits include writing, running, and lifting weights.

Marty Hogan is a legend in the racquetball world, having captured more than one hundred professional tournaments in his racquetball career, including five consecutive national singles championships. At the end of the 1986 season, he had been ranked No. 1 in the nation at some point during each of the last 11 seasons and finished runner-up the five times he didn't win the title. Marty has been playing racquetball for more than twenty years and is responsible for developing his characteristic "power racquetball" style that has changed the way racquetball is played.